Praise for
JJ Virgin's Sugar Impact Diet

"*JJ Virgin's Sugar Impact Diet* can help save your brain and your life. Numerous studies show that sugar can be addictive and pro-inflammatory and lead to a number of devastating illnesses. If you want a better brain, I highly recommend this book."
—Daniel G. Amen, MD, *New York Times* bestselling
author of *Change Your Brain, Change Your Life*

"Opens your eyes to how much sugar you're really eating, and provides an actionable plan to cut down on the sweet stuff and feel better fast."
—Mark Hyman, MD, #1 *New York Times* bestselling
author of *The Blood Sugar Solution 10 Day Detox Diet*

"In line with leading-edge science, JJ Virgin presents a radical and empowering new way to look at sugar."
—David Perlmutter, MD, FACN, #1 *New York Times*
bestselling author of *Grain Brain*

"Sugar is one of the most harmful elements of the American diet and one of our biggest contributors to obesity and disease. JJ Virgin has her finger on the pulse of the latest developments in diet and nutrition and I know *JJ Virgin's Sugar Impact Diet* will help a lot of people."
—Haylie Pomroy, #1 *New York Times*
bestselling author of *The Fast Metabolism Diet*

"Breaks through the myths and provides a clear and realistic path to health. This book is life changing!"
—Cynthia Pasquella, CCN, author of *P.I.N.K Method* and
The Hungry Hottie Cookbook, and founder of the
Institute of Transformational Nutrition

"Follow JJ Virgin's advice if you want to live longer, feel better, and be more vibrant. You will *never* look at sugar the same way again."

—Tana Amen, BSN, RN, *New York Times*
bestselling author of *The Omni Diet*

"In her newest book, *JJ Virgin's Sugar Impact Diet*, author JJ Virgin takes no prisoners. She delivers a hard-hitting, no-holds-barred, crystal clear message on how to identify and eliminate the astounding and myriad forms sugars have taken in our diets. Follow her advice and you will discover answers to why weight and health can prove so elusive despite the best intentions."

—William Davis, MD, #1 *New York Times*
bestselling author of *Wheat Belly*,
The Wheat Belly Cookbook, and
Wheat Belly 30-Minute (or Less!) Cookbook

"JJ Virgin understands how to get you thin and healthy. She is one of the leading voices in cutting edge science and her Sugar Impact theories will, once and for all, demystify the damaging effects of sugar and will, in turn, change your life!"

—Suzanne Somers, author, actress, entertainer

"In her groundbreaking new book, JJ Virgin definitively settles the debate on sugar and shows us how it wreaks havoc on our health and waistline. She provides simple yet novel strategies to remove the enemy and become the lean and energetic person you were meant to be. Highest recommendation."

—Sara Gottfried, MD, *New York Times* bestselling
author of *The Hormone Cure*

"Avoiding sugar is all the rage right now, and for good reason: sugar is wreaking havoc on our health! We're overweight, tired, and just plain sick—and that could all change once your Sugar Impact is lowered. Thanks to *JJ Virgin's Sugar Impact Diet*, you can banish the many hidden sources of sugar from your life, regain your vitality and finally lose the weight."

—Diane Sanfilippo, BS, NC, *New York Times* bestselling author of *Practical Paleo* and *The 21-Day Sugar Detox*

"*JJ Virgin's Sugar Impact Diet* offers a sensible, creative, doable program, which will rejuvenate desperate sugar addicts who are struggling with their weight. JJ shines the light on hidden sugars, misunderstood fruit juice concentrates, and misleading low-fat (but high-sugar), unreal foods. JJ will positively impact many lives with this book."

—Connie Bennett, bestselling author of *Sugar Shock* and *Beyond Sugar Shock*

THE SUGAR
IMPACT DIET

Also by JJ Virgin

The Virgin Diet Cookbook
The Virgin Diet
Six Weeks to Sleeveless and Sexy

THE SUGAR IMPACT DIET

JJ VIRGIN

headline

This book has been written by an American author, originally for a North American audience, and contains details of some nutritional values, recommended intakes and regulatory requirements that may not be relevant in the UK. The publisher recommends that the reader should check any such details against UK sources of such information.

First published in Great Britain in 2014 by HEADLINE PUBLISHING GROUP

1

Cataloguing in Publication Data is available from the British Library

Trade Paperback ISBN 978 1 4722 2638 9

Typeset in Bembo

Printed and bound in Great Britain by Clays Ltd, St Ives plc

Headline's policy is to use papers that are natural, renewable and recyclable products and made from wood grown in sustainable forests. The logging and manufacturing processes are expected to conform to the environmental regulations of the country of origin.

MIX
Paper from
responsible sources
FSC® C104740
www.fsc.org

HEADLINE PUBLISHING GROUP
An Hachette UK Company
338 Euston Road
London NW1 3BH

www.headline.co.uk
www.hachette.co.uk

For everyone who decided not to keep the good news to themselves . . . the movement you started is the reason the Sugar Impact Diet will help millions more people experience the power of reclaiming their weight, their health, and their lives—forever! Thank you, Virgin Diet tribe!

CONTENTS

Introduction

HOW LOWERING YOUR SUGAR IMPACT CAN CHANGE YOUR LIFE

When I wrote *The Virgin Diet*, I was on a mission. I had to help people with what I discovered: food intolerances were sabotaging their health and holding their weight hostage. You can be doing everything right, even eating healthy diet foods, and still not lose a pound. Eliminating seven foods unlocked the key to fast weight loss in just 3 weeks. It was so incredible to see people get their lives back—weight came off fast, and the fatigue, bloating, and aches that came with food intolerance disappeared. So people told their family and friends. I was amazed at the movement it started. By now it's helped hundreds of thousands of people finally lose the weight and feel better fast.

And as I watched people go through the program, I realized that one food was the biggest needle mover of them all: sugar. Reducing sugar is the one thing that can jump-start your weight loss or crack the code on breaking through a plateau better than any other, especially if you're not dealing with other intolerances. But—and this is a big but—not all sugar is created equal!

All of the sugar diets out there drive me crazy because they totally miss the point. You already know sugar is bad for you! Hardly anyone is gobbling up straight sugar anymore—consumption of table sugar is at an all-time low.

When many of my clients come to me, they're frustrated and ready to give up because they're already depriving themselves of candy, dessert, and a spoonful of sugar in their coffee. They're sweetening their oatmeal with honey, they're eating low-fat yogurt with fruit, they're fighting their hunger with low-calorie snack bars during the day, and they're living on salads, diet drinks, and "healthy" frozen meals. When a sugar craving hits and they slip, they beat themselves up for their lack of willpower. But after all the healthy low-calorie, low-fat, sugar-free eating, they end up with the same symptoms they'd get if they were eating a ton of sugar— weight gain, cravings, mood and energy swings, health issues like inflammation and insulin resistance, and maybe even diabetes. Sound familiar? So what the heck is going on?

NOT ALL SUGARS ARE CREATED EQUAL

These healthy diets are packed with *hidden* sugars, and these sugars are not harmless. I had to come up with a revolutionary new way to look at sugar to allow even more people to finally lose that extra weight and reclaim their health—and that's exactly what I've done. So let me shout this from the mountaintop—it's the *impact* of sugar that matters. You don't have to eliminate sugar completely, but you need to choose your sugars wisely. When you understand Sugar Impact, you'll know why I've declared sugar—especially sneaky sugars, which I'll describe in this book—public enemy No. 1. The high Sugar Impact of the seven foods I'm going to share with you is the single biggest factor when it comes to fatigue, obesity, diabetes, and a slew of other diseases, including cancer.

I've declared sneaky sugar public enemy No. 1.

Sneaky sugars hide in places you'd never suspect—whole foods, diet foods, packaged fruit, drinks, dressings . . . even sugar substitutes. Even the most health-conscious among us struggle to know everywhere they hide or how to avoid them. It can feel incredibly daunting. But I've found a way to make it easy. Once I give you the tools to drop these seven high Sugar Impact foods, you can cut out all of the hidden sugars that have been sneaking tons of sugar into your diet, causing you to gain weight, crave sugar, and feel terrible.

If you had success with the Virgin Diet but you're still looking to lose those last stubborn pounds—you've found your answer. You'll have even more success on the Sugar Impact Diet. It will change your life! People who've followed this program had incredible results—most lost 10 pounds in just 2 weeks! And they reversed inflammation and bloating, eliminated symptoms we're all told to believe are the normal signs of aging, and feel better than they have in years.

All that's waiting for you, too. You'll break free from the Sugar Impact of seven sneaky sugars that are making you weight-loss resistant—and you'll be surprised at how easy it is. I'll show you how to eliminate high and medium Sugar Impact foods—the biggest sources of hidden sugars holding your health and your waistline hostage—from seven food groups: grains; roots; packaged fruit; low and no-fat dairy and diet foods; sugary sauces, dressings, and condiments; sweet drinks; sweeteners, and added sugar. Just by dropping the high and medium Sugar Impact foods, you'll reset and retrain your taste buds—and, like my clients, you can lose up to 10 pounds in just 2 weeks.

TRACK YOUR IMPACT

It will blow your mind when you see how much sugar is sneaking into your diet—mountains of it, even in things you would swear have no added sugar. The average American eats about 22 teaspoons

Sugar is a chameleon—it has many different forms, hides under lots of different names, and slips into foods you'd never expect.

of sugar every day. Sugar is a chameleon—it has many different forms, hides under lots of different names, and slips into foods you'd never expect. There are more than 50 names for sugar! Studies have shown that the rising rate of obesity in kids today is coming from the foods they're eating at home, not the junk and sweets they're sneaking around eating after school. So you can't just shrug it off—you have to become a sugar sleuth!

But don't sweat it—I'm here to help. You'll find a cheat sheet in this book that lists different names for sugar and where it hides (see Sugar Hides In Plain Sight, page 35). I'll make sure you're armed and ready, because sugar is the number one topic of questions, concerns, and confusion I get from people, by far. *What if it's natural? What about honey? What can I substitute? What if I can't live without it? Help!*

And don't think you're better off if you're eating the calorie-free stuff. Artificial sweeteners are just the wolf in sheep's clothing.

Artificial sweeteners are just the wolf in sheep's clothing.

They let you think you beat the system by eating something sweet without the calories, but your body isn't in on the trick. It sets its sugar metabolism machinery in motion and screams for glucose, which means you'll probably just end up eating more.

So if you're like my clients—eating healthy but you just can't seem to lose weight (maybe you're even gaining weight), you've come to the right place. Lowering your Sugar Impact jump-starts fast fat loss, breaks through those weight-loss brick walls, reduces inflammation, balances hormones and mood, improves sleep, and reverses declining health more than any other change to diet or lifestyle.

There's even more good news—the Sugar Impact Diet isn't about eliminating sugar altogether; it's about eating the right sugar. The program I've created and outlined in this book is unlike any other. It lays out a step-by-step process to wean you off the foods with the highest and most damaging sugars—those with the highest Sugar Impact—so that you can lose weight, drop fat, and improve your health without feeling deprived. Learning how to swap good sugars for bad sugars for just 2 weeks will heal your body and transform your life *forever*.

> *Learning how to swap good sugars for bad sugars will heal your body and transform your life forever.*

By the end of the program, you'll not only have lost weight and reclaimed your life, you'll be armed with information and lots of great alternatives to satisfy your sweet cravings. I've built this program specifically to address the world we live in, to give you the tools and the strength to avoid the sugars that are hurting you. And if you have a sweet tooth (and yes, some people are born to crave sugar more than others), don't worry—you aren't doomed. There are ways to work with your genetics so that a lifetime in the grip of sugar isn't your fate. You'll change your taste buds and your sensitivity to sugar, so passing up cupcakes and ice cream will be a breeze, not a teeth-gnashing exercise in willpower.

Together, we're going to change how you think about sugar, so you can be clear about how to make the best choices for your weight, energy, mood, and life.

THE EVOLUTION OF HIDDEN SUGARS

We're genetically hardwired to want food that's sweet; our ancestors used to gorge on ripe summer fruit and the lucky honey find to "winter up" for the cold months ahead. Of course, back then, and even until fairly recently, sugar was never available in the forms or amounts it is today.

Living in a world that stresses us out constantly doesn't help. You're always on the run, work is crazy, you're shuttling kids everywhere, and the last person to get taken care of is you. Meals are whatever is convenient and fast.

Even though you don't have much time to think about what you're eating, guess who does? Food companies. They're busy, too, making sure that when you reach for that low-fat cookie, you keep coming back for more. Little by little, they're slipping more sugar into packaged foods, including diet foods, to keep up with the low-fat craze, and as food gets sweeter and sweeter, you want it even more. Yes, sugar is an addiction. When you eat a lot of sugar, you train your body to need it constantly, but getting rid of it is easier than you think.

Sugar is an addiction.

NEED OR WANT?

Did you know that we can't live without protein, fat, and water, but we *can* live without carbs? I know! Shocking, because I bet there are a lot of days during the week when you say to yourself, I just could not live without carbs. Well, that's what I used to say. No sourdough bread? I mean, come on! But yep, we can survive just fine on protein, fat, and water, since our bodies can actually create glucose on their own. It's just who wants to? Not me.

Besides, even though we can live without carbs, if we cut them out entirely we'll feel lousy and stress our bodies in the bargain. So let's do this right.

With the Sugar Impact Diet, you'll identify the right types and amounts of carbohydrates so that you always feel great and the weight keeps coming off. I want your body to get the food it needs to fuel and restore you, without putting you in a metabolic spin cycle. Foods with high Sugar Impact—specifically, foods with high amounts of a specific type of sugar called fructose—encourage your body to store fat without making you feel full. Talk about a bad combination! Throughout this book, I'll explain how to spot and avoid high Sugar Impact foods, and I'll teach you delicious low Sugar Impact swaps so that you can avoid the sugar roller coaster without feeling deprived. This is not about "living without." It's about the power of being informed to make good choices, knowing where there's wiggle room and how to step away from bad choices—the harmful, high Sugar Impact ones. You'll break through the sugar confusion to find the life that's waiting for you—you'll be leaner, more energetic, and healthier than you ever thought possible!

> *Avoid the sugar roller coaster without feeling deprived.*

SUGAR IMPACT TO THE RESCUE!

No other program looks at sugar as comprehensively, strategically, or innovatively as the Sugar Impact Diet does, and certainly no other comes close when it comes to ensuring your success.

Other programs set you up to fail by either focusing on only a single aspect of sugar measurement, like the glycemic index, or by asking you to take drastic and unrealistic measures, like giving up all carbs—right now! Well, how has that worked for you so far? You're sent on a roller-coaster ride—pumped up, then hungry and crashing—and still craving the sugar that sent you on the ride in the first place. That seems a little heartless of them to do to you, and more than a little unnecessary, don't you think? You can't go from a high-sugar diet to a low-sugar diet overnight without serious consequences.

MY IMPACT!

Mary Jo Bouman
Starting weight: 122 lbs.
Current weight: 112.4 lbs.
Total lost: 9.6 lbs.

I didn't realize the impact sugar
had on me until I did the Sugar
Impact Diet. I considered my diet
and lifestyle healthy. My kitchen was
stocked with fresh fruits and vegetables, healthy fats, gluten-free
grains and flours, olive oil and butter, good-quality meats and fish.
Most of my meals were home-cooked, my alcohol consumption was
low, and I rarely ate candy or drank soda. I usually had a cookie or a
sweet after dinner, and often had a craving for a treat midafternoon.

The reason I did the Sugar Impact Diet was to help my husband
and daughter who both are overweight. Wow! I feel like I have
been a catalyst for my family; the three of us have lost 49 pounds
combined, and another family member lost an additional 15
pounds. We are in this together and plan to continue until my
husband and daughter take off 50-plus pounds each. It feels great to
be working toward this goal together and to prepare and plan, cook
and eat together. The impact of fructose was a real eye-opener for
me. I was used to reading labels, but I look at them from a sugar
perspective now.

I work with energetic five-year-olds, and prior to the Sugar
Impact Diet I had been falling asleep early in the evening because
I was exhausted. Now I am awake and alert until 10 or 11 p.m.
Sleep is heavenly; I wake up feeling like I've been floating on
clouds all night. My energy is strong and steady during long days.
I also lost weight and inches. That wasn't really a goal for me, but
it feels great.

So let me set you up for the win. I'll give you the tools to evaluate where you're getting the most sugar in your diet and guide you through the transition from high Sugar Impact foods to low Sugar Impact foods. At the same time, you'll be retraining your taste buds to key back into the subtle sweetness of nature's treats.

I've developed the Sugar Impact Scale, which rates a food according to the amount of sugar in it and the effect it has on your body. It takes into account a food's fructose levels, nutrient density, fiber, and glycemic load. The Sugar Impact Scale, like everything else in my program, is simple and easy to understand. Sugars and carbohydrates are assessed as having a high, medium, or Low Sugar Impact. Think of them this way:

- High Sugar Impact—stop!
- Medium Sugar Impact—proceed with caution
- Low Sugar Impact—go!

The Sugar Impact Diet will help you avoid the highest Sugar Impact foods (and their negative health effects) by giving you simple swaps—nutritious, tasty trades with lower Sugar Impact. You'll probably like them even better!

RESET YOUR SWEET TOOTH—IN JUST 2 WEEKS!

In *The Virgin Diet*, I asked readers to give up seven foods for 3 weeks. If the Virgin Diet proved you can do anything for 3 weeks, 2 weeks will be a cinch! So prepare to be wowed. The simple three-step Sugar Impact Diet will deliver amazing results in the blink of an eye.

The three cycles will help you taper your Sugar Impact and transition you from high to medium to low Sugar Impact foods— slowly. You're not going cold turkey! Ever. I know that's conventional wisdom in certain diet circles, but how's that worked for you so far? Exactly. There are a few things I can guarantee going cold turkey will do for you, and losing weight isn't one of them. Instead, you'll be shaky, irritable, lethargic, starving, and craving sugar—not the outcome we're after.

First, you'll identify what sugars are undermining your weight and health. Where are the sugar land mines in your day? How much sugar are you really eating?

How much sugar are you really eating?

Then you'll shift from burning sugar to burning fat—which is just as good as it sounds! (More on this in Chapter 1.) I'll be with you every step of the way and I've put together a ton

You'll shift from burning sugar to burning fat!

of support and strategies for navigating any rough spots—including Sugar-Withdrawal Strategies (see page 180), Sugar-Attack Survival Strategies (see page 182), Speed-Healing Techniques (see page 223). You can also see my recommended Supportive Supplements at http://sugarimpact.com/resources. You're also going to read exciting stories and see the "before" and "after" photos of people who've already felt the impact and had incredible results. You'll be as amazed as I am. Best of all, you're next!

The Sugar Impact Diet Blueprint

Low Sugar Impact to a T

The strategic, step-by-step approach of the Sugar Impact Diet ensures your success by moving you through the program at your own speed, in tune with how your body responds to the changes in your diet. You have to know where you are when you start, gently remove high-impact sugars, shift from sugar burner to fat burner, and emerge on the other side, ready to chart your maintenance path forward.

Simply put, the journey to low Sugar Impact freedom is guided by the 4Ts: Test, Taper, Transition, Transformed! In just 2 weeks you'll drop 10 pounds, no longer wonder what it feels like to be bursting with energy, and be feeling better than ever.

CYCLE 1: TAPER

- Take the Sneaky Sugar Inventory to identify how much sugar you are actually eating
- Take the Sugar Impact Quiz to identify the impact sugar is having on you
- Trade your high Sugar Impact foods for medium Sugar Impact foods
- Take your starting weight and measurements
- Focus on following the portions of the Sugar Impact Plate and eating by the Sugar Impact Clock

CYCLE 2: TRANSITION

- Trade your medium Sugar Impact foods for low Sugar Impact foods and avoid any low Sugar Impact foods that are asterisked (i.e., most fruit)
- Hide or toss the medium and high Sugar Impact foods
- Take the Sugar Impact Quiz weekly
- Take your weight and measurements weekly
- Check in with the Sugar Impact Quiz at the 2-week mark to determine if you should stay in Cycle 2 or shift into Cycle 3

CYCLE 3: TRANSFORMED!

- Swap 3–4 low Sugar Impact servings for medium Sugar Impact servings; 1–2 of these servings should be from fruit
- Have one high Sugar Impact serving at the end of the week
- Weigh, measure, and retest at the end of the week. Decide whether you can stay in Cycle 3, or you need to return to Cycle 2

LOW SUGAR IMPACT FOR LIFE

Once a year, repeat Cycles 1 and 2 to ensure you're retaining your sugar sensitivity, and to bust any plateaus. You should also do Cycles 1 and 2 again if you "fall off the wagon."

When you complete this program once, you're good to go. Even so, I encourage you to redo Cycles 1 and 2 once a year, to take stock and take aim, especially if you have a new goal.

I know that the true test of a diet isn't just how much you lose when you're on it, but how successfully you can stay at your goal weight for good. Most programs yank the sugar and then leave you to your own devices—but too often that means you end up right back where you started. If you don't have a maintenance plan, you're bound to fail, and then you have to start again. When you have to do a diet over and over, it's fair to say it didn't work so well, isn't it?

Sugar is all around us. I'm going to help you make peace with it and understand it—especially the impact it's having on your weight and health. You have the power. You can do this! Plus, when you know what to eat and what swaps to make, you'll even learn to *enjoy* sugar again, without the guilt.

So if you're where I was, and where the thousands of men and women I've helped were, there's no need to be overwhelmed with despair. You can break free from sugar and lose 10 pounds in just 2 weeks!

PART I

SUGAR IMPACT:

The Hidden Cause
of Weight Gain

1

BREAK FREE FROM THE SUGAR TRAP

Welcome to the *Sugar Impact Diet*! Get ready to change your life in just 2 weeks! There are so many amazing benefits to eliminating high-impact, sugary foods. Yes, you're going to lose fat fast—on average, people lose 10 pounds in just 2 weeks! You'll also break free of your cravings, regain control of your appetite, and enjoy high, steady energy and laser-sharp focus. You'll finally ditch the constant bloat that makes you feel like you could be popped with a pin. You'll look and feel younger almost over-night, and you'll get rid of the nagging symptoms that make you feel crummy every single day—once and for all. And, more important, when you go low Sugar Impact (SI), you'll even begin to reverse chronic diseases like obesity, diabetes, and heart disease.

> *You're going to lose fat fast! You'll look and feel younger almost overnight.*

BECOME A FAT BURNER, NOT A SUGAR BURNER

One of the biggest benefits of the low SI diet is that you lose weight, fast. And I'm talking about that really stubborn, clingy weight... the weight you thought you were doomed to carry forever because you were told you'd be packing on a few as you got older. Don't believe that myth!

If you're carrying extra pounds, it's because when you weren't looking your body trained itself to burn sugar when it needed energy instead of fat. You became a sugar burner. Now your body doesn't even go near your fat reserves to look for fuel. It's gotten used to relying on a steady supply of carbs, so you need to keep snacking to give it fuel to burn, or you'll crash.

When you eat sugar or carbs, your pancreas releases insulin to pull the excess sugar, or glucose (blood sugar), out of your blood and restore balance. Glucose is a form of sugar in the food we eat. It's also our primary source of energy. It's packed away in your cells for quick-access fuel, and what's left over is stored as fat. If you eat lots of sugar and keep calling on insulin to lower your blood sugar all the time, you'll eventually lose your sensitivity to it, resulting in a condition called insulin resistance. Insulin resistance is a known cause of weight gain and can lead to diabetes.

One of the hallmarks of being a sugar burner is that while you're burning sugar and storing fat, you experience frequent drops in blood sugar that make your body scream for more sugar. You'll get crazy hungry if you go for a few hours without food or you skip a meal. And when this happens, watch out! You're irritable, foggy, totally preoccupied, and showing the fangs of cravings. So let's fix that! All it takes is 2 weeks to reap the benefits of being an Impact player! When you make just a few simple, tasty swaps for seven high-SI sugars, voila—with the new, low SI you will be burning fat and craving-free with sky-high energy.

ALL SUGAR IS NOT CREATED EQUAL

Let's start with one very important fact: all calories are not the same! The old mantra of "a calorie is a calorie" doesn't hold true. Isn't that liberating? No more counting calories! That's because food is information, and it has marching orders for your body. Different nutrients have different physiological effects and distinct roles within the body.

No more counting calories!

Food is information.

This makes sense, when you consider that you'd never say the calories in your spinach salad are the same as the ones in your Bananas Foster, would you? (Would you?) Maybe it's the guilt we associate with dessert, but we know some calories just feel different. The calories in the spinach will have a different effect on your body than the calories in that Bananas Foster. Let me tell you why.

Our bodies run on glucose. Our body can also metabolize fructose, the primary sugar in fruit and a main component of processed sugars like high-fructose corn syrup. But fructose is metabolized differently than other sugars. When most types of sugar enter your bloodstream as part of the digestive process, they elevate blood sugar levels, and your body then releases insulin to help lower those levels. But fructose bypasses this trigger by heading directly to your liver, the only organ that can metabolize it. Since it doesn't raise blood sugar levels, there's no real bump in insulin. When it hits your liver, it gets converted to glucose, and some of it is stored as glycogen, which is how we pack away carbs for energy use later. But another metabolic fallout from fructose metabolism is that the liver repackages excess fructose as triglycerides, or fat.

Of course, there are other forms sugar can take, like galactose, maltose, and lactose (milk sugar). Sugar is found in many plants, though most straight sugar as we know it comes from sugar cane and sugar beet. But no matter what source the sugar you eat comes from—whether it's high-fructose corn syrup, honey, or molasses—your body is going to break that sugar down until it has either glucose or fructose. And the end games for those two are not the same. Glucose gives you fuel; fructose gives you fat. That's what I mean by Sugar Impact.

Glucose gives you fuel; fructose gives you fat.

Fructose, as it exists in the natural whole foods we eat (like fruits and some vegetables), is all wrapped up in fiber and bundled with nutrients. When fructose is delivered to us that way, things change for the better—our digestion slows down, we burn some energy extracting the fructose, and fructose moseys to our liver in a steady stream rather than a torrent. But most of the sources of fructose in our diet are the ones that cause the Pavlovian response we know well…the cupcakes, ice cream, and crunchy candy bars. When fructose is freewheeling, or separated from its fiber source, like the high-fructose corn syrup in juice, sodas, and candy, it might as well be taking a laundry chute–like plunge to our liver…where its idea of a party is to start making fat.

Much of the credit for sounding the fructose alarm goes to Robert Lustig, MD, a pediatric endocrinologist and professor at the University of California, San Francisco. He ignited a very public conversation about sugar and the harmful effects of fructose metabolism with his YouTube video, "Sugar: The Bitter Truth." And I'm so glad he did. If you haven't seen it, it's definitely worth checking out.

In an October 2013 article in *The Telegraph*, Dr. Lustig reacted to a study in the journal *PLoS One*. The study, published February 27, 2013, looked at the rate of diabetes in 175 countries over a decade and linked increased consumption of sugar to higher rates of diabetes, independent of obesity. Dr. Lustig explained what that meant: the cause of type 2 diabetes isn't tied to the amount of calories you eat. It's more important where the calories come from. The study showed that when people ate more calories every day, yes, their rate of diabetes went up. But when they added the same number of calories and got them from added sugars like high-fructose corn syrup and sucrose, the rate went up a lot more. Dr. Lustig noted, "Added sugar is 11 times more potent at causing diabetes than general calories."

But we're not always *choosing* to eat more sugar; we're being dosed with it. Sugar is slipped into foods we'd never suspect, and often in combination with more than a dash of added salt, to keep us hungry and thirsty and coming back for more. No wonder you've

We're not always choosing to eat more sugar; we're being dosed with it.

been feeling like your health and waistline have been hijacked! Taking them back will be the most powerful part of your Sugar Impact transformation.

Eating too much of the wrong kind of sugar can also impact your appetite and hunger levels for the worse. When you eat lots of sugar, your insulin levels stay elevated. High insulin levels drown out the signals from the hormone leptin, otherwise known as the satiety hormone. Leptin is an important hormone produced in fat cells that tells you when you've had enough to eat. When leptin is working right, it tells you you've gotten enough energy and to stop eating, already. If things were working as they should, leptin would also keep its counterpart, the hunger hormone ghrelin, suppressed after a meal. Ghrelin is responsible for sending your brain the signal to eat when your stomach is empty or your blood sugar is low. Leptin should be the stopgap we need before we eat ourselves to death. Dr. Lustig calls leptin "the holy grail of obesity." When your brain ignores leptin (in a condition called leptin resistance), you eat more than you're supposed to, because ghrelin is never suppressed and your brain still thinks you're starving.

Sugar fractures your ability to control your appetite.

So, in essence, sugar fractures your ability to control your appetite. But you're not doomed to live with it as a permanent condition, something another anti-sugar crusader, David Gillespie, points out in an interview about his book *Big Fat Lies*: "Remove [fructose], and the appetite control system goes back to working as designed and starts moderating the amount of everything you consume. Slowly but surely, your weight returns to the normal weight range, and it stays there."

Isn't that great news? You can fix it, and fast. But not by counting calories. Even if you make an extreme cut to the calories you consume, research shows that if most of your calories come from fructose, you're wrecking your metabolism and satiety signaling and paving the way for insulin resistance, gastrointestinal disorders, obesity, and diabetes. The key is lowering your SI—making simple swaps that deliver huge rewards.

If most of your calories come from fructose, you're wrecking your metabolism.

High–impact sugars have also been found to play a role in a serious condition called metabolic syndrome, a combination of risk factors including excess abdominal fat, high blood pressure, and high triglycerides. In fact, Dr. Richard Johnson, author of *The Fat Switch*, squarely points the finger at a high-fructose diet as increasing the risk of developing metabolic syndrome. Metabolic syndrome raises your risk of diabetes, heart disease, and other chronic health conditions. It's the disease equivalent of being run over by a truck. He also suggests that consuming high amounts of fructose is connected to chronic inflammation and uric acid buildup, which can also cause you to gain more weight.

One of Dr. Johnson's key contributions to our understanding of fructose metabolism is that he discovered it actually throws a pretty significant metabolic switch in your body. Flip the switch, and you store fat! He found that fructose activates an enzyme, fructokinase, which then activates another enzyme, aldolase, that throws the switch and causes cells to accumulate fat. This process can be life-saving if you're a bear preparing for hibernation. It's what allows animals to beef up for a long winter snooze—or add fat when food is scarce. Once they need access to their reserves, the enzyme is blocked, and they burn fat to survive. But it doesn't do your waistline any favors if you don't have a five-month sleep in your future!

BECOME A FAT BURNER, NOT A SUGAR BURNER

Now that you understand the ways different sugars react in your body, you can see why SI is the key to freeing yourself from

Sugar Impact is the key to freeing yourself from the sugar trap.

the sugar trap—and the jelly belly, bloating, and fatigue that come with it. Some sugars cause a higher SI than others. By tapering you off high SI foods and transitioning to a diet filled with low SI foods, the Sugar Impact Diet pulls you out of that sugar-burning, fat-storing cycle and transitions you to being a fat burner, which is exactly what you want to be to lose weight fast and keep it off. Reducing the SI in your diet will reset your body's toxic habit of pounding you for a quick hit of fuel. You'll move off burning sugar, and as more good fats and clean, lean protein take center stage in your diet, you'll burn a steady, high-energy flame all day long.

Becoming a fat burner is exactly how it sounds—you burn fat! So you drop weight fast. And you stay in power weight-loss mode because once your SI is under control, your hormones will work with you to lose weight and stay lean. You'll finally be hearing leptin bark out the order that you're full and you should stop eating. Ghrelin will be back in check, so you'll actually know what it feels like to feel full again!

You'll also have more energy, because when you fuel your body with low SI foods and burn your stored fat for energy, you avoid those awful energy slumps that come with a high SI diet (you know those sugar crashes all too well!). And here's a bonus—you'll even burn more fat as you sleep!

LOW SUGAR, NOT NO SUGAR

We're designed to eat sugar; our genes tell us so. But getting it in the right amounts and from the right sources is the real secret.

Don't worry. I'm not saying you have to totally give up sugar! It's important to remember this is a *low* SI diet, not a no-sugar diet. We're designed to eat sugar; our genes tell us so. But getting it in the right amounts and from the right sources is the real secret. The Sugar Impact Diet will do all that for you and more. Just by transitioning to a low-SI diet, you'll see big shifts in your weight, energy, bloating, joint pain, and all-around *joie de vivre*. And there's lots more wind at your back in the way of Supportive Supplements (visit http://sugarimpact .com/resources), Speed-Healing Techniques (see page 223), and strategies to beat back cravings and cope with withdrawal. You're not in this alone! I've not only helped myself dig out of the sugar trap, but I've helped thousands of people do the same. In fact, you can read some of their inspiring stories in this book. I hope their success with the Sugar Impact Diet will be all the motivation you need!

WHAT'S WITH THE CRAVINGS?

This program is designed to help you win the battle against high-impact sugar—and a key part of that is staving off the intense cravings that can derail your best intentions.

Cravings can have their roots in everything from ancestry to lifestyle choices, and you have to know where they're coming from to break their grip. So let's dig in to find out the source of yours. Just so you know, these causes aren't like coupons—you're not limited to just one! Knowing what kind of cravings you're dealing with could be the key that finally helps you break free of your sugar addiction.

Let's start with two of the most common causes of cravings: genetics and a low-fat (read: high-SI) diet. We all have sweet-seeking behavior as part of our evolutionary beginnings. But cravings could be part of your unique genetic wiring, and that's something different. No surprise to you! Because if you've got a sweet tooth, you know it.

Just one change to a single gene could explain why you break into a sweat trying to resist dessert, while your friend could care less about the hot lava cake topped with whipped cream. Research shows that a difference in DNA could mean some people are less sensitive to the taste of sugar, so they chase sweeter and sweeter foods to get the reward—foods the average person would find way too sweet.

The other major cause of cravings comes from eating high-impact sugars. They give you quick energy fixes, but ultimately set off a vicious circle of cravings for the very foods that *create* cravings. These two sources of cravings may seem pretty far apart—one you inherit and one you create—but your body responds to both the same way. The insulin spikes and blood sugar dips that come on the heels of eating sugar make you a metabolic rag doll, with your hormones and defense system being thrown all over the place, at the mercy of whatever you've eaten, and how much.

> *You may not even be aware you're eating much sugar.*

You may not even be aware you're eating that much sugar. Labels don't make it easy to spot. Sugar is sneaky, and it's often not even listed as sugar on the ingredients list. It may be hiding there with names like maltodextrin, barley malt, or fruit juice concentrate. If you believe you're making all the right food choices and eating healthy, but you're still dealing with the frustration of...

Bloating, gas
Cravings
Increased appetite
Poor mood (focus, irritability, depression)
Low or unstable energy
Stubborn belly fat
Inability to lose weight

...it's likely you're getting way more sugar in your diet than you want or need.

Those symptoms may also be telling you that extra sugar has led to a stealth attacker—Candida Albicans, or Candida, a systemic fungal overgrowth. Candida is a condition that thrives on sugar and makes you crave it. You could also be struggling with small intestinal bacterial overgrowth, an overgrowth of bad gut bacteria fed by all of that sugar (see page 221–222). These bacteria actually cause you to extract more calories from the food you eat and store them as fat. Talk about unfair!

Or you may be dealing with leaky gut syndrome, which results when the tight junctions in your intestinal wall have become loose from repeated attack due to stress, fructose, gluten, toxicity, and certain medications. That increased permeability lets undigested food particles and toxic waste slip into your bloodstream, triggering an immune response and inflammation. You feel all that internal warfare as brain smog, headaches, bloating, gas, cramps, food sensitivities, and general aches and pains. All of these conditions make it hard, if not impossible to lose weight.

The important thing to remember is that you're not powerless against the forces of sugar. When you lower your SI and reset your sensitivity to sugar, your metabolic balance is restored, which paves the way for you to drop weight and feel better fast.

> *You're not powerless against the forces of sugar.*

Sneaky Sugar

You may be eating more sugar than you realize. Here are some sneaky sources that might surprise you.

Medium muffin (113 grams)—61 grams carb/37 grams sugar

Orange juice (12 ounces)—39 grams carb/33 grams sugar

Apple juice (12 ounces)—42 grams carb/39 grams sugar

Oriental Chicken Salad—42 grams carb/18 grams sugar

FAGE Total 0% Apple Cinnamon Raisins (6 ounces)—17 grams carb/16 grams sugar

Starbucks Caffè Vanilla Frappuccino Blended Beverage (16 ounces)—72 grams carb/69 grams sugar

Starbucks Hot Chocolate (16 ounces)—50 grams carb/43 grams sugar

Jamba Juice Banana Berry Smoothie (16 ounces)—68 grams carb/60 grams sugar

Jamba Juice Mango-A-Go-Go Light Smoothie (16 ounces)—42 grams carb/37 grams sugar

Coca-Cola Classic (12 ounces)—39 grams carb/39 grams sugar

Dunkin Donuts Cinnamon Raisin Bagel—66 grams carb/14 grams sugar

---

SUGAR ADDICTION

That same survival circuitry that told us to eat sweets whenever we could find them has turned into an addiction pathway in a world of sweet abundance. We're still driven to find it and eat it, in case it's our last chance to have it for a while. If only that were the case!

A sugar high is a real thing, as is sugar addiction. As Dr. Pamela Peeke, author of *The Hunger Fix*, explained it to me, "Animal studies have shown that refined sugar is more addictive than cocaine, heroin, or morphine. An animal will choose an Oreo over morphine. Why? This cookie has the perfect combination of sugar and fat to hijack the brain's reward center."

A bag of chips or chocolate bar sends a rush of sugar that alerts the reward center in your brain to release feel-good neurotransmitters like serotonin, dopamine, and beta endorphin. These endorphins are made in your pituitary gland and hypothalamus and are released in response to dietary triggers—mainly foods with that powerful combination of fat and sugar. The endorphin surge gives you intense pleasure and blocks pain, the same as if you had just injected heroin. Yep, this is your brain on sugar. A 2001 study published in the journal *NeuroReport* states that "palatable food stimulates neural systems implicated in drug dependence."

But you probably don't need to be told about serotonin or dopamine or opioids to know you're hooked. Just think about the way you feel when you have to do without it: you're tired, cranky, irritable, lethargic, and craving it. That's called withdrawal. So you get your hands on it (finally!) and you binge. Ahh. You feel so good. Then you feel so lousy. And guilty.

But it's not your fault! Don't beat yourself up for your lack of "willpower." When your blood sugar gets low, you crave something that will give you a quick hit of energy, which is nothing short of a survival mechanism. Those cravings are your body's way of getting what it needs to rescue your blood sugar. Sugar does that for you. Of course, once you have sugar, you're back on the sugar-high/energy crash ride that started your cravings to begin with!

We can't deny the mounting evidence of sugar's toxicity. But if we're sugar addicts, we're patients first, and we need to heal ourselves above all else.

THE IMPACT OF STRESS

Sometimes those sugar cravings are a result of low blood sugar, but it's no surprise that cravings strike even when you're not hungry. We also turn to food for comfort when we're stressed or upset.

When we're stressed, we don't crave wild salmon or grass-fed beef. We crave sugar. And you don't have to take my word for it. Researchers at the University of South Florida found that when people are stressed, they crave foods that are higher in sugar and fat. But ironically, sugar actually stresses your body further, shooting it full of short-term energy, sending your hormones into a spin cycle, and causing your blood sugar to spike and then plummet. So our go-to crutch actually leaves us more jittery and crankier than before. Not to mention that it causes weight gain, fatigue, brain fog, hormone imbalance, and worse. I'd consider *that* pretty stressful!

The good news is that going low SI is the soothing change your system needs to pull you out of the cravings/crash cycle—in just 2 weeks.

SUGAR AND YOUR HORMONES

One of the reasons stress has you jonesing for chocolate chip cookies instead of Brussels sprouts is that stress puts a big dent in the level of your don't-worry-be-happy hormone, serotonin. Serotonin is one of the feel-good endorphins released when you eat sugar.

There are lots of ways other than sugar to address chronic stress and stimulate your brain's pleasure center, but unfortunately few offer the immediate relief of a "drug" like fudge. The serotonin hit you get from sugar quiets the noise and gives you a little pleasure—even if it's not for long. Soon as you crash, you're plagued with guilt and remorse, and you beat yourself up and reach for some munchies to self-soothe. Incidentally, antidepressants do what sugar does—they get available serotonin into your brain. That idea of self-medicating isn't so far off, is it?

IT'S TIME TO HEAL

Now you know how bad sugar is for you. Don't despair—there's a solution! The key is to avoid drastic measures. If you try to cut out sugar cold turkey, you'll go into withdrawal, just as you would with any addiction. That's why you're going to taper and transition, nice and easy, from high- to medium- to low-SI foods. It's a process that sets you up for success and prevents the cravings that can set you back. I'm also going to give you strategies to help you fight any and all symptoms that pop up as you make the shift to low-SI living. I'll hold your hand and help you ease off the high-SI foods that are hurting you—so you can seize the vibrant life that's waiting for you!

As you heal, you're going to retrain your taste buds. Yes, even if you have a genetic sweet tooth! Just as you trained your body to become insensitive to sugar and want more of the sweet stuff, you're going to teach it to once again to be sugar-sensitive.

Being sugar-sensitive means you'll finally get rid of your cravings. You'll appreciate the exquisite subtle sweetness of fruit like raspberries and blackberries, spices like vanilla and cinnamon (which helps control blood sugar)—things you hardly

You'll finally get rid of your cravings.

notice or appreciate as a sugar addict. You'll even become aware that some foods are "too sweet." Yes, I'm going to ruin them for you!

LESS IS LESS, MORE IS MORE

When you give your body healthy substitutes for its addiction to carbs, it will begin to crave those foods instead. So pile on the clean, lean protein, stock your fridge with fresh veggies and hummus, and keep nuts and seeds at the ready on your countertop. They'll keep your serotonin levels even and will help keep your amped-up food-reward cycle in check. A steady supply of sugar to the brain from slow carbs actually helps your mental clarity and focus.

And as your taste buds come alive again, I'll help you work more spicy and savory foods into your diet using Cajun spices, salsas, garlic, and onions. You'll ratchet up the flavor in your foods until you can appreciate the way they burst! As a sugar addict, you may not even realize that your diet is bland. But it is! Not only because you're eating one-dimensional high SI foods, but because you've also lost your ability to truly taste. And you're missing out on a lot. You're missing bitter, like the nuance in dark chocolate, and tart, like the party on your tongue after you eat Greek yogurt. These foods and flavors will all help you transition beyond craving sweet, and only sweet.

Don't worry about letting go of your favorite foods—remember we're swapping delicious, familiar lower-SI foods for the high-SI foods you've been eating, so you won't even miss them. I'm willing to bet you like the swaps even more—for the way they taste, and the way they make you feel.

MY IMPACT!

Lorrie Valinsky
Starting weight: 180 lbs.
Current weight: 165 lbs.
Total lost: 15 lbs.

For the past 11 years, following a radical colon cancer surgery, I had to adapt my social life due to my gastrointestinal (GI) issues, especially after eating. I would meet my girlfriends for lunch, but instead of continuing the afternoon with after-lunch activities, I would beg off and head home. I was fatigued and in need of being close to a bathroom. The same held true when my husband and I went out with other couples in the evening. I could join for dinner, but not the "ands"...and a movie, a play, a concert, drinks. I accepted this as a small price to pay for having my life.

About a year ago, I was flipping TV channels and heard a woman discussing *The Virgin Diet*. I stopped flipping and started listening, and I liked what I heard. It made sense. Immediately, I downloaded the book, *The Virgin Diet,* and started my journey with JJ. I lost 32 pounds rather quickly and had improved energy and decreased joint pain. All was well until I hit the dreaded plateau. I still wanted to lose another 20 pounds, but nothing was happening. I kept eating according to the Virgin Diet, but instead of staying the course, being the sugar addict that I am, I let sugar back in my diet. I was frustrated and thought...what harm can a little sugar do? The answer is...a lot!

My joint pain returned. My energy level took a nosedive in the late afternoon. I gained back 20 of the 32 pounds I had lost. And worst of all, my chronic GI problems became increasingly debilitating. How could such a sweet, natural, innocuous thing like sugar wreak all this havoc?

I decided that I needed to get this addiction under control, once and for all. I committed to the Sugar Impact Diet and steeled myself for the inevitable headaches and moodiness that have always accompanied my previous sugar withdrawals. I started the program a week before Halloween. I wanted to challenge myself with all that good chocolate around. So I stayed in Cycle 1 for 2 weeks. The headaches and moodiness never appeared. Once I started Cycle 2, my energy level was high and even all day long, my joint pain was greatly reduced, and my GI issues improved radically. My intense sugar cravings were gone, and within 4 weeks, I lost 15 pounds and five inches each from my waist and hips!

Somewhere during Cycle 2 of the Sugar Impact Diet, I also realized that after lunch with a friend, I wasn't feeling the need to run home. I had abundant energy and no GI problems. Then my daughter came home for Thanksgiving. We decided to jump into the fray and do Black Friday at a local shopping area. We shopped for 2 hours, had lunch, then shopped for another 5 hours! We had a blast! When we got home, it dawned on me what I was able to do. When I pointed it out to my daughter, she flew across the room and hugged me saying, "That's right! I can't believe I have my old mom back!"

I am back. I feel like my old self! The Sugar Impact Diet has given me all the "ands" back in my life. This is huge!

EVERYTHING YOU NEED TO SUCCEED

You'll have everything you need to be successful on the Sugar Impact Diet, even beyond the food. This program is designed to take you through three cycles (see page xxiii–xxiv for a refresher) so that you can transition to a low-SI diet without shocking your body or succumbing to nasty cravings. If any withdrawal symptoms hit, don't try to tough them out. You don't have to! I've got lots of helpful strategies in Chapter 8 and in the Resources section on my website (http://sugarimpact.com/resources) to help get you through the first week until the withdrawal passes and you feel better than you've ever felt! In Chapters 8 and 9, I include fool-proof menu plans and delicious recipes that make it easy—and tasty—to follow the program. I've also got your back with strategies on how to handle stress (see the Supportive Supplements online at http://sugarimpact.com/resources) and eating out (see Chapter 12), and how to support your transformation with powerful exercises (see Chapter 12) that don't require hours out of your week or a gym membership.

I've designed this program to win your fight against sugar—so you can't fail! This program will help you heal your body, shatter those weight-loss plateaus, kick fast fat loss in high gear, and get you over the withdrawal hurdle, fast. Your inflammation will let up, your hormones will swing back into balance, your mood will level out, you'll finally sleep, and you'll wake up with enough energy to conquer the world. Most people feel so good they want to stick with it for life. I'm pretty sure you'll never go back, either.

2

TRACK YOUR IMPACT

Remember when you showed up to class and the teacher served up a surprise quiz that day? Arriving at this chapter may bring back that feeling. But not to worry, it will be quick and painless, and this quiz is the beginning of the path to sugar freedom.

Take a couple of minutes to fill out the Sugar Impact Quiz. This quiz has you measure some of the most common symptoms of a high Sugar Impact (SI) diet. We're going to use your score as a baseline to start the Sugar Impact Diet and for progressing through the cycles, so you'll see improvement no matter where you start. We'll also come back to it later for a reassessment to see how far you've come.

Sugar Impact Quiz				
Rate each category from 1 to 5, with 1 meaning that for you the area is a nonissue, and 5 that it's a big problem.				
Low or unstable energy 1	2	3	4	5
Sugar and carb cravings 1	2	3	4	5
Appetite 1	2	3	4	5

Poor mood and focus	1	2	3	4	5
Gas and bloating	1	2	3	4	5
Difficulty losing weight	1	2	3	4	5
Belly fat	1	2	3	4	5

If your total score is 20 or above, or you score at 4 or higher on 2 or more symptoms, you may have to extend Cycle 1 by a week to ease your transition to Cycle 2. Also consider using one or more of the Speed-Healing Techniques in Chapter 10 (page 223).

If you're struggling with chronic health conditions you also may need to spend a second week in Cycle 1 and taper more slowly so you'll be able to go through Cycle 2 with ease. Use the Sneaky Sugar Inventory in this chapter (pages 26–30) to identify where medium and high Sugar Impact foods are sneaking into your diet on a regular basis, and make these the first ones you swap out during Cycle 1.

If you're starting from the ideal place of a score of 2 or less per symptom, and 12 or less overall, good for you! You'll still see a benefit from the program, and you'll avoid these symptoms becoming an issue for you later on.

When your symptoms are right there in front of you, in black and white, it speaks volumes, doesn't it? For a lot of people, this quiz is really a wake-up call. The good news is that wherever you're starting from, the Sugar Impact Diet can help you heal and conquer sugar for good!

THE SUGAR IMPACT SCALES

I've created the Sugar Impact Scales to be your cheat sheets and take the thinking out of this for you. You can eat and shop with blissful abandon, knowing I've got your back.

The Sugar Impact Quiz no doubt made it very clear that now is the time for a change. You're not feeling as good as you could, and you're carrying around stubborn extra pounds you can't hide, pounds that take their toll on your self-esteem every day. Without making a change, your situation won't change, either, and it could very well get worse. Every journey begins with the first step. And the first step here is to figure out where the sugar in your diet is coming from.

The Sugar Impact Scale takes into account a food's fructose (in grams), nutrient density, and fiber, as well as its glycemic load, a measurement of how the food affects your blood sugar levels (more on the glycemic index and glycemic load on page 32). Fiber and nutrients are positives that can downshift the effects of high fructose and glycemic load. And, of course, dose matters—the glycemic load is also based on average serving size.

This scale is a simple and easy way of categorizing foods according to their overall impact on your blood sugar—high, medium, or low. Think of low-SI foods as "green." You're good to go on these foods; eat them regularly. Consider the medium-SI foods yellow, so proceed with caution and incorporate only the amount you can have and still feel great. (I'll walk you through the best way to taper medium-SI foods out of your diet in Cycle 1, and then I'll explain how to figure out the right amount for you to eat long term in Cycle 3.) When it comes to high-SI foods, you guessed it—stop! Think of them as red. Eat and drink them as a rare treat, and even when you do, you're likely to feel it. And not in a good way.

Here's the shorthand:

- High SI—stop!
- Medium SI—proceed with caution
- Low SI—go!

I've also pinpointed seven food groups where hidden sugars tend to be an issue. Some of these may surprise you:

- Grains
- Roots
- Packaged fruit
- Low and no-fat dairy and diet foods
- Sauces, dressings, and condiments
- Sweet drinks
- Sweeteners and added sugar

Within each of these seven categories, I've ranked foods according to the Sugar Impact Scales, so that you'll know just which high-SI foods to trade for low- to medium-SI options. I go into more detail about the seven foods and provide Sugar Impact Scales for each food in Part II of the book. (They are also available online at http://sugarimpact.com/resources.)

HOW THE PROGRAM WORKS: UNDERSTANDING THE THREE CYCLES

The Sugar Impact Diet is designed to help you gradually shift from a high-SI diet to a low-SI diet. It's essential that you transition your diet gradually to avoid withdrawal and cravings that can set you back, which is why there are three cycles in the program. Here's how they work.

Cycle 1—Taper

The first step is to identify what's sabotaging your weight and health. Where are the sugar landmines in your diet? You'll figure that out by taking the Sneaky Sugar Inventory (pages 26–30). Once you pinpoint the sneaky sugars that are sabotaging your health, this cycle will help you step away from them slowly, easing you from high-SI foods to medium-SI foods.

Be prepared: the Sneaky Sugar Inventory is an eye-opener. It even shocked me. And I thought I had my SI in check! But there it was...piling up in my diet in innocent-looking fruit, sundried tomatoes, and balsamic dressing.

What's great is that it doesn't matter where you start out—you can always improve. You'll make a big jump or a lot of little ones, but any size step makes a difference, especially when it comes to everyday habits. And remember—you're not going cold turkey! You're going to *trade and taper* with swaps. Nothing is cut from your diet without being replaced. Don't be surprised if you like the swaps better anyway—doesn't a sauce made with fresh tomatoes, basil, and olive oil sound a heck of a lot better than a sugar-filled jar of boring marinara?

Depending on where you start on the Sugar Impact Quiz, you'll spend 1 or 2 weeks in Cycle 1. This time is necessary to lay the groundwork for Cycle 2. As you swap high-SI foods for medium-SI foods, you'll begin your shift from sugar burner to fat burner—and seeing the change in your energy levels and on the scale will be the motivation you need to stay on the plan until you're ready to move to Cycle 2.

Cycle 2—Transition

These are the weeks you'll see the weight fall off and you'll truly reset your body and taste buds after years of eating the wrong way. During Cycle 2 you'll swap medium-SI foods for low-SI foods, and your metabolism will shift from burning sugar to burning fat! And to keep your motivation high, you'll be losing weight— specifically losing fat— quickly.

> *Your metabolism will shift from burning sugar to burning fat!*

The average person loses 10 pounds during these 2 weeks! As the weight melts off, you're letting your taste buds come back to life and you're retraining them to appreciate what natural sweetness really means.

Cycle 3—Transformed!

By the time you get to Cycle 3, you'll feel like a new person— you'll be lighter, more energetic, and more in tune with how your body is designed to eat. Many of my clients feel so great by the time they get to Cycle 3 that they don't want to reintroduce any high-SI foods! But the last thing I want is for you to gradually slip back into your old high-SI habits over time, and that's where Cycle 3 comes in. This cycle is all about customizing the program to your body and your long-term goals. Using the Sugar Impact Quiz, you'll determine how much sugar you can handle on a daily basis without unraveling all your progress and without losing the great feeling that comes with low-SI living. Your quiz results will help you create a maintenance program that works specifically for you and builds on your success going forward.

SUGAR HIDE AND SEEK

To begin your Sugar Impact Diet journey, you'll need to take stock of where you are. Your starting place will help map a path forward that's tailored specifically to your needs. So go through this Sneaky Sugar Inventory and make a note of which foods you eat regularly. Once you've identified them, you'll use the Sugar Impact Scales to swap them out. In just 2 weeks, you'll see weight come off fast, and you'll be on your way to reclaiming your health and life. Pencils ready? Go!

Sneaky Sugar Inventory		
Circle any food or food ingredient eaten in the last week.		
Acesulfame-K	Amaranth flour	Asian dressing
Agave	Animal crackers	Aspartame
Almond milk ice cream	Apples	Baked beans
Amaranth	Apricots	Balsamic vinaigrette

Balsamic vinegar

Banana

Barley

BBQ sauce

Bean chips

Beer

Beet juice

Beets

Biscotti

Black bean flour

Blue cheese dressing

Brandy

Bread and butter
    pickles

Breakfast bars

Brown rice

Brown sauce

Brown sugar

Buckwheat

Buckwheat flour

Caesar dressing

Cakes and pies

Candy

Cane syrup

Canned fruit cocktail

Capri Sun

Caramel sauce

Carnation Instant
    Breakfast

Carrot juice

Catalina dressing

Cereals

Champagne

Cherries

Chocolate syrup

Cocktail sauce

Coconut milk creamer,
    sweetened

Coconut milk ice cream
    (sweetened)

Coconut palm sugar

Coconut sugar

Coffee creamers
    (refrigerated or dry)

Commercial "smoothies"

Cookies

Cool Whip and Lite
    Cool Whip

Corn

Corn cereals

Corn chips

Corn syrup

Corn tortillas

Cornstarch

Couscous

Crackers

Cream cheese spread

Cream of Wheat

Creamsicles

Crystal Light

Crystalline fructose

Cyclamates

Dates

Diet soda

Dried fruit snacks

Energy bars

English muffins

"Enhanced" waters
    (with sweeteners)

Ensure

Farro

Fat-free baked chips

Fat-free muffin mix

Fat-free or sugar-free
    Jell-O

Fat-free pudding

Fat-free Twizzlers

Fava bean flour

Fermented soy

Fish sauce

Flavored almond milk
    yogurt

Flavored coconut
    yogurt

Flavored kefirs

French dressing

French fries

Fresh figs

Frozen yogurt

Fruit added cream
    cheese

Fruit juice concentrates

Fruit juice Popsicles

Fruit juices

Fruit leather

Fudgesicles

Fuze

Garbanzo flour

Gatorade

Gelato

Gin

Glazed nuts

Glucose

Gluten-free beer

Gluten-free flour

Graham crackers

Granola bars

Grapes

Green curry sauce

Grits

Half-and-half

High-fructose corn syrup

Hoisin

Honey

Honey mustard

Honey mustard dressing

Honey roasted peanuts

Honeydew

Hot and sour sauce

Hot cocoa

Ice cream

Ice cream sandwiches

Instant oatmeal

Instant rice

Italian dressing

Jams

Ketchup

Kiwi

Kombucha tea

Kool-Aid

Lentil chips

Low-fat cheeses

Low-fat cream cheese
    spread

Low-fat graham crackers

Low-fat or fat-free ice
    cream bars

Low-fat or fat-free Ice
    Dream

Low-fat or light frozen
    dinners: Lean Cuisine,
    Lean Pockets, Lean
    Gourmet, etc.

Low-fat Oreos

Low-fat plain yogurt

Macaroni and cheese

Maltodextrin

Mango

Mannitol

Maple syrup

Marinara sauce

Marshmallows

Mashed potatoes

Matzoh

Milk chocolate

Millet

Millet flour

Mixed drinks

Molasses

Mousse

Muesli

Muffins

Mung bean noodles

Nectar

Neotame

Nestlé's Quik

Neufchatel cheese

Non-fat cheeses

Non-fat cream cheese

Non-fat plain yogurt

Nut chips

Oyster crackers

Papaya

Parsnips

Part-skim mozzarella

Part-skim ricotta

Pastas

Peanut sauce

Pears

Pickle relish

Pineapple

Pineapple cottage
    cheese

Pita

Plain coconut yogurt
    (sweetened)

Plums

Polenta

Pomegranate

Popcorn

Pop-Tarts

Port

Potato chips

Potato starch

PowerAde

Preserves

Pretzels

Pudding

Puffed millet

Puffed rice

Quick breads

Quinoa flakes

Quinoa flour

Quinoa pastas

Ranch dressing

Raspberry vinaigrette

Red curry sauce

Reduced-fat cookies

Reduced-fat crackers

Reduced-fat macaroni and cheese

Reduced-fat peanut butter

Reduced-fat Pringles

Rice cakes

Rice chips

Rice crackers

Rice flour

Rice pasta

Rice syrup

Rice tortillas

Risotto

Rockstar energy drink

Root veggie chips

Rum

Rutabaga

Saccharin

Scones

SlimFast

Snack packs

SnackWells low-fat and fat-free cookies and treats

Sobe

Soda

Sorbet

Sorbitol

Soy cheeses

Splenda

Sprouted whole grain breads

Steak sauce

Strawberry cream cheese

Sucralose

Sun-dried tomatoes

Sweet chili

Sweet pickle relish

Sweet pickles

Sweet potato fries

Sweet potatoes

Sweet tea

Sweetened coconut water

Sweetened cows' milks (vanilla, chocolate)

Sweetened dairy-free milks

Sweetened nut butters

Sweetened whipped cream

Tangerines

Tartar sauce

Tequila

Teriyaki sauce

Thousand Island dressing

Tomato juice

Tomato paste

Tomato sauce

Tortillas

Unsweetened rice milk

Unsweetened soy milk

V8 juice

Vitaminwater

Vodka

Wasa crackers

Water crackers

Watermelon

Wheat breads

Whipped cream cheese

White flour products

White potatoes

Whole grain cereal

Wine

Worcestershire sauce

Yams

Yogurts with sugar or artificial sweeteners

<85% dark chocolate

94% fat-free microwave kettlecorn

94% fat-free microwave popcorn

HOW DID YOU DO?

Now that you've given it the once-over, tell me—how many foods on this list are you eating every week? Every day? Well, guess what? You're far from alone.

After decades of a misguided information-assault and billions of dollars in advertising that seems to find us when we sleep, here's a look at a day in the life of "healthy" eating as an average American:

Yawn, stretch. What's for breakfast? Oh, look! It's instant oatmeal or fruit yogurt with wheat toast and orange juice. Yum. Maybe a snack mid-morning, but just a protein bar. So far so good. And for lunch, it's a salad. How about the one with raspberry vinaigrette, glazed walnuts, dried cranberries, and a pita wedge? And, of course, diet soda. Dinner? Everyone loves pasta! Thank goodness there are healthy pasta choices. Whole wheat pasta and canned marinara sauce it is.

During a day like that, this is what the average American body registers:

Breakfast—sugar
Lunch—sugar
Dinner—sugar

If there were a sugar seismograph in your body, it would be scratching out a catastrophic event at every meal. But how could you know? That's the way we've all been taught to eat for most of our lives. It's just one more reason it's so important to understand where sugar hides, how it's metabolized and, most important, that you can actually reset your sugar sensitivity. When that happens, you'll be more attuned to subtler, naturally occurring sugars, and your cravings for sickeningly sweet sweets will be gone for good.

You can reset your sugar sensitivity.

GAUGING SUGAR'S IMPACT

If anyone ever tries to tell you "sugar is sugar," you can leave them where they stand, right there in 1999. All sugars are not created equal, especially when it comes to the major differences in how your body processes each one.

Unless you only eat meat (and I don't recommend that, you're not a jungle cat), you're going to get some sugar in your diet. And not just from sweet things. Even green, non-starchy veggies and raw nuts contain a little sugar. Ideally, you should focus on eating whole foods, which means there are no added sugars. For processed foods, my rule is that food should have no more than 5 grams of *added* sugar per 100-calorie serving (and the less the better, of course). And, of course, it goes without saying (but I figured I might as well) that I mean the healthier, least-processed choices here.

As you learned in Chapter 1, food is information, and from here on out you're going to look at carbohydrates differently. All carbs except straight fiber will end up as sugar. You're going to evaluate them based on their overall impact on you: Do they create steady, sustained energy, or spike and crash it? Do they slowly raise blood sugar or send it on a ride? Do they keep you satisfied or make you hungrier?

The SI of a food is determined by a variety of factors: its glycemic load (a measure of how much a serving of food changes your blood sugar levels—see page 33 for more on this), fructose levels, nutrient density, and fiber. The Sugar Impact Scales take all of this into account. Your body's response to a high-SI food, in turn, is governed by your metabolic health, which is directly a result of how high an SI diet you've been eating and for how long. That's what influences your degree of sugar sensitivity.

And, by the way, no one is immune from sugar's impact—given enough time and exposure, we'll all

No one is immune from sugar's impact.

become insensitive to it. You can take measures to protect yourself with quality sleep, good stress management, and regular exercise. But the single most effective thing you can do to reverse the damage sugar has already done and to increase your immunity to it going forward is to make sure you eat food that's low on the SI Scales. When you do, you'll reset your sugar sensitivity—in just 2 weeks!

THE GLYCEMIC INDEX

The foods you eat on the Sugar Impact Diet create a slow, steady rise in blood sugar. Among other things, they've been chosen based on the source of the sugar in them, which will give you some information about its impact. That brings me to the glycemic index (GI).

The GI is a rating system designed to measure how much the food you eat affects your blood sugar levels. Pure glucose is ranked highest, at 100, and all other foods are measured accordingly. The higher its glycemic rating, the greater the effect a food will have on your blood sugar. The best choice to keep your blood sugar levels balanced is to stick to lower glycemic foods.

Some fruits, most veggies, lentils, and hummus with raw vegetables are all low on the GI scale. Higher-glycemic fruits like bananas and grapes can raise blood sugar pretty quickly because they have more sugar and less fiber than other fruits, like berries.

So the glycemic index can be useful, within limits. The problem is that the GI makes fructose look like an angel. That's because fructose doesn't raise your blood sugar or insulin, so according to the GI it should be a great and healthy choice. But we know it's anything but.

The glycemic index also doesn't take quantity into account, which is an issue. All foods on the glycemic index are measured using the same amount—it doesn't use realistic serving sizes. Potatoes, beets, and carrots are all high on the glycemic index. But it's easier to eat a lot of potatoes in one sitting than a lot of carrots, right? That's why the glycemic load is a better tool.

THE GLYCEMIC LOAD

The glycemic load (GL) uses the glycemic index as its foundation. Then it takes serving size—the amount you eat—into account. That makes perfect sense, right? The amount of a food you eat also matters.

GL, like the GI, uses a numerical ranking system to assess how much a food will raise your blood glucose level after eating it. It's calculated by multiplying the GI of a food by the amount of carbohydrate being consumed, and dividing the total by 100.

Let's say a carrot has a GI of 92 and 6 grams of carbohydrates. Its GL, then, is 92 × 6/100, or 5.52. Mashed potatoes, on the other hand, have a GI of 83 with 20 grams of carbohydrates, so the GL is 83 × 20/100, or 16.6. Just as with the GI, the lower the GL, the better.

Now, at least, we're taking the dose of sugar into account. But we're not there yet.

FRUCTOSE HAS US PEGGED

The amount of fructose in a food can have a big influence on its SI. When you eat fructose, you bypass every one of your body's satiety safety nets, and your system functions in reverse. Your appetite switch is pegged in the on position, and it causes you to overeat. And worse yet, you're storing that fructose as fat. So now you're fat, overweight, *and* hungry! I assume you don't want to be good at storing fat and being hungry, right? What a nightmare! Let's put that thought right out of our minds.

The good news is that the less fructose you eat, the less fat you store! When you reduce fructose, you can restore your sugar sensitivity very quickly, which means you'll get rid of your cravings, you'll appreciate the natural sweetness of whole fruits, and you'll naturally want to avoid foods that taste too sweet. Best of all, you'll get those results fast.

FIBER AND NUTRIENTS

I'll get more into the nutritional role of fiber in the next chapter, but let me touch on its role in SI here. Consider the difference between a carrot and carrot juice, an orange and orange juice. Don't you think the sugar in the juices will have a slightly different impact on your system than the whole food? Of course it will!

A cup of blueberries has 15 grams of sugar, and that's a lot (by comparison, a cup of raspberries has just over 5 grams and the same amount of strawberries has about 7 grams). But berries are low on the glycemic index, and provide a slow, steady rise in blood sugar that won't trigger a dramatic insulin response. How's that possible? The answer is fiber.

Nature packed blueberries and other fruits with nutrients, fiber, antioxidants, and all kinds of other goodness that cumulatively lower the SI on your body. The fiber and nutrients in blueberries are the reason they're relatively low on the glycemic index, despite their sugar content. In fact, studies show blueberries can actually help normalize blood sugar levels and reduce your risk for diabetes. In 2006, a study in the journal *Phytomedicine* demonstrated that extracts of the Canadian blueberry have promise as a complementary anti-diabetic therapy. Vitamin C in fruit acts as an antioxidant that specifically improves insulin sensitivity and insulin's ability to get glucose out of the bloodstream.

The phytonutrients and fiber in nature's foods change the way your body deals with sugar.

The phytonutrients and fiber in nature's foods change the way your body deals with sugar. Even high-GI fruits like dates and watermelon and higher-sugar tubers and starchy carbs like sweet potatoes and beets have phytonutrients and fiber, so you don't want to cut them out of your diet completely. I'll arm you with all the info you need on how much of them you can eat, and how often, in Part II with my at-a-glance Sugar Impact Scale lists.

SUGAR HIDES IN PLAIN SIGHT

Sugar is right under our noses, popping up on labels with more than 55 "fake IDs." That hardly seems fair! Here's a look at some of the masqueraders.

The Many Names for Sugar

Barley malt	Fructose
Beet sugar	Fruit juice
Brown sugar	Fruit juice concentrate
Buttered syrup	Galactose
Cane juice crystals	Glucose
Cane sugar	Glucose solids
Caramel	Golden sugar
Carob syrup	Golden syrup
Castor sugar	Grape sugar
Confectioners' sugar	High-fructose corn syrup
Corn syrup	Honey
Corn syrup solids	Icing sugar
Date sugar	Invert sugar
Demerara sugar	Lactose
Dextran	Malt syrup
Dextrose	Maltodextrin
Diastatic malt	Maltose
Diatase	Maple syrup
Ethyl maltol	Molasses

Muscovado sugar

Panocha

Raw sugar

Refiner's syrup

Rice syrup

Sorbitol

Sorghum syrup

Sucrose

Sugar

Treacle

Turbinado sugar

Yellow sugar

The Many Names for Artificial Sweeteners

Acesulfame potassium

Alitame

Aspartame

Aspartame–acesulfame salt

Cyclamate

Isomalt

Neohesperidin
     dihydrochalcone

NutraSweet

Saccharin

Splenda

Sucralose

You can make huge gains toward your health and weight-loss goals just by identifying added sugar in the food you're currently eating and beginning to cut those foods—and that sugar—out.

> *You'll notice a visible difference in the way you look and feel in just 2 weeks!*

When you also manage the amount of naturally occurring sugar you're eating, mostly in fruits, juices, roots, and grains, you're going to shoot your energy and weight loss to the next level, fast. On my plan, you'll notice a visible difference in the way you look and feel in just 2 weeks!

NO-SUGAR-ADDED AND SUGAR-FREE FOODS

Let's be honest. You get excited when you see that sparkly starburst on the box telling you there's been no sugar added to those fruit roll-ups. Well, I'll be delicate here. They're taking some poetic license—with your health. Manufacturers give you some credit, and they know that if you saw a box that read "21 teaspoons of added sugar for your metabolic upheaval!" you might think twice. So they've spent a lot of time and money testing ways to get around your sensible objections so they can manipulate you into buying as much of what they're selling as possible, guilt and worry-free. They've made all your favorite treats "without added sugar," so you could have your cake and eat it, too. It's a little like the magician's equivalent of "Look over here at this shiny object!"

And just because a manufacturer labels a food or drink "no added sugar," that in no way means that it doesn't *contain* sugar. No added sugar does not mean sugar-free. It can also mean they've used fruit juice concentrate as their sweetener. That's essentially fructose without the fiber. And remember, white flour will end up as sugar anyway, so many of the ingredients in your no-sugar-added cookie will turn into sugar as soon as you start munching.

> *No added sugar does not mean sugar-free.*

> *Many of the ingredients in your no-sugar-added cookie will turn into sugar as soon as you start munching.*

Labels can be misleading. You don't see labels on fruits and vegetables or nuts and seeds, do you?

MY IMPACT!

Pia Civiletti
Starting Weight: 143 lbs.
Current Weight: 130 lbs.
Total Lost: 13 lbs.

Wow, I used to eat so much sugar, and food in general, and

I did not even realize it. I was diagnosed with hypoglycemia in 1996 and have struggled with the daily ups and downs of how my body processed sugar. If I ate a heavy lunch, my head would practically be on my desk by 3 p.m. I typically would eat constantly, but even if I was eating healthy foods, it was way too much food for my body, leaving me chubby and lethargic. I had frequent gas and bloating, and I had trouble digesting some vegetables. My endocrine system was burning out. I just felt big, fat, and tired.

Eating very low amounts of sugar has allowed my body to go back to doing what it needs to: get rid of extra weight and digest foods better. I don't really miss the sugar either—that includes the bread, pasta, and fruit. I am not craving anything, so I don't feel deprived. Losing weight has been easy and pretty effortless, and I've really enjoyed it. I feel light, sexy, and younger. I am wearing clothes that I would never even pull out of the closet. I am wearing my skinny jeans and can see my hip bones!

I was tickled pink the other day when my son said he noticed how skinny I was getting. Friends are noticing that I am losing weight and saying how great I look. My energy and ambition has increased and I just want to go, go, go…make some changes and get moving. Sitting on my big butt really had me sitting on my proverbial butt as well.

Sugar really had a hold on me, but now I am the boss, and my body knows it. I don't feel fat anymore, nor do I feel like an aging woman having to accept the extra weight and Rubenesque look I was sporting. I have done a lot of diets and detoxes and also hold a certification in health coaching, but this program holds a crucial piece of the puzzle. There is something about the Sugar Impact Diet that just makes it so easy to lose the weight. The other diets make you dread having to give something up. On this program, I don't feel like I'm giving anything up—except the unwanted pounds!

VOLUME AND IMPACT

No doubt you're dying to know: How much sugar am I *really* eating? And you're probably wondering how much you *should* be eating.

Well, to really make the about-face in your weight, your energy, and the symptoms of inflammation and depression you battle every day, you're probably catching on that it's not only the amount of sugar you're eating that should concern you. You also need to make the kinds of sugars you consume and their impact a priority.

The American Heart Association says added sugars should only be 5% of your daily discretionary calories. In a measurement that's a bit easier to understand, in 2009 a paper published in the journal *Circulation* established the limit as 5 teaspoons of added sugar for women and 9 teaspoons for men. The important distinction here is *added* sugar, which means they aren't including refined grains, fruit juice, and other foods that have a high SI.

The reality is that, according to National Health and Nutrition Examination Survey data published in *JAMA*, any given one of us is averaging 21.4 teaspoons of added sugar a day (and the 2009 *Circulation* paper cites a survey that put it at 22.2 teaspoons a day). Sadly, the highest consumption is among 14- to 18-year-olds, who average a *yikes*-inducing 34 teaspoons every day. Not so coincidentally, children are now being diagnosed with diabetes at an astronomical rate. It's jumped more than 20% since 2001. A SEARCH for Diabetes in Youth Study funded by the Centers for Disease Control and Prevention found that of almost 3.5 million people under 20 years old in 2009, just over 7,500 had diabetes, including 6,668 with type 1 diabetes and 837 with type 2 diabetes.

The good news is that symptoms of type 2 diabetes can be (totally!) turned around. Those children—and you—can avoid a miserable lifetime battle with weight, debilitating conditions, and medications with just a few simple changes to what you eat.

According to Dr. Robert Lustig, the pioneer in fructose research we introduced in Chapter 1, 50 grams of sugar (10 teaspoons), with 25 grams being fructose from fruits and vegetables, is a reasonable daily amount. Ideally that comes from whole foods. Remember, you have to count all the sugar you're consuming, not just the extra table sugar you're sprinkling on your cereal!

Even if you're a vegetarian, which is regarded by most measures as a pretty healthy way of eating, you're often consuming exponentially more sugar than you know, especially if you're also trying to follow a low-fat diet. You're probably opting for high-carb options in the absence of meat, and high-carb is high sugar. (Don't stress if you're a vegetarian—you can get great results from this program, too!)

High-carb is high sugar.

CHANGE YOUR IMPACT!

You've tracked your impact—now it's time to change it. Don't panic! Remember, this program isn't about deprivation, and you'll be gradually decreasing your SI to avoid feelings of withdrawal and cravings. You'll begin by simply trading high-SI foods for medium-SI choices, and then medium-SI for low-SI foods. You'll make the most sizeable impact when you switch away from the foods with added sugar or sweeteners, but I'll also be here to help ensure you don't fall prey to the trap of believing all whole foods are created equal, either. I'll guide you to the best choices, keep you away from the worst, and let you know how much you can have of each, so you see a big difference—fast!

3

THE SUGAR IMPACT PLATE

I'm all about giving you the tools you need to succeed. Getting you off high Sugar Impact (SI) foods is too important—in fact, it's no exaggeration to say it's a matter of life and death. So you bring the commitment, I'll bring the strategies, and together we're going to crush

Together we're going to crush your sugar addiction.

your sugar addiction, get rid of the extra pounds you've been lugging around, and get you back in the game, feeling great.

One of the most powerful tools is the Sugar Impact Plate. It's set up to improve satiety, reduce hunger between meals, create steady sustained energy and focus, and help you burn fat for fuel. It's your first step in transitioning from a sugar burner to a fat burner. I'll get into each part of the plate in detail later so you'll understand its purpose.

When you eat according to the Sugar Impact Plate, with balanced meals of clean, lean protein, healthy fats, colorful non-starchy veggies, and some slow carbs, you're not going to be chased by cravings all day, and you'll eat less overall. Plus, what you do eat will be food that heals and honors your body, and burns fat fast.

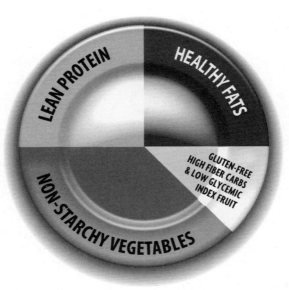

The Sugar Impact Plate

UNDERSTANDING THE SUGAR IMPACT PLATE

I've talked a lot about how this book will help you transition from higher-SI foods to lower-SI foods. But food quality matters, too. And it's worth understanding how all of the major food players work together to support you and get you to the finish line faster.

Each macronutrient—protein, fat, or carbohydrate—creates its own hormonal response, depending on the quality, timing, and amount you eat. Carbs are a source of energy, and they trigger the release of insulin to help absorb glucose from your blood and move it into your cells, where it's stored as glycogen or fat. Proteins are the building blocks of lean muscle tissue, and they support satiety by slowing down stomach emptying, which keeps ghrelin, the hunger hormone, suppressed. Fat releases chemicals in the small intestine that tell your brain you are full.

But we don't typically eat foods in isolation, so what really matters is what happens when those macronutrients are combined. That's why the Sugar Impact Plate is so important. You may remember that refined sugar by itself is a bad thing (especially liquid sugars like juice and soda), but you should avoid processed foods with added sugar and fat *together* at all costs—it's a fat-storing, metabolically toxic combo.

> *Sugar and fat together in processed foods is a fat-storing, metabolically toxic combo.*

Meanwhile, your body's reaction is further impacted by your own personal chemistry lab. If you're diabetic or insulin-resistant, eating certain foods can change you chemically for the worse in a hurry. The good news is that the Sugar Impact Diet will heal your metabolism quickly—all by eating from the Sugar Impact Plate and living by the Sugar Impact Clock, a guide for meal timing to keep your blood sugar nice

> *The Sugar Impact Diet will heal your metabolism quickly.*

and even (more about the Sugar Impact Clock later in this chapter). Your body is amazing, and it will heal fast with the right input!

PROTEIN: THE BUILDING BLOCK YOUR BODY NEEDS

One of the fastest ways to calm your sugar cravings is by eating protein. It's fairly common knowledge that protein is great for filling you up and keeping you satisfied, but did you know that it can actually decrease your cravings, too? It puts the brakes on our neuronal reward system, the brain chemicals that make us feel good and motivate us to get more food, even when we're not hungry. When we're low in protein, cravings take over and crack the whip in search of a quick fix.

Protein is made up of amino acids, the building blocks your

body needs to make muscle, hormones, and neurotransmitters, and that help you have great hair, skin, and nails and healthy bones. They're in every tissue in your body. Your body is able to create some amino acids on its own, but there are key amino acids in protein—called essential amino acids—that can only come from food, which is why protein is so important to your health and such a key part of the Sugar Impact Diet.

When a sugar craving hits, your body is really crying out for protein. Many times when a sugar craving hits, your body is really crying out for protein. When you're low in protein, your system knows it needs energy, and you crave foods that will give you fuel fast. But a refined high-carb treat is only going to raise your blood sugar and trigger an insulin response, which shuts off fat-burning. If you reach for protein instead, it will actually help curb cravings for sweets by giving your body the kind of sustained energy it really needs. By eating protein, you can outsmart your sweet tooth!

Protein only minimally impacts blood sugar and doesn't create a big insulin spike. That's because when you eat protein, your pancreas responds by releasing the hormones glucagon and insulin, which help stabilize blood sugar. Insulin's job is to lower your blood sugar by driving glucose into your cells. Once it's done its job, glucagon makes sure your blood sugar doesn't get too low (and you don't get too cranky) so it raises your blood sugar by driving glycogen, or stored sugar, out of your cells. That's what you want!

GETTING ENOUGH PROTEIN

Even if you're eating enough protein, you may not be assimilating it well. You can interfere with its absorption if you're a speed eater, if you drink too much fluid with your meals, if you don't chew enough, or if you've got low stomach acid. Low stomach acid is a real concern if you're over 30 or under stress or—worse yet—both. And if you're taking acid blockers, you're lowering the stomach acid needed to break down your protein.

So clearly, your goal is to be sure you're eating enough protein and digesting it well. I'll get into specific portions for women, men, athletes, and vegans and vegetarians in Chapter 8, but in general, every meal should include 1 serving of clean, lean protein (4–6 ounces of fish, chicken, turkey, or grass-fed beef for women, 6–8 ounces for men). Vegans and vegetarians—hang on, I'll be back to you in a moment.

In general, the average woman should get 75–80 grams of protein a day, and most men should get 100–120 grams a day. This is based on average size—160 pounds for a woman and 200 pounds for a man. Your protein requirement isn't static, though. Your weight and body composition will influence the amount of protein you need. It will increase if you're under stress, if you're healing, and if you're doing some heavy resistance training (I'm talking to you, CrossFitters!).

The best protein sources are animal protein, and not just any animal protein. Choose organic, free-range, cage-free, grass-fed, and no-hormones-added sources whenever possible. When you choose fish, avoid farm-raised fish and fish at risk for medium or high levels of the toxic heavy metal mercury, like orange roughy and swordfish (see page 170 for a helpful list).

YOU ARE WHAT YOU EAT

One of the things you'll notice about this program is that it's going to encourage you to eat more whole foods, the way nature intended. But sadly, not all of the meat, fish and poultry you eat today—foods you might consider to be healthy, natural foods—are as healthy for you as you think they are. You not only are what you eat, but you are what you eat, ate.

I'll use grass-fed beef as an example. Cows are biologically designed to eat grass and forage. That's it. So when you buy and eat meat from a cow that's only ever been fed what it's naturally meant to eat, you benefit from the purity of the food in that chain. When you don't ensure your cow was grass-fed, it's more than likely that you're getting your meat from an animal that was fed corn, a foreign food source for them. In fact, they're fed corn specifically to fatten them up. Big leap coming here—what do you think that corn in their diet is doing to you?

And many corn-fed cows aren't just fed any corn, they're munching on genetically modified corn that has been altered to withstand pests and pesticides. So there goes any diligence you've had about keeping genetically modified organisms (GMOs) out of *your* diet. Many are also being pumped full of antibiotics to protect them from the damage their overly acidic diet is doing to their gut and to keep them from succumbing to disease in the filthy close quarters some of them are forced to endure. Plus they're often given growth hormones so they produce more meat and get to the dinner table faster. Make no mistake about it—their stress becomes your stress. And this is true for all factory animals. When they're stressed, their stress hormones increase and end up in the meat you eat.

Grass-fed cows get better food and have a higher quality of life, which equates to less stress for them and you. They also have higher omega-3 fatty acids, higher levels of B_{12}, other B vitamins, and trace minerals like magnesium and calcium. Just by letting a cow be happy and allowing it to eat what it wants to eat, you'll get all that goodness in you. So always choose meat from an animal that was fed its native diet—it's best for you, too. And supporting farmers who treat their animals humanely is simply the right thing to do.

IF YOU'RE VEGAN OR VEGETARIAN

I've included vegetarian/vegan protein powder on my list of protein sources, but unless you're a vegetarian or vegan for spiritual reasons, I personally don't advocate getting all your protein from plant-based sources. When you do, you have to eat either a lot of carbohydrates or a lot of fat to get the protein you need. If you can't be swayed, be extra diligent about including protein powder, legumes (especially lentils), quinoa, nuts, or seeds at each meal. Also, please be sure to take a B_{12} supplement (B_{12} is only available to us naturally in animal-based food) and an algae-based omega-3 DHA/EPA supplement as well.

Protein
JJ's Top 10
1. Wild salmon
2. Wild Alaskan halibut
3. Grass-fed beef—all types
4. Virgin Diet All-in-One Shake or protein shake powder per my specifications—see page 176
5. Sardines
6. Wild scallops
7. Pastured eggs
8. Grass-fed bison
9. Grass-fed lamb
10. Pastured chicken breast

Food Intolerances

If you have a food intolerance, you may lack an enzyme to digest a certain food well, as with lactose intolerance. Or you may just have a sensitivity to a food, so it creates low-grade symptoms over time, such as fatigue, digestive unrest, and joint pain. Food intolerance is very different from a true food allergy, which is rare but can cause an immediate, scary physical reaction, as happens when someone allergic to peanuts takes a whiff of one and their throat starts closing up.

Some foods are more notorious for causing food intolerances, like eggs, dairy, and gluten. I've listed pastured eggs as a good source of clean protein, and I've included dairy foods in this book in the recipes, but you know your body best. If you suspect that you have any issues eating these foods, avoid them! Choose another option—it's as simple as that.

JJ's Worst 10

1. Commercial hot dogs
2. Soy burgers
3. Soy hot dogs
4. Factory-raised 80% ground beef
5. Commercial bacon
6. BBQ-sauced pork ribs
7. Honey-glazed ham
8. Chicken fingers
9. Farmed salmon
10. Bologna

Do You Need Enzymes?

If you have digestive issues like heartburn or gas and bloating after you eat, you may need the support of a digestive enzyme supplement. Our body's own digestive enzymes, especially our stomach's hydrochloric acid secretion, slow down by the time we're in our thirties, which means we have more problems breaking down our food. If you're experiencing the fallout from that with symptoms after you eat, you may be tempted to self-medicate. Let me tell you, you're not doing yourself any favors by popping antacids. Overuse of antacids can push your hydrochloric acid levels even lower and make your digestive issues worse. When you're not digesting your food well, you're also not absorbing nutrients, so you can be setting yourself up for vitamin deficiencies, too.

Highly reactive foods, especially high-SI foods, trigger indigestion, leaky gut, inflammation, bloating, cramping, and other gut-related issues. You need to give your gut a chance to heal. Moving to low-SI foods will help you do that, but you might need some reinforcements, including probiotics, antimicrobial herbs, fermented foods, and digestive enzymes to attack your symptoms and get your digestion humming again.

FAT: YOU NEED TO EAT FAT TO BURN FAT

Fat doesn't make you fat; sugar makes you fat. So connect those dots—a high-sugar diet is actually a high-

> *Fat doesn't make you fat; sugar makes you fat.*

fat diet. I'm not asking you to tattoo that somewhere, but you should know it as if you had. There are many reasons to start calling fat your friend. For one, it helps curb your cravings for sugar and fast carbs.

Here's another big reason—fat doesn't raise your insulin levels at all. As you just learned, protein can raise insulin a little, and fast carbs can raise it a whole lot more. But insulin doesn't acknowledge fat, and that's just the way you want it. When your body digests fat, it breaks it down into monoglycerides and free fatty acids, which are absorbed by your small intestine and then connected to form triglycerides. Just as oil and water don't mix, triglycerides slide through your bloodstream without being absorbed. They connect to other fat, protein, and cholesterol molecules to form lipopro-teins or water-soluble molecules that act as shuttles moving these triglycerides around. Once the lipoproteins arrive where they're meant to be, they break down in one of three ways:

1. they become stored as fatty acids in your liver
2. they become a source of energy for muscles
3. they get stored as fat.

HOW TO GET RESULT #2

The quick answer is to eat the right kind of fats! Healthy fats like avocado and olive oil reduce your appetite and stabilize your blood sugar by slowing the release of sugar into your bloodstream. Because you don't trigger a surge of insulin, your blood sugar doesn't drop too low. That means you're not starving and tortured by more cravings almost as soon as you've eaten, like you are when you eat sugar. When fat moves through your small intestine, it triggers satiety signals that tell your brain you're full.

Our bodies thrive on good fats; they've been an essential com-ponent to our diet—and brain health—for millions of years. When you're on a diet rich in healthy fats, you'll lose more weight, lower your triglycerides, raise your large fluffy HDL cholesterol, and reduce inflammation, which means you're lowering your risk for chronic disease.

But watch out for fats that take aim at your health and waistline, like damaged fats and trans fats. I think of trans fat as the artificial sweeteners of the fat world. They're manufactured by pumping hydrogen ions into polyunsaturated fats to make them shelf sta-ble (getting suspicious yet?). These modified fats actually increase your small dense LDL particles, or bad cholesterol, and reduce your large dense HDL particles, or good cholesterol—the exact opposite effect you get from good fats. They've been linked to heart disease, as have the processed foods you find them in: cookies, crackers, cakes, donuts, chips, microwave popcorn, and so on....basically anything you have to get by shoving your fingers in a box or bag.

If it's made to last on a shelf, chances are good that it has trans fats in it. So read your labels, and when you see the words "partially hydrogenated vegetable oil," which is code for trans fat, run away, far away!

The other kind of fats to watch out for are damaged fats. These are fats that have been altered by heat, light, or air and have become rancid—think of the "bulk buy" vegetable oils in your local grocery store. I call them "damaged" because that's how they'll leave you. Instead, choose organic, cold-pressed oils in dark bottles and store them in a cool place.

HOW MUCH FAT DO YOU NEED?

Ideally, you should have 2–3 servings of healthy fats at every meal. Men and athletic women can go up to 4. This is where the Sugar Impact Plate will come in really handy, because it will lay it out for you. You'll meet the mark with things like 1 tablespoon olive oil, ¼ avocado, 4 ounces cold-water fish, 5–10 nuts, 1 tablespoon nut butter, or 10 olives. If you're having grass-fed beef or fish, you'll want to count the fat in that as a serving, too, so you're not doubling up.

Fats

JJ's Top 10
1. Grass-fed ghee
2. Macadamia nut oil
3. Avocado
4. Walnuts
5. Chia seeds

6. Freshly ground flaxseed meal

7. Malaysian red palm fruit oil

8. Grass-fed beef

9. Wild salmon

10. Sardines

JJ's Worst 10

1. Margarine

2. Processed peanut butter

3. Honey-roasted nuts

4. Corn oil

5. Cottonseed oil

6. Thousand Island dressing

7. Honey mustard dressing

8. Raspberry vinaigrette

9. Butter substitutes

10. Cooking sprays

WHEN FAT MAKES YOU FAT

I can see that you're flipping back a few pages to the sentence that read, Fat doesn't make you fat, sugar makes you fat. Well, that's true. *Unless...* you serve it up with some sugar.

Remember, fat in and of itself doesn't trigger an insulin response. But when it's combined with high-SI foods, insulin skyrockets in response to the sugar or fast carbs. Insulin triggers fat-storing enzymes *and* decreases fat-burning enzymes—a knock-out punch for anyone trying to lose weight. And if you're under chronic stress, ka-boom. Other chemical reactions come into play that ensure you've mixed the perfect fat-storing cocktail.

For those already dealing with high blood sugar or insulin resistance, fat will slow the speed of blood sugar entering the bloodstream by slowing down stomach emptying, and that's important for all of us—especially if you're diabetic. But if you eat sugar and fat together all the time, the combined sugar and fat load in your diet will eventually come home to roost, and lead to lots of extra pounds.

THE BASICS ON SUGAR, STARCH, AND FIBER

First, know this: sugar, starches, and fiber are all carbohydrates. Of the three, only fiber isn't a source of sugar for your body. We don't have the digestive enzymes to break fiber down into sugar, so fiber scrubs its way slowly through our digestive system and provides huge benefits of its own, including keeping your blood sugar stable and helping you feel full longer. More on this in a bit.

Now for the other two: sugars and starches. All sugars are carbs, but not all carbs *start* as sugars. Both end up as sugar, though—they get converted into glucose, which every cell in your body uses as fuel. And that process starts as soon as food hits your tongue. Digestive enzymes in your saliva, like amylase, begin to break down any sugar or starch that isn't already glucose or fructose.

FAST CARBS

You may have heard sugars being called simple or complex. But that's not the way I look at sugar, because, frankly, it misses the point. It's not important to be concerned about the molecular makeup of carbs (though I'll share a little of that with you). It's really about SI—how high they raise your glucose and insulin or how fast they hit the liver and start making fat. That's what determines whether you're lean, sharp, and full of energy, or exhausted, overweight, and foggy. So I want you to look at carbs as fast or slow, depending on how they affect you. That said, here's a little of the biochemistry.

Fast carbs are made of one or two sugar molecules, called monosaccharides (like glucose and fructose) and disaccharides (like sucrose, which is table sugar). Notice the -ose ending—it tells you something's a sugar. Another example is lactose, the sugar found in milk. When eaten, the monosaccharides are absorbed right into your small intestine without having to be broken down further. Disaccharides are snapped apart quickly before they're absorbed. So mono- and disaccharides are fast carbs.

When you eat refined sugar or fast carbs, whether it's in a soda or maple syrup, you get a quick shot of energy from the injection of glucose. Your insulin wire is tripped, and it mobilizes to get that blood sugar stored. Ideally, it's packing the blood sugar away in your muscles and liver to use as fuel for your next workout, but when you run out of storage there, there's only one option left—it gets stored as fat. Usually around your belly.

STARCHES

Starches, on the other hand, are slow carbs and are digested very differently than their fast counterparts. They're plant-based, so they occur naturally in unprocessed whole foods, and they're made up of long chains of sugar. The starch is broken down into maltose in your mouth, and then into glucose in your intestines.

Slow carbs take longer to digest because your body has to work harder to break down all the links in the chain to get the glucose it needs. After that, the glucose is metabolized the same way it is in refined sugar digestion; it's used as energy or stored as glycogen or fat as a reserve fuel source. But because the process of getting to glucose takes longer, your blood sugar rises more slowly, so the insulin cavalry responds lower and slower too (a good thing).

But here's something to file away: starches aren't all the same. If starches have been processed, as is the case with some flours and cereals, they can behave more like fast carbs and have a more immediate impact on blood sugar and insulin response. That's also true of white rice and white potatoes; they're made up of long chains of glucose that are more easily broken down by our digestive system, so they raise blood sugar faster than the starches I consider slow carbs. So instead of refined and high-SI carbs, choose less processed grains, lower-SI roots, vegetables, and legumes like black beans, quinoa, artichokes, spinach, lentils, and wild rice, and cruciferous veggies like broccoli and cauliflower. More on these in a bit.

FIBER CHANGES EVERYTHING

Fiber is a carb, and it's the only carb our body doesn't turn into sugar. It's the part of plant-based foods that our bodies can't digest, and it doesn't provide us with any nutrition or calories. It's simply roughage. High-fiber, water-rich foods slow down stomach emptying and take longer to move through our digestive tract, so they make us feel full on fewer calories than foods with very little fiber, like refined grains.

Fiber does some other good deeds, too, like helping fat move smoothly through our digestive system without loitering, so less of it is absorbed. Fiber also keeps blood sugar on an even keel, which helps feed a steady supply of energy to your brain. And fiber feeds the healthy bacteria in your gut, which supports a strong immune system and beats back the bad kinds of bacteria.

When sugar is served up in a healthy fiber wrap, as with the pulp in an orange, that fiber is designed to slow down our absorption of sugar and have us burn some energy in the bargain as our metabolism works to get at the sugar it wants. Whole foods are also rich with protective antioxidants, such as vitamin C, which combat free radicals to stave off the effects of accelerated aging. I'll take that!

Things change dramatically when whole food is "unwrapped" from its fiber packaging; the amount of sugar we get from that food soars (as does the speed at which it spikes our insulin), and there is often added sugar in processed foods, to boot. So it's safe to say that the 15 grams of sugar in a processed protein bar has a completely different effect on your blood sugar levels than natural, whole foods with the same amount. Seemingly healthy foods like dried fruit or fruit juices also count as processed food. Why? Even if you get a little fiber in them, you're not getting enough nutrients and antioxidants to offset the impact of concentrated sugar on your insulin.

Fiber is a fierce secret weapon for balancing your blood sugar and helping you break free from the vise grip of sugar. My goal is for you to eat 50 grams of fiber a day. That might sound high, mostly because if you're like most people,

Fiber is a fierce secret weapon.

you're probably currently only getting 5 to 14 grams a day. Be patient and increase your fiber intake slowly, and drink plenty of water while you do—it may take you 1 to 2 weeks to get there. If you ramp up too fast, you could find yourself dealing with gas, bloating, diarrhea, or constipation.

LIFE IN THE SLOW LANE: SLOW, LOW CARBS

I want you to eat more slow, low carbs and non-starchy veggies. Eating a small amount of slow, low carbs and non-starchy veggies every day gives you sharper focus, better bowel movements, and higher energy, while revving your metabolism. That should keep you in a good mood!

The more non-starchy veggies you eat, the better, considering all the phytonutrients, fiber, and bulk they'll get into your diet. Shoot for 5 to 10 or more servings a day. At a minimum, I want you to get 2 or more servings at every meal (using ½ cup cooked or 1 cup raw as a serving size). Also aim to get 1–2 servings of high-fiber starchy carbs per meal or snack (using ½ cup cooked as a serving). Larger or more athletic men can have 3 servings per meal.

Here's one simple way to bump your fiber intake—eat more whole foods and fewer processed foods. The Sugar Impact Diet is all about getting as close to nature as possible, minimizing the amount of fructose you consume, and reducing your glycemic load. Nuts and seeds, legumes, wild rice, quinoa, berries (except in Cycle 2), and non-starchy vegetables are all awesome sources of fiber. Here's another idea—toss a fiber blend, chia seeds, or freshly ground flaxseed meal into your breakfast shake. Those two tips alone, if you do them consistently, should get you to 50 grams of fiber a day pretty easily.

I always encourage you to buy organic whenever possible. Even so, it's not necessary that all your fruits and vegetables be organic, so if you're on a budget or just need help making choices, check out this website: www.ewg.org/foodnews/summary.php. It's the Environmental Working Group's complete list of both the "Dirty Dozen Plus" (a list of the most pesticide-laden fruits and veggies) and the "Clean Fifteen" (just the opposite). And always wash your fruits and veggies before you eat them. Even organic fruit can be coated with dirt and germs, or carry pesticide "drift" from nearby farms.

Dirty Dozen Plus		
Apples	Hot peppers	Spinach
Celery	Nectarines	Strawberries
Cherry tomatoes	(imported)	Sweet bell peppers
Cucumbers	Peaches	Kale/collard greens
Grapes	Potatoes	Summer squash

Clean Fifteen		
Asparagus	Eggplant	Onions
Avocados	Grapefruit	Papayas
Cabbage	Kiwi	Pineapples
Cantaloupe	Mangoes	Sweet peas (frozen)
Sweet corn	Mushrooms	Sweet potatoes

Non-starchy vegetables should take up the most space on your Sugar Impact Plate, and considering the major role they play in your fast fat loss, don't be shy about piling them high. Mix it up at each meal with creative and colorful choices—look how many you have to choose from!

Non-Starchy Vegetables

Here are your best choices:

- Artichokes
- Arugula
- Asparagus
- Bamboo shoots
- Bean sprouts
- Beet greens
- Bell peppers (red, yellow, green)
- Bok choy
- Broccoli
- Brussels sprouts
- Cabbage
- Carrots
- Cassava
- Cauliflower
- Celery
- Chicory
- Chives
- Collard greens
- Coriander
- Cucumber
- Dandelion greens
- Eggplant
- Endive
- Escarole
- Fennel
- Garlic
- Green beans
- Jalapeno peppers
- Jicama
- Kale
- Kohlrabi
- Leeks
- Lettuce
- Mushrooms
- Mustard greens
- Okra
- Onions
- Parsley

- Radicchio
- Radishes
- Shallots
- Snow peas
- Spaghetti squash

- Spinach
- Sugar snap peas
- Summer squash
- Swiss chard
- Turnip greens

- Water chestnuts
- Watercress
- Zucchini

Slow, Low Carbs

- Adzuki beans
- Berries (blackberries, blueberries, boysenberries, elderberries, gooseberries, loganberries, raspberries, strawberries, acai)
- Black beans
- Chickpeas (garbanzo)
- Cowpeas
- Cranberries
- French beans
- Grapefruit
- Great Northern beans

- Groats
- Guava
- Kabocha squash
- Kidney beans
- Leeks
- Lentils
- Lima beans
- Mung beans
- Navy beans
- Nectarines
- Oatmeal (steel-cut or rolled)
- Okra
- Oranges

- Passion fruit
- Peaches
- Persimmon
- Pinto beans
- Pumpkin
- Quinoa
- Split peas
- Squash (acorn, butternut, winter)
- Star fruit
- Tomatoes
- Turnip
- White beans
- Wild rice

Slow, Low Carbs

JJ's Top 10

1. Black beans
2. Butternut squash
3. Cranberries

4. Hummus
5. Kabocha squash
6. Lentils
7. Quinoa
8. Raspberries
9. Tomatoes
10. Wild rice

JJ's Worst 10

1. Apple juice
2. Agave nectar
3. Baked beans
4. Cornbread
5. Flavored rice cakes
6. French fries
7. Fruit leather
8. Granola bars
9. Kettle corn
10. Root veggie chips

Non-Starchy Veggies

JJ's Top 10

1. Artichoke
2. Arugula
3. Broccoli
4. Brussels sprouts
5. Cabbage
6. Cauliflower
7. Garlic
8. Kale

9. Red peppers

10. Spinach

JJ's Worst 10

NONE!

One important note as you increase your fiber, though—you have to also increase the amount of water you drink. It's critical in order to keep everything moving smoothly through your digestive pipes.

MEAL TIMING: EATING BY THE SUGAR IMPACT CLOCK

If you're dragging yourself through the day, caffeinating and snacking every 2 hours to pull yourself through stretches of plummeting energy, you're compensating for blood sugar spikes and crashes brought on by your high-SI diet. No doubt your fatigue is crippling you, and your insulin levels, your immune system, and your metabolism are all taking a beating, too.

So one of the very important shifts you'll be making on the Sugar Impact Diet is to change from eating every 2 hours to eating every 4–6 hours. (I'll give you details on how to make this happen in Chapter 8.) You'll move from those high-SI foods to medium- and low-SI foods, so you're eating blood sugar–balancing foods that are high in fiber along with protein and good fats. You'll be amazed at the difference this is going to make for you! When you stabilize your blood sugar, you'll stay full longer, so stretching out the time between meals is a breeze.

As you make this move, you're going to drink plenty of water between meals. It will help stave off hunger pangs, and—surprise—you may find that when you think you need to eat, you could just be thirsty. I have some tips on that coming up.

THE SKINNY ON SNACKING

Snacking is pretty polarizing in fitness and nutrition camps, and as someone who wants to lose weight, facing completely opposing opinions can be pretty frustrating when you just want the answer with no fuss, no muss. Advocates argue snacks or "mini-meals" throughout the day can curb appetite, stabilize blood sugar, and help you eat less during meals.

However, based on my research and experience helping people who struggle with weight loss, especially people who just can't seem to shake those last few stubborn pounds, I'm in the anti-snacking camp. There's just no getting around the fact that it sabotages fat loss and fast metabolism. All it does is give you permission to eat more than you need. Every time you eat, you raise your insulin levels. So snacking keeps insulin levels elevated and the fat-burning doors locked. Taking a food break between meals encourages your body to reach into those fat stores to burn what you've already got.

Snacking sabotages fat loss and fast metabolism.

Sweet and salty snacks also increase cravings, so that snack pack has the dark power to make you reach for seconds, even if you just had one. Snacking becomes a mindless, many-times-a-day habit, and the repercussions land on your waistline. Junk food manufacturers love this vicious circle: you're snacking throughout the day and never really satisfied, but still reaching for more.

A study published in the *American Journal of Physiology: Regulatory, Integrative, and Comparative Physiology* found evidence suggesting that young women who snack at nighttime prevent fat breakdown and increase their obesity risks. Another study published in the journal *Obesity* showed that mice fed a high-fat diet before sleep gained about 48% body weight compared to mice that ate the same amount at other times of the day (they only gained 20%, but I should point out, they still gained!).

That makes sense, right? Those calories have to go somewhere, and unless you're doing sprints in your sleep, chances are they'll land around your middle.

If you're an after-dinner snacker, you're missing out on the significant fat-burning benefits of fasting. It's not about starvation or deprivation, but when you simply cut out after-dinner snacks, your body goes into fat-burning mode for about 12–14 hours until the next morning's breakfast. That's going to help transform you into a fat burner!

In Case of Emergency

I want you to carry emergency foods to prevent you from going off the rails in a moment of weakness, or when bad choices are the only ones you've got. If your blood sugar crashes or you're in airport hell, one of these little goodies will save the day.

They're fast, easy, tasty options to grab and go (you may recognize a few from the smart snack list). They make being armed and ready so simple.

- Aseptic-packed wild salmon
- Celery with almond butter
- Hard-boiled eggs (if not intolerant)
- Hummus with veggies
- Kale chips
- Low-roasted or dehydrated nuts and seeds
- Nitrate-free, no-sugar-added jerky
- Raw veggies with black bean dip
- Shaker carry cup with protein powder (just add water!)
- Virgin Diet bar or other approved bars (see Resources at http://sugarimpact.com/resources)

Finally, add high-quality supplements—a multivitamin and mineral complex, essential fatty acids, and a high-potency antioxidant blend—and you'll be armed against sugar wherever you go, all day long.

Help—It's Midnight, and I'm Hungry!

Well, this might help blunt that hunger fast: snacking at night isn't just fat storing, it's age-accelerating. Ack!

Eating sugar can make proteins sticky and "gum up" the works, preventing those proteins from doing their jobs in a process that results in what are called advanced glycation end products (AGEs—and yes, they do!). This process is exacerbated at night, because when you snack on something sugary before bed, your body is less likely to utilize that sugar and it has a higher chance of being stored as fat and wreaking metabolic havoc.

But even if you've done everything right, you may still find yourself gnashing your teeth, completely preoccupied with food, and scrambling for some fast relief. As with most solutions, this one is simple, and it's right under your nose. It's...water. A study at the University of Washington showed that *everyone* who drank just eight ounces of water before bed curbed their hunger completely. Everyone!

And here's another tip—tossing 5 to 10 grams of fiber powder into a glass of water 30–60 minutes before you eat will make you much less likely to reach for seconds.

Believe it or not, as simple as water seems, it can be a powerful weapon in your battle against the bulge. Read more about how in Chapter 6.

Lemon-Aid

There's an old wives' tale that lemon juice lowers blood sugar. Well, it turns out, there's some truth to it! My hero Tim Ferriss, infamous biohacker and author of *The 4-Hour Body*, experimented with it and discovered that having 3 tablespoons of lemon juice when he ate lowered his blood sugar peaks by about 10%.

Choose "Lemon-Aid" once or twice a day to ease your hunger pangs and keep hydrated. Here's how to whip it up:

Juice and zest of one lemon (or lime)
½ thinly sliced lemon
32 ounces water
1 teaspoon glutamine (an amino acid) powder
Stevia, monk fruit, xylitol, or erythritol as needed (use as little as possible).

Combine the juice and zest of one lemon or lime with the water. Add the glutamine powder and sweetener (only if needed). Stir well and gently stir in lemon slices.

You may have noticed one of the secrets of the Lemon-Aid recipe in the ingredients list—a teaspoon of the amino acid glutamine. Remember when I mentioned that protein can reduce reward (i.e., sugar) seeking behavior? Well, a little glutamine, an amino acid that helps your body synthesize protein, can also alleviate sugar cravings and support gut healing at the same time. Plus, the sour taste of lemon can curb your sweet tooth, so be sure to sweeten as little as possible.

To kick it up another notch, add a little fiber. I use either a fiber blend or chia seeds. Fiber helps keep ghrelin suppressed so you aren't as hungry, and it reduces the absorption of fat at your next meal.

JOIN THE SMART SNACKING CLUB

It's safe to say I made the case against snacking, right? But it's a challenge, no lie. Those sugary treats—and their well-funded marketers—are a formidable opponent. So rather than deprive yourself, just pivot. Reward yourself with something other than food. Take a spa time-out if you can afford it, enjoy a hot bath, or walk through the park to reduce your stress and bring yourself back to feeling good.

Still, I get it: sometimes there's no way around it—you have to have a snack. And I can help you make a better choice than microwave popcorn. Check out the tasty options in Chapter 8. They'll support you as you condition yourself to shift to 4–6 hours between meals.

TOO MUCH HEALTHY FOOD IS UNHEALTHY

You can actually get too much of a good thing. Too much food is always going to be too much food, whether it's healthy or not. You only need so much to keep your engine running, and any extra will be packed away in the storage closet of your hips or your belly. So, less is more, even when it's low SI.

When you're eating balanced meals of clean, lean protein, healthy fats, non-starchy veggies, and some slow carbs, you only need three meals a day, and possibly a snack if you're going to have to wait more than 4 to 6 hours between meals. That's enough to keep you humming between feedings and burning fat. More meals just means more chances to overeat.

Here's how the timing of those three meals breaks out:

- Eat a substantial breakfast within 1 hour of waking up. No skipping! Skippers spike their blood sugar and tend to be fatter and less healthy than people who regularly eat breakfast.

- Eat every 4 to 6 hours, and have a snack if you need it.
- Close the kitchen and stop eating 3 hours before bed (no, you cannot just go to bed later!). Ideally, I'd like you to have at least a 12-hour span between dinner and breakfast to allow insulin to return to fasting levels so your body can use stored fat for fuel.

EAT BY THE PLATE

I designed the Sugar Impact Plate to make sure you're getting all the nutrition you need and engaging your fat-burning machinery at every meal. When you eat according to the Plate, you'll have a full and happy tummy for longer stretches, so you can eat three balanced meals every 4 to 6 hours without feeling deprived of a thing.

In addition to 1 serving of clean, lean protein and 2–3 servings of healthy fats, each meal should include 2 or more servings of

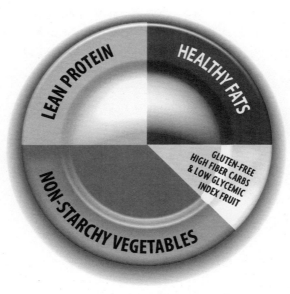

The Sugar Impact Plate

non-starchy vegetables—and the more the better; my goal for you is 5–10 servings per day (yes, 10!)—and up to 2 servings of high-fiber starchy carbs like beans or quinoa. As you now know, getting enough fiber is critical to fast fat loss. As you move from high-SI foods to low-SI foods, your fiber is going to trend the other way, from low to high.

When your diet is full of lean protein, plenty of non-starchy veggies, fiber-filled slow carbs like lentils and beans, and good fats like avocado or olive oil, you'll lose weight fast, have to-die-for energy, and your blood sugar levels will be nice and stable. That's a pretty good return on just changing what you eat!

PREPARE TO CHANGE YOUR LIFE

You're almost there. Soon you'll have all the tools you need in your arsenal to lower your SI and lose fat fast—in a *healthy* way. In the following chapters, I'll walk you through the seven most common high SI foods, and I'll outline the simple swaps you can make to bring your SI down. When you do, you'll drop the weight, boost your energy, and feel better than ever—in just 2 weeks!

PART II

SEVEN FOODS TO SWAP

4

BE GONE, GRAINS, ROOTS, AND FRUIT

Now we're getting into the nitty gritty. Let's dig into my seven high Sugar Impact food categories to get a better understanding of what impact each is having on you and how you can make better choices. Keep in mind that your primary goal will always be to eat as close to nature as possible. Whole foods that are closest to their natural state give you more nutrients than food with a label.

LOSE THE HIGH SUGAR IMPACT GRAINS

They're the medicine you need to lose weight, fight disease, and slow down aging. What's not to love?! The problem with many grains is that we don't eat them the way nature intended us to. To lower your SI, you'll swap grains—especially refined grains (a top ingredient in many processed foods)—for natural, whole foods like beans, nuts, and seeds.

Grains weren't part of our ancestors' diet, so we don't need them to survive. But we've been told that whole grains like wheat, barley, and rye are healthy and good for us, and to eat more of them. Compared

Don't buy into the myth of whole grain goodness.

to more processed, refined grains, they are healthier—but don't buy into the myth of whole grain goodness.

By the time grains make their way into our diet, they're usually refined, meaning pounded into powder with all the nutrients and fiber sucked out of them. That's even worse than it sounds, which I'll explain in a bit. On the other hand, beans, nuts, and seeds are nutrition powerhouses, dense with protein, healthy fat, fiber, antioxidants, vitamins, and minerals.

ENERGY IN THE FORM OF STARCH

Grains and beans are packed with energy in the form of starch. The starches in plants are mostly made of long strings of glucose, which we easily break apart for fuel. *All* starch turns into glucose. But not all sugar is created equal. Starch is metabolized differently than, say, sucrose (table sugar), which is half-glucose, half-fructose. When you eat sucrose, you're actually ingesting glucose and an equal dose of fructose. You know the domino-like effect fructose can have on your health and weight.

Starches, or slow carbs, take longer to digest than fast carbs, as their names would suggest. Plus, your body uses enzymes to break down slow carbs and get to the glucose, so you burn some energy during that process. That digestive process begins in your mouth with enzymes in your saliva—right then and there, starch starts turning into sugar.

How fast that happens depends on how the food was processed and prepared and its molecular makeup. So whether it's raw or cooked, whole or processed, liquid or solid determines how quickly it will turn into sugar. Cooked foods are more easily digested than in their raw form, so the sugar in cooked foods is more accessible to your body and hits your body faster. And, of course, when you eat whole foods, the fiber in it slows the rate at which sugar hits your bloodstream, whereas processed food and liquids don't have the fiber and give sugar a free pass.

The good news is, grains, beans, nuts and seeds are loaded with fiber. Fiber puts the brakes on stomach emptying, which keeps you full longer. It helps feed the good bacteria in your small intestine and improves nutrient absorption. It also pushes food through your intestinal tract (scrubbing all the way) and provides bulk to the stool so that you produce poops you can be proud of (yep, I really said that).

But wait, there's more. Fiber prevents free fatty acids from accumulating in your bloodstream. You want and need this. Your body should metabolize and use those free fatty acids; they shouldn't be hanging out in your blood! Free fatty acid buildup can create insulin resistance and diabetes, and they're often elevated in obese people.

Your colon also puts fiber to good use: it converts it to short-chain fatty acids, which gives it the energy it needs to keep metabolic machinery humming along.

SHOW ADDED SUGAR THE DOOR

Obviously, eating as close to nature as possible is the deal. If you're serious about wanting to lose weight fast and shift your health back to great, you've got to eliminate foods that contain added sugar, as well as refined grains like bread and pasta. It's the path toward the light, out of that dark diet maze, and the key to throwing off the cloak of conditions that keep you from really living and loving your life. If you struggle with eliminating sugar and refined grains completely, you'll find that once you go through Cycle 2 you don't even miss them, especially when you discover low SI swaps you like even better (promise!). Most people who bought into the "high-carb, low-fat" myth have wrestled with their weight and health but have no idea what they're doing wrong. And, sadly enough, they feel like they've failed, when they're just following the wrong set of rules.

Clearly there's a lot to be gained by eating the right kinds of foods, but the right amounts matter, too. The problem is that when you overdo the carbs, you can prevent fats from being used for energy *and* stimulate an increase in fat production and storage. Your body has a limited capacity to store excess carbohydrates. That's one of the reasons elevated blood sugar follows overeating: more is more, and lots of carbs equals lots of blood sugar. If you're eating too many carbs and you're not able to immediately use all the sugar you eat—and you're not likely to unless you've got some seriously intense physical activity going on—there isn't any more room to store it as glycogen.

So one of the ways your body avoids dangerously elevated blood sugar is by converting those surplus carbs into fat, usually around your belly. Not pretty!

> *Your body converts surplus carbs into fat, usually around your belly.*

Here's how it works. Any carbohydrate not immediately burned by your body as fuel is stored in the form of glycogen, a long string of glucose molecules linked together. Your body has two primary storage sites for glycogen: your liver and your muscles. Once the glycogen levels are filled in both your liver and muscles, surplus carbs are converted to fat and stored in your adipose, or fatty, tissue.

> *The fact that carbs are considered "fat-free" is, at best, misleading.*

So the fact that carbs are considered "fat-free" is, at best, misleading. Worse yet, they can sneak into your diet in huge amounts if you're eating processed and packaged foods, or if you're a mindless muncher. Here's a tip and some label-reading shorthand to prevent that from happening to you: when you see refined grains on a food label, think of them as "hidden sugar," and when you see sugar, think of it as "hidden fat." Bye-bye, pretzels!

Even a meal or snack high in slow carbs like beets or yams is packed with those long chains of glucose molecules that raise your blood sugar, regardless of whether they're mitigated by fiber. To compensate, your pancreas secretes insulin, which then brings your blood sugar back down. The problem is that insulin is essentially a storage hormone, and its primary function is to hoard carbohydrate calories in the form of fat. Excess carbs keep insulin busy padding you with as much fat as you're willing to make available. Sure, that was great when our ancestors were wandering the savannah hoping to hunt or gather something. But today, scarce calories—and the savannah—are not everyday issues in our world, are they? As a result, this protective mechanism actually sabotages your health. When you eat too much sugar, bread, pasta, or any other processed grain products, you're sending a hormonal message, via insulin, to your body that says "store more fat, please!"

But that's not even the worst of it. Insulin triggers the release of the hormone leptin, which comes out of your fat cells to tell you you're full. Chronically high insulin from excess carbs means your leptin never comes down, either. When leptin stays elevated, your appetite control center eventually tunes it out and no longer hears the message to curb hunger. And you go crazy trying to figure out why you still feel like you're starving after you've just eaten. So excess carbs help make you fat, and tell you to eat more. Devious!

REACH FOR THESE CARBS

I'm not saying that you should avoid carbs completely. I eat carbs, too! Processed sugary carbs are the culprit in obesity and insulin resistance, not nutrient-dense carbs. Nutrient-rich slow carbs don't spike your blood sugar and accelerate fat storage the way empty fast carbs do. Stay close to nature and you'll be fine. Whole, unprocessed carbs come packaged with immune-supporting, anti-aging nutrients and blood sugar–balancing fiber. Besides, nobody ever got fat eating asparagus.

My personal top slow, low carb faves are quinoa, hummus, wild rice, black beans, and lentils. Stick with those and you'll be making nutritious choices that aren't the blood sugar equivalent of a Taser. Also check out the great swaps I have for you later in this chapter (see page 82). Make those easy trades and you'll never feel deprived. Instead, you'll just feel energized and giddy about thinking clearly, the weight falling off, your skin looking brighter, and your aches and pain evaporating.

GONE WITH GLUTEN

Some grains deliver more starch than others. And several, such as wheat, barley, and rye, also contain the sticky protein gluten.

Wheat may as well be the devil in disguise.

We get a lot of our gluten from wheat. Wheat sounds wholesome enough, but don't be fooled by the halo—it might as well be the devil in disguise. Wheat serves up a platter of diseases, conditions, and weight-gain cocktails, and it's slipped into thousands of things we eat. Today's wheat is essentially an engineered food product created (yes, I said created) within the last 50 years that has an entirely different effect on our digestive system than the wheat your Great Aunt Betty ate.

This newer dwarf wheat has been genetically manipulated to endure harsher conditions than its natural predecessor so that it delivers a higher yield. But what's good for agriculture isn't necessarily good for us. This genetically engineered wheat contains much more gluten and starch, including a compound called amylopectin A. According to Dr. William Davis, author of *Wheat*

Belly, amylopectin A is a complex carbohydrate unique to wheat. Wheat's amylopectin A is more digestible than other amylopectins in unprocessed carbs like legumes. He writes: "Because wheat carbohydrate, the uniquely digestible amylopectin A, causes a greater spike in blood sugar than virtually any other food—more than a candy bar, table sugar or ice cream—it also triggers greater insulin release."

To drive the point home, Dr. Mark Hyman, author of *The Blood Sugar Solution*, calls amylopectin A a "super starch." He says amylopectin A is behind those big, fluffy slices of wheat bread we love to slather with PB and J. And as a super starch, it doesn't just bump your blood sugar. Dr. Hyman says "two slices of whole wheat bread will raise your blood sugar more than two tablespoons of table sugar."

The food business is a mega-machine, and gluten has become its go-to ingredient in everything that sits on a shelf. While gluten may be getting applause for its sticky, stretchy ability to shape muffins, it's not being so helpful to you, unless you appreciate how it helps you store belly fat. People with a condition called celiac disease—a severe reaction to gluten—get sick if they eat even a small amount of gluten. But even in people without celiac disease, gluten can also trigger leaky gut and inflammation (and the onslaught of conditions that follow).

Odds are you're being negatively affected by gluten. It's estimated that 30–40% of Americans have a sensitivity to it. I find that estimate to be just *a little low*; about 90% of the people I pull off gluten feel enormously better without it (and I'm convinced the other 10% didn't really get it all out). If you haven't identified gluten as a problem for you yet, maybe this will help: symptoms of intolerance include weight gain

> *About 90% of the people I pull off gluten feel enormously better without it.*

or inability to lose weight, cravings, digestive upset, headaches, joint pain, anxiety, depression, brain fog, and especially leaky gut. Hmmm.

GLUTEN AND LEAKY GUT

Gluten can trigger the release of the protein zonulin, which regulates the permeability of your intestines. When zonulin is out and about, it loosens the tight junctions in your gut. Suddenly, proteins and toxins not meant to penetrate your gut wall slip into your bloodstream and incite an immune response. But the manifestation of that response—as joint pain, brain fog, gastrointestinal problems, anxiety, depression, and more—can be delayed hours or even days. So you can give yourself a break for missing the connection between the headache you have one morning and the wheat pasta you ate the night before. Leaky gut has also been linked to chronic conditions like rheumatoid arthritis and diabetes, in addition to gastrointestinal issues.

Gluten can even sneak into foods that are naturally gluten-free. Oatmeal is a great example. Oats are not a grain that contains gluten, so oatmeal shouldn't contain gluten, either—and pure oatmeal doesn't. But commercial brands of oatmeal are often cross-contaminated in the facilities where they're made, so they can contain little bits of wheat, barley, or rye. If you're hankering for some oatmeal in the morning, make it pure steel-cut or rolled for the lowest SI. Flavored instant oatmeals are always a bad choice; they're just reservoirs of added sugar.

CUT THE CORN

Then there's corn. The "vegetable" we all grew up loving at backyard parties and barbecues. There we were, zinging it along our teeth, feeling truly American. The trouble is, corn is not a vegetable. Corn is a grain, and a very starchy one at that. It turns to sugar right there in your mouth and becomes a gusher headed for your bloodstream. Yep, corn = sugar.

Corn = sugar.

That's one of the reasons industrial farms feed their cows and pigs corn—to make them fat, fast! Knowing that, it's a little hard to believe it's doing anything different to you. To heighten the concern here—and it should be heightened—the corn (and other grains) that many factory-farm animals are fed is often genetically modified, which means you end up eating those GMOs, too. (And remember, you are what you eat, ate.)

GMOs are plants that have been genetically altered to increase crop yield or shelf life. They're engineered by inserting foreign genes into the DNA of the plant. Even scarier, according to the American Academy of Environmental Medicine, there are serious health risks associated with genetically modified food.

Studies show there's a direct through line to obesity when you eat GMO corn or GMO corn-fed animals. And there's mounting evidence that GMO crops are connected not only to obesity, but also to immune issues and a host of gastrointestinal problems like leaky gut.

China and most of Europe already require GMO labeling, but in the United States we have to work a little harder to figure out how to dodge GMOs in our food. Until GMOs are on our labels and highlighted in red, it's worth the additional legwork to sleuth them out. GMOs are in as many as 80% of the processed foods available in the United States. For more information and a complete list of where they might be slipping onto your plate, visit www.respon sibletechnology.org/buy-non-gmo and download the non-GMO shopping list. Also, look for the certification of the nonprofit organization Non-GMO Project; it puts its seal on brands it verifies as GMO-free, so you can buy worry-free.

SAY NO TO SOY

For years, a lot of us have been led to believe soy is a health food. Nothing could be further from the truth. That pretty glow around soy was put there by (you guessed it!) soy companies. So let me be the one to break it to you—there's no joy in soy! Here's its rap sheet: soy has been linked to impaired thyroid function, reproductive disorders, cognitive decline, digestive problems, and lower sperm count. In evolutionary terms, it's relatively new to our food supply, so many people respond to it as an allergen. And nearly all soy has been genetically modified, which means it's likely to contain high amounts of pesticides. It also contains the anti-nutrients phytates and lectins.

PHYTATES AND LECTINS: ANTI-NUTRIENTS

Phytates can block mineral absorption, leading to nutrient deficiencies, including iron-deficiency anemia. Lectins can cause leptin resistance and result in increased hunger. I'm guessing the last thing you want is to eat food that makes you hungrier, am I right? Lectins are part of a plant's defense mechanism, so they're born to fight. Lectins in grains, beans, nuts, seeds, and other plants have been shown to damage intestinal cells, leading to leaky gut. Read on to learn how to eat beans, nuts, and seeds without worrying about lectins.

IMPORTANCE OF SPROUTING, SOAKING, DEHYDRATING, AND SLOW-ROASTING

Nuts like almonds, walnuts, and Brazil nuts and seeds like pumpkin and hemp are rich sources of protein, fiber, healthy fats, antioxidants, and vitamins and minerals. And they can be healing.

They're also effective soldiers against free radicals, inflammation, and aging, so even though they have phytates and lectins, I want you to incorporate some of them into your diet. The key is to soak and sprout them to lower the antinutrient load, so you get all the good without the bad. The same goes for grains. All grains can raise your blood sugar and insulin, so go easy on them, but when you do indulge, the most ideal choice is sprouted grains, which have been soaked and germinated and are more nutritious and less refined than others.

How does this help? Sprouting reduces lectins in beans and seeds, because once the seed starts to germinate and form a wee plant, a lot of the lectin gets broken down to feed the growing baby (some of it hangs behind to protect the seedling).

Or, if you can, buy your beans (and grains) dry, and rinse and soak them before cooking them. They'll be more nutritious, lower in salt, and less expensive than canned beans. Soaking also ensures they'll cook evenly and cuts down on the gas they generate.

There are two main ways to soak beans: the long soak method, and the quick soak method. To long soak, rinse the dried beans, put them in a bowl, and add enough water to cover them by about 3 inches. Then just put them in the fridge overnight, and they'll be ready for you to drain, rinse, and cook in the morning. When you're in a hurry, pour the beans into a large pot and add water until they're covered by about 3 inches. Boil for 1 minute, then cover and let stand for an hour. When the beans are tender and have doubled in size, they're done and ready to drain.

Slow-roasting nuts and seeds is essentially the same process. You soak them overnight in a bowl with water that covers them by about 3 inches. In the morning, with most of the work done, you drain them, spread them out on a baking sheet (or place them in a dehydrator), and bake them at 140° for 8 hours.

YOUR SUGAR IMPACT SWAPS: GRAINS

These swaps will help you effortlessly reduce the impact starchy grains are having on your metabolism, digestive tract, and fast weight loss. They're just as tasty as the high-SI choices, and I guarantee you'll like them even better, knowing they're releasing you from the grip of foods that are sabotaging your health and holding your weight hostage. Don't feel limited by this list, though—experiment with your own, then let me hear about them!

Swap Your...	For...
BBQ beans	Pinto beans
Bran cereal	Quinoa flakes
Corn soup	White bean soup
Cornstarch	Arrowroot powder
Creamed corn	Black beans
Instant oatmeal	Long-cooking oatmeal
Mashed potatoes	Mashed cauliflower
Nutella	Almond butter
Pasta	Spaghetti squash, shirataki noodles
Peanut butter	Cashew butter
Potato chips	Kale chips
Tofu	Lentils
Tortilla chips	Bean chips or kale chips
Tortillas	Lettuce wraps or coconut wraps
Trail mix	Slow-roasted nut mix
White rice	Wild rice
Whole wheat pasta	Corn-free quinoa pasta

YOUR SUGAR IMPACT SCALE: GRAINS

Let me introduce you to the Sugar Impact Scale for grains. Remember, the framework for these categories is based on the amount of sugar in them and the impact they'll have on you: how much they'll spike your blood sugar and insulin and send your body the message to store more fat. So get excited about stopping that message in its tracks!

In Cycle 1, you're going to swap high–SI foods for medium–SI choices, then in Cycle 2 you'll swap the medium SIs for lows. Ready? Go!

LOW SUGAR IMPACT

Lentils	Hummus	Flaxseeds
Black beans	Wild rice	Chia seeds
Black turtle beans	Groats	Sesame seeds
Boston navy beans	Long-cooking	Hemp seeds
Broad beans	oatmeal (rolled or	Pecans
Cannellini beans	steel-cut)	Brazil nuts
Chickpeas	Shirataki noodles	Cashews
Fava beans	Lentil soup	Hazelnuts
French green beans	Chili (homemade, no sugar	Macadamia nuts
Great Northern	added)	Walnuts
beans	Coconut wraps	Almonds
Green beans	Coconut flour	Pine nuts
Kidney beans	Dehydrated unsweetened	Pistachios
Lima beans	coconut	Poppy seeds
Mung beans	Roasted chestnuts	Peas
Pinto beans	Almond flour	Unsweetened nut
Wax beans	Pumpkin seeds	butters
Quinoa	Sunflower seeds	Peanuts*

Ideally, choose tree nuts rather than peanuts for their superior fatty acid profile and lower allergenicity potential

Mistaken Identity

Peanuts are not nuts at all. In fact, they're legumes! Legumes are plants with seeds that grow inside pods. Nuts are grown on trees, but peanuts are part of the pea family and grow underground.

MEDIUM SUGAR IMPACT

Rice pasta
Arrowroot
Amaranth
Buckwheat
Millet
Rice tortillas
Sprouted whole grain breads
Brown rice

Fermented soy
Ezekiel brand sprouted cereal
Quinoa flakes
Quinoa pasta
Chili (store-bought, sugar added)
Amaranth, rice, millet, or buckwheat flour

Garbanzo flour
Quinoa flour
Fava bean flour
Black bean flour
Rice crackers
Rice chips
Bean chips
Lentil chips
Nut chips

Note: if a small amount is used in a recipe (e.g., 1 tablespoon for 4 servings), this is safe for Cycle 2.

HIGH SUGAR IMPACT

Gluten-free flour blend
Mung bean noodles
Honey-roasted peanuts
Cornstarch
Potato starch
Glazed nuts
Sweetened nut butters
Instant oatmeal
Instant rice
Baked beans
Puffed rice
Puffed millet
Rice cakes
Polenta
Corn
Cornbread
Wheat bread

Pasta
Tortillas
Couscous
Soy cheese
Muffins
White flour
Cakes and pies
English muffins
Scones
Biscotti
Cream of Wheat
Pop-tarts
Grits
Macaroni and cheese
Matzoh
Pita

Risotto
Muesli
Quick breads
Sugar cereals
Edamame*
Barley
Farro
Graham crackers
Water crackers
Animal crackers
Wasa crackers
Oyster crackers
Popcorn
Corn tortillas
Corn chips
Cookies
Crackers

This is low sugar, but high in lectins that can cause leptin resistance; choose only organic fermented soy.

I hope you can already see how fun and easy this is going to be. Pretty soon you'll also see results! Now that you have a grip on grains, it's time to kick roots to the curb.

GIVE HIGH SUGAR IMPACT ROOTS THE BOOT

Now let's swap those high-SI roots for low-SI veggies and squashes. This closer look at roots and vegetables is all about shifting the balance on your plate away from those high-SI carbs you're relying on, like mashed potatoes, to lower-SI carbs like pumpkin and non-starchy veggies like Brussels sprouts and red peppers. Do you remember how big the non-starchy section of your Sugar Impact Plate is? You've got some filling to do!

And my guess is that right now the slow, low carb and non-starchy vegetable sections of your plate are parked in each other's spaces. But there's no need to overthink how you'll flip the equation; this is an easy category. Focus on eating from the rainbow. Let color be your guide. And I want you to go hog wild on the low-SI veggies—there's no limit to how many you can have! *Try* to overdo it. I've yet to get an SOS call from someone who has binged on broccoli.

Root Vegetables

Root vegetables are the edible underground part of a plant, but they're not always literally roots. They store their energy in the form of carbohydrates in that tube you yank out of the ground. Think potatoes, carrots, parsnips, radishes, beetroot, sweet potatoes, yams, and turnips. There are also different categories of root vegetables—taproots (like beets and jicama), tuberous roots (like sweet potatoes and turnips), tubers (yams), and bulbs (like garlic and onions).

Root vegetables are typically starchy, and most (though not all) are high on the glycemic index. Potatoes have the highest glycemic index of any vegetables, so the carbs in them turn into sugar and get absorbed into your blood fast. (Don't worry—I've got plenty of swaps on page 89 so that you don't miss your mashed potatoes.)

I want you to be aware of which roots impact your blood sugar and insulin—and your energy, mood, weight, and more—for better or worse. Of course, the Sugar Impact Scale will be your guide for that.

Non-Starchy Vegetables

Non-starchy is essentially the name given to veggies that don't contain much starch. They're usually lower in sugar and higher in fiber than starchy vegetables, and many of them are green and juicy. Why are you always being told to eat your veggies, and why am I saying you can have as many as you want? Impact, impact, impact. As a rule, you can eat more non-starchy vegetables and get fewer carbs (and calories) than when you eat fruits, whole grains, or starchy vegetables. That results in less of an impact on your blood sugar, insulin, and, ultimately, your weight. They're a great source of fiber, so pile them on your plate to hit that goal of 50 grams a day (for a list of your best choices, see page 90). Plus, non-starchy veggies are loaded with phytonutrients. (More on that in a bit.)

You can eat more non-starchy vegetables and get fewer carbs (and calories) than when you eat fruits, whole grains, or starchy vegetables.

Beet This

In some circles, beets and carrots have gotten a bad rap because they're higher on the GI than other vegetables. But as you know, the GI doesn't tell the whole story.

Carrots have a GI rank of 39—but their GL is only 2. So please, munch on. The same green light goes for beets. While they have a pretty high glycemic index—with a rank of 64, their glycemic load is only 4. Compare this to a russet potato with a GI rank of 111 and a GL of 33.

The amount of carbs in carrots is so low, you'd have to eat more than 4 cups of them to get 50 grams worth of carbohydrates. That's a lot of carrots! Eating that much in one sitting hardly seems possible. But there are 50 grams of carbs in just one large potato; I'm guessing you've hardly thought twice about that, until now.

Vitamins and Minerals

Non-starchy vegetables are also vitamin and mineral rock stars. They're packed with the energy-providing, bone-building nutrients we need to keep our metabolism revved and humming, like the finely tuned machines we're meant to be.

Vitamins don't yield energy directly when they're broken down; instead, they work in concert with enzymes to release energy from carbohydrates, proteins, and fats. For example, green leafies like spinach give us B vitamins that support energy metabolism and nerve function, and colorful red bell peppers and tomatoes give us vitamin C to promote a healthy immune system, collagen synthesis, and help iron absorption.

Non-starchy vegetables also provide sodium and potassium, which help maintain electrolyte balance, and magnesium, which helps maintain healthy blood sugar levels and is involved in hundreds of essential metabolic functions. Of course, many non-starchy veggies and herbs like artichokes, parsley, spinach, and broccoli can also be a rich source of iron, which is an essential part of the process of carrying oxygen to your cells. That's always nice to have.

Phyto Superstars

Non-starchy vegetables are also universally high in phytonutrients (literally nutrients "from plants"), making them the most nutrient-dense foods on the planet. Phytonutrients are bioactive chemicals that support a plant's immune system by warding off bacteria, viruses, bugs, and other threats to a plant's survival. Fruits and starchy vegetables are also high in phytonutrients, and they're found in grains, nuts, and seeds as well.

Studies over the past 30 years have confirmed the benefits of eating 5 servings of fruits and vegetables a day. The Harvard-based Nurses' Health Study and Health Professionals Follow-Up Study tracked the dietary habits of almost 110,000 men and women for 14 years. People who averaged 8 or more servings of fruit and vegetables a day were 30% less likely to have had a heart attack or stroke. Evidence also suggests fruits and vegetables protect against a laundry list of other diseases and chronic health conditions, including high blood pressure and diabetes.

The phytonutrients in cruciferous vegetables such as broccoli, cauliflower, and Brussels sprouts make them disease-fighting warriors. They contain sulforaphane, an antioxidant and natural detoxifier, which studies suggest has powerful cancer-fighting properties. Cruciferous veggies are also high in indole-3-carbinol, another potent anticarcinogen.

Of the many classes of phytonutrients, there are two that pack a real punch: carotenoids and flavonoids.

Carotenoids

There are more than 600 carotenoids, which give fruit and vegetables their red, orange, and yellow color—think carrots, bell peppers, tomatoes, and pumpkin, to name a few. Carotenoids like the beta carotene in carrots are thought to protect against certain cancers, heart disease, and vision loss. Studies show that people who frequently eat spinach or collard greens, plants high in the carotenoid lutein, have a decreased risk of age-related macular degeneration compared to those who eat them infrequently. Are you beginning to see why I want you to eat a rainbow? You knew it wasn't just so your plate will look pretty (though it will!). Eating a variety of colorful veggies gives you an infusion of immune-boosting phytonutrients.

Eating a variety of colorful veggies gives you an infusion of immune-boosting phytonutrients.

Flavonoids

Flavonoids include catechins (found in green tea and known for their anti-cancer potency) and flavonols. Flavonols like quercetin are found in onions, apples, berries, and some other plant-based foods. Quercetin has been linked to reduced risk of certain types of cancer and cardiovascular disease.

YOUR SUGAR IMPACT SWAPS: ROOTS

Now, the moment you've been waiting for—specific swaps for roots. I promise you'll never miss those mashed potatoes!

Swap Your...	For...
Beet juice	Beets
Beets	Cucumbers
Carrot juice	Green juice
Cooked carrots	Raw carrots
French fries	Baked butternut squash fries
Mashed potatoes	Mashed cauliflower
Parsnips	Cauliflower
Potatoes	Turnips
Sundried tomatoes	Fresh chopped tomatoes
Veggie chips	Kale chips
Yams	Pumpkin

YOUR SUGAR IMPACT SCALE: ROOTS

Here's the complete Sugar Impact Scale for roots. Remember, these lists categorize foods as low, medium, and high SI for a reason—they're moving you away from high-SI carbs that spike your blood sugar and keep you burning, and craving, sugar. Instead, they'll load you up with heaps of low SI, non-starchy veggies that will keep you full, energized, and burning fat. Go to town on the Lows!

LOW SUGAR IMPACT

Acorn squash	Escarole	Pumpkin
Artichoke	Ginger root	Radicchio
Asparagus	Jicama	Radish
Bok choy	Kabocha squash	Snow peas
Broccoli	Kale	Spaghetti squash
Brussels sprouts	Kale chips	Spinach
Butternut squash	Leeks	Sprouts
Cabbage	Lettuces	Sugar snap peas
Carrots	Maca	Turnips
Cauliflower	Mushrooms	Water chestnuts
Celery	Mustard greens	Watercress
Chard	Okra	Zucchini
Cucumber	Onions	
Eggplant	Peppers	

MEDIUM SUGAR IMPACT

Beets	Rutabaga	Yams
Parsnips	Sweet potatoes	

HIGH SUGAR IMPACT

Beet juice	Mashed potatoes	Sweet potato fries
Carrot juice	Potato chips	White potatoes
French fries	Root veggie chips	

FORGO FORBIDDEN FRUIT

Surprise! Yes, fruit. It may not shock you that fruit is full of sugar, but I bet you didn't think it was one of the foods that could be contributing to your sugar addiction, slavery to cravings, and inability to drop that unwanted weight. What?! It's natural! It seems so healthy! True, some of it really is. But spreads, juices, and sorbets all slapped with a "made with real fruit" label aren't necessarily the healthy choice they appear. Some are loaded with added sugar and sabotaging your weight and health.

Here's another blow: fruits we're told to eat every day—like apples—can actually be some of the worst offenders for sneaking more sugar into your diet than you ever imagined, especially because you're probably giving yourself a pass to eat up. Don't despair, though—you don't have to give them up entirely. I'll help you take back your fruit. You'll make some simple swaps to get you on course for fast fat loss and feeling good. You're going to ditch the juice, jam, and dried fruit for berries, grapefruit, and other low SI fruit. As a bonus, you'll retrain your taste buds to once again truly appreciate the exquisite sweetness of whole fruit.

THE BIG PICTURE

First, a look at fruit from 5,000 feet. What we call a fruit is normally the fleshy (or dry) part of a plant that contains the seed, and it's usually edible in its raw state. Plants want the seeds in their fruits to live on and prosper, and they're very crafty about making them attractive and delicious so we animals will eat and deposit them elsewhere. We mostly think of fruits as being sweet, but that's not always the case—think cranberries and coconuts. Believe it or not, avocados are considered fruits, too, as are olives and tomatoes.

Who Knew?

Who knew fruits could be so confusing? Did you know a tomato is technically a fruit, but commercially it's considered a vegetable? Is it only a fruit if the seeds are on the inside? What about strawberries?

I'm about making things simple and easy, to set you up for success. So let common sense rule: if you eat it and use it as a fruit, it's a fruit (think "culinary fruits"). If you think of it as a veggie, it's a veggie. Officially cucumbers are fruit, and so are zucchini and pumpkin—but you'd never think of them that way. So I've kept them in veggies. I want you to keep your eye on the main thing—focus on SI, not becoming a fruit nerd.

Fruits are a crazy good source of vitamins, minerals, and other nutrients, like antioxidants. Antioxidants boost our immune system and fight off carcinogens and predators that we ingest or that are in our environment. Colorful fruits like blueberries and blackberries get their pigment from the antioxidants anthocyanins. Others, such as apples, give us antioxidants like quercetin through the chemical defenses in their skin. Studies show that a diet rich in antioxidants and anti-inflammatory agents may slow cognitive decline and the risk of developing chronic disease.

Fruits can be wet and juicy and filled with water, so they count as hydrating; they're great at satisfying your thirst as well as your hunger. They can also be an amazing source of fiber. Fruits can deliver an experience when you eat them, too. You know what I'm talking about! Some are succulent and tender and transport you to the tropics. Others are exotic and weirdly shaped and take you to the far-off place they grow.

I'm not here to deny much of the goodness that is fruit, unless you're talking dried fruit or fruit juice, which are different things entirely—and we'll get to those in a bit—but only to make some fine distinctions. As with most things, some fruits are simply better for you than others, and you should know which are which.

FRUCTOSE

Too much sugar is never a good thing, even from foods we consider healthy. The increased sugar load you punish yourself with when you eat a three-banana smoothie doesn't behave any differently in your system than it would if you ate a candy bar. And if too much sugar is bad, too much fructose is worse. In Chapter 1, I explained why fructose can be so damaging. Despite having the lowest GI ranking of any sugar, fructose is more easily and quickly turned into fat (usually belly fat) than glucose.

Fructose is naturally occurring in many foods, and it's the

primary (but not the only) sugar in fruit. Our consumption of it went up 19% from 1970 to 2005. That's dramatic, and it's not because we're inhaling 19% more fruit. You'd be surprised at the ways fructose may be sneaking into your diet. Fruit juice concentrates are one of the most popular sweeteners on the market. You may be fooled into thinking you're choosing a "no-sugar-added" product, only to find that it contains fruit juice concentrate.

Remember, when you connect the dots between what you eat and the result you get, it's simple—a high-sugar diet is a high-fat diet. So if you want to lose weight, a good place to start is to cut way (way) back on fructose. And you'll feel better, too, because in a bit I'll share with you the other damage fructose does to you besides making you jiggle around the middle.

Just as not all sugars are created equal, not all fruits have equal amounts and kinds of sugar. Most foods that contain fructose have about an equal amount of glucose. But many fruits have more fructose than glucose, and some have even more than others. Plums have less than half as much, but apples and pears have significantly more fructose than glucose—in fact, *twice* as much. That's one reason their juices are worse for you than full-sugar sodas—they have more sugar in them than the equivalent amount of drinks made with high-fructose corn syrup. They're pure liquid fructose bombs!

MAKE ROOM FOR MORE

Your capacity to absorb fructose increases the more you eat it. If that sounds like your body doing the good work you want it to do (you don't want that gastrointestinal distress!), not so much. When you eat more and more fructose, the building blocks of a transport system for it, known as Glut 5, also increase. So you just get better and better at sending it sailing to your liver, making sure all the extra fructose gets stored as fat, fast. And your fructose absorption really shoots up when fructose is paired with glucose. So when you eat fruit, which has both, you absorb a lot more fructose than if you were just to eat fructose alone.

It's not that you can never enjoy fruit again (although thinking about that last bit of information may make it a little less appealing), it just makes it mission-critical that you sleuth out and ditch all the worst-offending fruit sugar in your daily diet. Fruit based sauces, jams, and juices, which have a ton of added sugar, should jump to the top of your list. It's also important to know which whole fruits (and how much of them) are okay on a regular basis, and I'm going to help you with that.

NOT-SO-HEALTHY SWEETENERS AND SWEETS

It's really common for me to hear fruit juice and fruit juice concentrates recommended as "healthier sweeteners." In reality, they're often worse than other sweeteners. They're extremely high in fructose, and they don't have any nutrients or fiber, so that fructose barrels into your liver like a freight train.

Then there's dried fruit. I know you want to consider it the same as fresh, whole fruit. It's tidy and bite-size, and you don't need napkins or to eat it over the sink. The problem is that when food companies remove the water, they condense the sugar, and they often add other things, whether it's sulfur dioxide to preserve color or syrup to make it even sweeter. And in that case, it's just flat-out candy. Plus, if it's not organic, those little raisins could be pesticide pellets. Even if it is organic and nothing is added, dried fruit has the same amount of sugar and calories as its water-logged counterpart, but the pieces are so much smaller you're guaranteed to eat more (and get more sugar) than you would with whole fruit. I suppose you could argue that it's better than fruit cocktail drowning in heavy corn syrup, but it's close enough. Give dried fruit the red X.

DON'T DRINK YOUR SUGAR

Above all, don't drink your sugar. When you turn fruit into juice, you basically unwrap it from its fiber and set it free to give you a big sugar hit, fast. That includes those cool, funky juices that scream healthy and jump up and down about being made with real fruit. Fruit juices and sugary (sometime fruit-based) drinks are often infused with added sugar or high-fructose corn syrup, which is a lot sweeter than sugar, setting up a vicious cycle of craving and addiction that ensures high volumes of fructose get to take a shot at your weight and health with every drink. The fructose and glucose in high-fructose corn syrup aren't bound together, and without having to be broken apart, they work fast once they're ingested. The fructose races to your liver, and glucose almost instantly spikes your blood sugar and insulin.

MY IMPACT!

Lynn Kelly
Starting weight: 204 lbs.
Current weight: 194 lbs.
Total lost: 10 lbs.

I am a family practice nurse practitioner with no education regarding diet—hard to believe! The Sugar Impact Diet explicitly spelled out for my husband and me how to live in the real world and still take care of our nutritional needs.

I am diabetic and have heart disease. I now know that my body's responses to sugar and gluten are similar. My glucose has improved dramatically, and my goal is to get off many of my medications. I really have hope for that now. I feel so much better and have much more energy!

When I started the Sugar Impact Diet, I felt insecure about yet another "plan," even though I had done the Virgin Diet and trusted JJ. Now my husband and I are both singing JJ's praises!

Peers have always told me that I'm a gifted teacher, and I'm hoping to use that on this very subject with family, friends, at my church, and at an underserved clinic where I volunteer! The Sugar Impact diet changed my life—now all I want to do is share it with others!

YOUR SUGAR IMPACT SWAPS: FRUIT

With the Sugar Impact diet, you'll swap your juice, jam, and dried fruit for low–SI, whole fruits. And here's a simple rule to live by, or at least stick on your fridge: if it tastes sweet, don't eat!

Swap Your...	For...
Apple chips	Kale chips
Apples	Jicama
Canned fruit cocktail	Plain Greek-style yogurt
Dried cranberries	Fresh cranberries
Dried fruit	Freeze-dried berries
Fruit juice	Lemon-Aid
Fruit juice concentrate	Monk fruit, stevia
Fruit-sweetened or non-fat yogurt	Plain Greek-style yogurt *
Grapes	Blueberries
Jamba Juice smoothie	Sugar Impact Shake
Jams	Almond butter
Juice bar	Popsicle made with coconut milk, berries, and vanilla protein powder
Mangos	Guavas
Pineapple	Grapefruit
Raisins	Grapes
Sorbet	Coconut milk ice cream (1g of sugar sweetened)
Sun dried tomatoes	Fresh tomatoes
Tomato bisque	Gazpacho

*If you're not dairy-sensitive.

YOUR SUGAR IMPACT SCALE: FRUIT

The Sugar Impact Scale for fruits will help you navigate your transitions and swaps for high SI fruits. Look them over while you're here and reference them often during your cycles. See you back here soon!

LOW SUGAR IMPACT

Acai berries (no sugar added)
Avocado*
Blueberries
Cantaloupe
Cranberries
Gazpacho*
Grapefruit
Guava
Lemons*
Limes*
Nectarines
Olives*
Oranges
Peaches
Persimmon
Raspberries
Star fruit
Strawberries
Tomatoes

* 0–1 grams fructose—safe for Cycle 2.

MEDIUM SUGAR IMPACT

Apples
Apricots
Bananas
Cherries
Dates
Fresh figs
Grapes
Honeydew
Kiwi
Mango
Papaya
Pears
Pineapple
Plums
Pomegranate
Sun-dried tomatoes
Tangerines
Tomato juice
Tomato paste
Tomato sauce
V8 Juice
Watermelon

HIGH SUGAR IMPACT

All dried fruit
Fruit leather
Fruit juices
Jams
Preserves and conserves
Nectar
Sorbet
Fruit juice concentrates
Canned fruit cocktail
Fruit juice Popsicles

I hope you can already see how fun and easy this is going to be. Pretty soon you'll also see results! The Sugar Impact Diet will redefine your relationship with food to food, with benefits. The swaps for grains, roots, and fruit are delicious and give you a huge bang for your lower-impact buck. This is clearly not a diet that tells you what to give up and wishes you luck!

5

DITCH THE LOW-FAT AND NO-FAT DAIRY AND DIET FOODS

I can't wait for you to kiss that jelly belly goodbye. And I'm willing to go out on a limb and bet this category will make more of a dramatic shift in uncovering the secret channels of sugar in your life than any of the others. It's the giant leap you've been waiting for to jump-start fast fat loss and bring you back to life!

Low-fat labels are wicked, aren't they? They can set off a Pavlovian response that you may not even catch until you've got your hand on the carton. It's because in the 1970s, fat became the villain. Now it's as if there's some DNA programming we need to undo to help the truth sink in: a low-fat diet is a high-sugar diet! Period, end of story.

A low-fat diet is a high-sugar diet!

This low-fat brush fire was actually sparked in the 1950s by Ancel Keys, an epidemiologist from Minnesota who convinced us, based on some suspect science, that fat was the villain behind weight gain and heart disease. Poor fat! Just as it got scarlet lettered, high-fructose corn syrup swooped in to steal the limelight. In combination, those two incidents served up a mushroom cloud attack on American health. When we started pulling fat—meaning taste—out of all our food, food marketers had a bit of an issue. High-fructose corn syrup saved their bacon by filling in the taste vacuum to make food super sweet, and cheap. But when fat came out, the fiber did, too, so low-fat foods became sugar vessels without brakes.

IT'S A BIG TENT

Think about the wide swath covered by low-fat and non-fat food products—from dairy to frozen meals and meal replacement bars, to processed boxed and bagged junk food. Low fat is represented on product labels as "fat-free," "low-fat," "light," and "reduced-fat." That clears everything up, right? According to the Food and Drug Administration and the US Department of Agriculture, here's what they mean:

- "Fat-free" foods have less than 0.5 grams of fat per serving.
- "Low-fat" foods have 3 grams of fat or less per serving.
- "Reduced-fat" foods have at least 25% less fat than their full-fat counterparts.
- "Light" foods have either one-third fewer calories or 50% less fat.

As appealing as they've been made to sound, those low-fat labels spell trouble. Not all low-fat foods help you lose weight—far from it. They don't give you a pass on developing heart disease or gaining weight; probably just the opposite. And they certainly don't keep your cholesterol down, either. We're

Those low-fat labels spell trouble.

going to shine a spotlight on anything with a low-fat label and shame it right out of your kitchen.

GOOD FAT: YES, THERE IS SUCH A THING

So the focus here will be to help you identify and eat more of the good, life-sustaining fats that are fundamental to weight loss and a strong, healthy metabolism, and to dump the bad fats that are fueling inflammation and weight-loss resistance. The good fats keep you mentally sharp, your moods stable, and your energy high, and they play a huge role in weight control. They're the monounsaturated and polyunsaturated fats and omega-3 fatty acids in foods like avocados, olives, olive oil, nuts, grass-fed dairy, and wild, cold-water fish.

Cholesterol is a kind of fat, and it's not the bad guy you think it is. Cholesterol is essential to so many functions in your body that without it, you'd be dead. So your body doesn't leave it to chance that you'll get enough from what you eat. Instead, it goes ahead and makes its own—which is used for everything from hormone production to the manufacture of cell membranes and vitamin D. Yes, there's a bit of a distinction between kinds of cholesterol particles, and you want to eat foods that raise the number of good particles and lower the bad. More on that coming up. But don't avoid otherwise healthy foods because they have a little cholesterol.

WHEN THEY'RE BAD, THEY'RE HORRID

Bad fats are a very different story. And your body lets you know that by responding to them with increased inflammation, weight gain, and conditions that raise your risk of chronic disease. One kind of bad fat is the saturated fat found in factory-farmed meats like beef and pork. When animals are fed GMO corn and soy, it changes their fatty acid profile, and not for the better. Plus, that fat is often loaded with hormones, antibiotics, and pesticides, to boot.

Not all saturated fats are bad, though. It's all about the quality of their source. When you choose butter or meat from grass-fed cows or high-quality coconut oil, sure—you'll get some saturated fat. But make no mistake about it, it's not the pro-inflammatory fat you get from those factory-raised animals or potato chips.

The oils sitting on the supermarket shelf have been robbed of their nutrients (which have been sold off to supplement companies) and highly processed in their journey to the plastic bottle you find them in. They're exposed to heat during travel, light on the shelves, and air every time you open them, all of which helps them oxidize and turn rancid. So the value jugs of vegetable oil are anything but. They're damaged fats that have an effect similar to trans fats, and you don't want them in your body.

As you can see, the distinction isn't small. The wrong fats can make you gain weight and increase the risk of disease, but the rich, good fats you'll get in natural, organic whole foods offer a ton of benefits for your health and weight, mostly *because* the fats are in the food. Remove those fats, and everything they offer is turned on its head.

DAIRY

It might never occur to you that dairy should headline the low-fat category. But one of the long-standing nutritional recommendations from the US Department of Agriculture is that we eat 3 cups of dairy a day. When low fat became the rage, it meant nutritionists were recommending only skim or 1–2 percent milk, low-fat yogurt, and low-fat cheese to hit that mark. Everyone reasoned that because full-fat dairy products are higher in calories, their low-fat counterparts would allow kids (and the rest of us) to benefit from their calcium, vitamin D, and other nutrients without becoming obese.

It turns out, though, that may have been exactly the outcome they engineered. Not only was the focus on calories completely misguided, we now believe low-fat milk products may actually drive weight gain and the very health risks the low-fat versions were meant to help us avoid.

Low-fat milk products may actually drive weight gain and the very health risks the low-fat versions were meant to help us avoid.

When the fat is pulled out of dairy, both the flavor and that food's ability to make you feel full and satisfied are yanked, too. Plus, without the fat, guess what's left? You guessed it—the sugar! That's why skim milk is especially wicked.

Skim milk can also be highly processed. The high heat used in making skim milk kills all the beneficial bacteria in it. And the skimming process not only strips the milk of essential healthy saturated fats and vitamins, but some manufacturers even add powdered non-fat milk. So it's got none of the healthy fats you need for hormone synthesis, fewer of the vitamins and minerals essential for a high-functioning metabolism, and more lactose, or sugar, than full-fat milk.

Lactose is made from the sugars galactose and glucose. The enzyme lactase breaks down lactose into those sugars during digestion. Without fat to slow the absorption of glucose and galactose, low-fat dairy spikes your blood sugar and insulin response the same way any high-sugar processed snack does.

Low-fat dairy spikes your blood sugar and insulin response the same way any high-sugar processed snack does.

Granted, if you're dairy-sensitive, you can have other things going on, too. You can respond badly to casein, the primary protein in dairy. It's similar to the protein gluten found in grains, since both can have a drug-like effect on the brain. Casein peptides in dairy products can react with opiate receptors, mimicking the effects of opiate drugs like heroin and morphine. As a result, your brain responds to dairy just like it would to any drug. It's no surprise that cheese is loaded with casein. Anyone addicted to cheese? Anyone?

When casein breaks up during digestion, the morphine-like compounds it produces are called casomorphins. Dr. Neal Barnard, author of *Breaking the Food Seduction: The Hidden Reasons Behind Food Cravings—and 7 Steps to End Them Naturally*, says "Since cheese is processed to express out all the liquid, it's an incredibly concentrated source of casomorphins—you might call it dairy crack." Here's a news flash—skim milk contains more casein than whole-fat milk! See, there's no such thing as a skinny latte. And cheese has an even higher concentration of caseins than milk, so that low-fat cheese on your pizza is not your friend—it's your fix.

But one of the biggies of dairy sensitivity, of course, is intolerance to lactose. Lactose intolerance is usually a result of not having enough lactase, the enzyme produced in your small intestine that helps you digest the sugar in dairy products. Populations around the world vary in their ability to tolerate lactose, but it seems Europeans are the genetic winners, with the most people able to handle it. It's believed that many Europeans produce lactase as adults because their ancestors used milk from cows, goats, and sheep as food throughout their lives.

Still, the population of people who can't break down lactose is huge. If you're one of them, lactose travels intact to your gut and fertilizes gas-producing bugs, which leads to diarrhea, gas, bloating, and other gastrointestinal distress. The good news is that you're not doomed to suffer every time you have dairy. You can control your lactose intolerance by being very selective about the kinds and amounts of dairy you consume.

So, if you're intolerant to dairy and you're desperate to have a little dairy now and then, I'm about to serve up some great news. There are some really amazing choices out there that won't wreak havoc on your system. How is that possible? Because there's a nutrient gulf between the good options and the low-fat dairy from factory-farmed cows you've been reacting to up until now.

FERMENTATION

Fermented dairy products are also known as cultured dairy. Fermenting has been around for thousands of years, and traditional cultures, including some in Russia and Europe, still rely on it heavily. The fermentation process increases the shelf-life of dairy products, makes them much more tasty (no comparison, truly), and makes them a whole lot easier to digest.

Once Americans enthusiastically embraced pasteurized dairy products over raw or fermented forms in the early part of the twentieth century, we lost a lot of powerful, immunizing probiotics and enzymes right along with any potential pathogens. Too bad, because fermentation, in particular, has some near miracle druglike powers—it can make food that was once inedible or even dangerous not only edible, but nutritious.

Raw milk is fermented either by allowing it to sour naturally or by adding the milk-loving bacteria lactobacillus to it. Lactobacilli are generally benign and exist naturally in small amounts in our gut. They feed on the sugar and starch in the milk, creating lactic acid and preserving the milk in the process. They also beat back bad bacteria and release beneficial enzymes, vitamins, minerals, omega-3 fatty acids, and various strains of fabulous probiotics. And remember the protein casein? These good bacteria also help break down casein so we can digest it. Wow, right?

But back to the big headline—the bacteria also feed on sugar. The fermentation process eats up the lactose, so it takes that problematic sugar right out of the equation for anyone who's lactose-intolerant. In doing so, it also decreases carb content. And since labels are made before fermentation, fermented dairy actually has fewer carbs than you see on the label. Win!

So exactly how does fermenting dairy products improve their nutritional content and digestibility—and ability to detoxify? By preserving the enzymes lactase and lipase, which help you absorb more of fermented dairy's (increased) nutrients. Fermenting dairy tends to increase B vitamins including folic acid, important in the fight against heart disease and cancer. It also boosts the detoxifying powerhouse amino acid glutathione and many essential amino acids, and, of course, probiotics, the healthy bacteria in your gut.

Probiotics balance the ecosystem in your gut and earn fermented dairy a gold-star reputation for improving digestion and strengthening immunity. There's evidence they can also slow or reverse some diseases.

So, as you can see, if you aren't dairy-intolerant, I'd have you get some raw, grass-fed, fermented dairy into your diet. That's the trifecta. You don't always have to have all three, but check off as many of those boxes as you can. It will allow you to enjoy the richness of dairy again without the guilt, or the proteins and sugars that make you suffer with the symptoms of intolerance and extra pounds. Imagine!

Here are some sources I recommend:

- Crème fraiche
- Cultured buttermilk
- Cultured cheeses (especially goat cheese)
- Cultured cottage cheese
- Cultured sour cream
- Grass-fed butter (such as Kerrygold)
- Grass-fed ghee
- Kefir
- Yogurt

I find that even people who react to dairy can often eat some of these foods, especially the nutrient powerhouse grass-fed ghee. It doesn't have any dairy protein particles, so it's safe even if you're dairy-intolerant, like me.

YOU ARE WHAT YOU EAT

As I explained in Chapter 3, you are what you eat, ate. That doesn't just apply to protein—it applies to dairy sources, too. If you reach for dairy that comes from factory-farmed animals, you're increasing your risk of ingesting all the hormones, antibiotics, and stress in those horribly treated cows, goats, or sheep. And those animals are fed corn or soy-based feed, which is likely to be genetically modified, so they also produce more inflammatory omega-6 fatty acids than pastured animals.

Go for raw, grass-fed, full-fat dairy. It's so much better for you and for the animals that produce it. It's a win–win: happy cows, happy humans. If you can't get your hands on raw, grass-fed, high-fat dairy, at least make certain to choose full-fat, organic, and hormone and antibiotic-free.

FULL-FAT, FULL-TIME—AVOIDING LOW-FAT SNACKS AND DESSERTS

The low-fat dairy umbrella covers its processed cousins, like frozen desserts and those little alien sticks in plastic. If low-fat milk, yogurt, and cheese are no good, low-fat packaged cheese wands are worse, since they can have preservatives and anti-caking agents as well. (To be fair, there are full-fat versions, but it's unlikely they're from grass-fed cows, and they're certainly not raw or fermented.) How about other dairy treats like reduced-fat cheese cubes or low-fat fro-yo? I'm hoping I don't have to cover Cheese Whiz Light here, but the appeal of "low-fat dairy" goodies cannot be underestimated.

Packaged dairy snacks and desserts branded "low-fat" are meant to appeal to anyone who's been brainwashed to believe fat is the enemy (namely, everyone!). Once those addictive foods get their hooks in you, your brain works you over, telling you they're healthy and to give them a free pass because, hey, if they don't have fat, you can't gain weight. Sorry to break it to you, but there's no such thing as a healthy ice cream sandwich. These snacks are loaded with added sugar (usually high-fructose corn syrup) to make up for their terrible, low-fat taste. The added sugar contributes to their addictive quality, making you come back for more and more, when all they are doing is sabotaging your efforts to trim down and feel better. Frankenfood isn't the answer. I've got plenty of delicious Sugar Impact Swaps for you (see page 110) that will help you cut the cravings for low-fat dairy and lose fat fast.

You can see that pulling the fat out of dairy snacks does a lot more than just kill the taste. It also removes a very important pathway that protects you from weight gain. When you eat healthy fat with low Sugar Impact, naturally occurring sugar—think full-fat Greek yogurt with raspberries versus a candy bar—you slow down the release of food from your stomach, which mitigates blood sugar spikes and the insulin surge that goes with it. It helps you feel full and get by for longer periods of time without eating again. Sugar in non-fat yogurt hits your bloodstream a whole lot faster than the sugar in full-fat yogurt, and you're scrounging for another snack before you know what hit you.

FAT AND HAPPY

I don't want to mince words here. Low-fat diets—or rather, high-sugar diets—raise triglycerides through fructose metabolism in the liver. Those elevated triglycerides, which get stored as fat, are a risk factor for cardiovascular disease and an indicator of metabolic syndrome, a precursor to obesity and diabetes. Many studies on the effect of low-fat diets on the risk of heart disease show they not only don't lower risk, they contribute to it!

Low-fat diets actually lower your large HDL particles, or what's known as "good" cholesterol, the one you're trying to keep high. High levels of large HDL particles are associated with a reduced risk of heart disease. Essential fatty acids, especially omega-3s, can elevate large HDL particles, improve cholesterol levels, and protect your heart.

A diet without good fats also increases small, dense LDL particles—the part of cholesterol that's considered "bad." A high level of LDL particles puts you at greater risk for heart disease. Studies show that low-fat diets contribute to an increase in these harmful LDL particles.

Healthy fats are also essential for testosterone levels, and this is not just a guy's thing. It's important news for everyone. Testosterone is made from cholesterol. A drop in testosterone can lead to decreased muscle mass, increased body fat, osteoporosis, and low libido.

Eating a diet without enough fat can also create issues with the absorption of the critical fat-soluble vitamins A, D, E, and K. Your body needs healthy fats to help those vitamins get absorbed; otherwise, they're excreted. And you need them to keep your immune system strong and repair your cells.

Besides, a diet without delicious, healthy fats is just depressing. It's not just a bummer to eat food that's only edible because it's been drowned in manufactured sugars. Worse, when essential fatty acids are missing—and those are fats your body can only get from food—it might truly impact your mental health. Omega-3s and some 6s are necessary for hormone synthesis and brain chemicals, and play significant roles in mood and behavior.

Healthy fats like eggs (if you're not intolerant), avocado, olive oil, coconut oil, sustainably raised palm oil, wild salmon, and organic, grass-fed dairy are sources of healthy, brain-feeding fats that keep your blood sugar stable and regulate the amount of insulin released after you eat. In other words, these delicious foods tee up fast fat loss by making you feel good, filling you up, and helping you keep a handle on your cravings.

It's time to put that old low-fat chestnut to bed and embrace the light of the new full-fat day. Taste and nutrition, welcome back.

YOUR SUGAR IMPACT SWAPS: LOW-FAT AND NO-FAT DAIRY AND DIET FOODS

We love our swaps, and there's no end to the list of delicious (and more nutritious) choices to replace your low-fat crutches. Here are a few tasty treats to try:

Swap Your...	For...
Butter substitute	Coconut cream
Cool Whip	Full-fat coconut milk (whipped)
Fat-free pudding	Mousse made with avocado, coconut cream, and coconut milk
Frozen "light" dinner	Lentil soup
Frozen yogurt	Sugar Impact Shake
Fruit on the bottom yogurt	Plain full-fat Greek-style yogurt *
Fudgesicle	Homemade protein Popsicle
Ice cream	Monk fruit–sweetened coconut ice cream
Light cream cheese	Avocado
Low-fat crackers	Bean chips
Low-fat pita chips	Olives
Low-fat potato chips	Kale chips
Margarine	Grass-fed butter
Microwave light popcorn	Crudités
Pretzels	Roasted Brussels sprouts
Protein bar	Wild salmon jerky
Skim milk	Full-fat grass-fed milk
Snack packs	Baggie of low-roasted nuts
Sweetened creamer	Coconut milk creamer (unsweetened)
Sweetened soy milk	Unsweetened coconut milk

*If you're not intolerant.

Choosing Protein Powder

Protein shakes can be a great and easy way to make sure you're eating by the Sugar Impact Plate, even at breakfast. Here are some general guidelines to follow so you don't get confused when you shop for protein powder.

- Ideally, choose a high-quality protein base: de-fatted beef, or plant-based powder made from rice, pea, chia, chlorella, or cranberry protein, or a blend of these.
- Look for GMO-free and hormone-free (meaning no recombinant bovine growth hormone, or rGBH) if choosing beef-based powders.
- Avoid soy, egg, or milk protein powders, and artificial colors and sweeteners such as aspartame and sucralose. If there is an added sweetener, it should be no more than 5 grams per serving and not come from fructose or high-fructose corn syrup.
- When making your protein shakes, use 1–2 scoops of protein powder, according to the package directions.
- For some of my favorite brands and best recommendations, check out the Resources section on my website http://sugarimpact.com/resources.

YOUR VIRGIN SUGAR IMPACT SCALE: LOW-FAT AND NO-FAT DAIRY AND DIET FOODS

When I discovered I should be eating more healthy fat and ditching low-fat diet foods, it was like being set free. I wanted to "Mmmm" out loud with every rich spoonful of organic, plain, full-fat Greek-style yogurt—and I can't wait for you to feel the same way! Without the added sugars of low-fat foods, these delicious low-SI choices won't spike and crash your blood sugar . . . they'll just leave you satisfied and smiling.

LOW SUGAR IMPACT

Flax milk (unsweetened)

Full-fat cheeses (avoid blue cheese due to gluten)

Full-fat cream cheese

Full-fat grass-fed milk

Full-fat organic milk

Full-fat plain cottage cheese

Monk fruit sweetened coconut ice cream

Mozzarella

Coconut creamer (no sugar added)

Coconut, cashew, or almond milk (no sugar added)

Cultured coconut milk (no sugar added)

Nut cheese

Organic creamer

Organic, plain full-fat Greek-style yogurt

Plain cultured coconut yogurt (no sugar)

Plain dairy or coconut kefir

Protein powder (following my parameters)

Ricotta cheese

MEDIUM SUGAR IMPACT

Cream cheese spread (low-fat or full-fat)

Half-and-half

Low-fat cheese

Neufchatel cheese

Organic low-fat or non-fat plain Greek-style yogurt

Part-skim mozzarella

Part-skim ricotta

Plain coconut yogurt (sweetened)

Soy cheese

Sweetened coconut milk creamer

Unsweetened rice milk

Whipped cream cheese

HIGH SUGAR IMPACT

94% fat-free microwave kettle corn

94% fat-free microwave popcorn

Almond milk ice cream

Blue cheese

Breakfast bars

Carnation Instant Breakfast

Coconut milk ice cream

Creamsicles

Dried fruit snacks

Ensure

Fat-free baked chips

Fat-free muffins

Fat-free pudding

Fat-free, sugar-free Jell-O

Fat-free Twizzlers

Flavored almond milk yogurt

Flavored coconut yogurt

Flavored kefir

Frozen yogurt

Fruit-added cream cheese

Fudgesicles

Gelato

Granola bars

Hot cocoa

Ice cream

Ice cream sandwiches

Lite Cool Whip

Low-fat and fat-free cookies

Low-fat graham crackers

Low-fat or fat-free ice cream

Low-fat or fat-free ice cream bars

Low-fat or light frozen dinners

Low-fat Oreos

Low or reduced-fat crackers

Mousse
Nestlé's Quik
Non-fat cheeses
Non-fat cream cheese
Pineapple cottage cheese
Pretzels
Protein bars
Pudding
Reduced-fat macaroni and cheese
Reduced-fat peanut butter
Reduced-fat Pringles
Snack packs

Snackwells low-fat and fat-free cookies
   and treats
Sorbet
Strawberry cream cheese
Sweetened coffee creamers
Sweetened cow milk (vanilla, chocolate)
Sweetened dairy-free milks
Sweetened whipped cream
Unsweetened soy milk*
Yogurts with sugar or artificial
   sweeteners
Whey Protein Powder

Low in sugar, but high in lectins that can cause leptin resistance—choose only organic fermented soy.

Now that we've all finally emerged from the haze of the low–fat/ no–fat craze, we can once again take pleasure in the brain-fueling, fat-burning food nature has given us—guilt-free. Removing low-fat and no-fat diet foods goes a long way in reducing the hidden impact of sneaky sugar. The fact that it's also tastier is just an awesome bonus!

6

SO LONG, SWEET DRINKS
AND DRESSINGS

Sometimes it's not the meal itself that's sabotaging you, it's what you're having with it, even if it's something you've been led to believe is a healthy choice. A fresh salad packed with veggies becomes nothing more than a sugar delivery vehicle when it's drowned in "low-fat" dressing. What you're sipping matters, too, whether your drink is sweetened with added "natural" sugar or high-fructose corn syrup or it's a "diet" version. Drinks and dressings aren't usually given as much thought as what to order off the menu, but just because they fly under the radar, they're by no means innocent. My guess is that you're about to be surprised by the Sugar Impact (SI) of these sneaky sugars and their stealth attack on your waistline and health.

CAN THE SUGARY DRINKS

There's a reason the saying isn't, "Eat, and be merry!" We've arrived at liquids. Let's give them the respect they deserve, considering you can fast without food for a day or even more, but go without water, and you'll feel it fast—your mouth dries up, and you'll get nauseous, light-headed, and maybe even have heart palpitations.

But choice is not to be taken lightly in this category. There's a huge divide between beverages that give you incredible health benefits, like boosting your immunity and brain function, and those that wreck your blood sugar levels and leave you fatigued and frustrated. I'm going to make sure you're always reaching for drinks that do triple duty to fuel your fast fat loss, sky-high energy, and peace of mind. You can do this!

THINK ABOUT IT

When you drink throughout the day, more than likely you don't give it a second thought. It's less about choice than habit, isn't it? Once you're a sweet tea or soda drinker, it can become a habit that you haven't given thought to in years—until you go to break it. Then you may find you get a serious wake-up call that makes it hard to deny the hold some of these sugary, jolt-inducing concoctions have over you.

The mindless funnel of liquids with and between meals is one of the biggest ways sugar sneaks into your body and wreaks havoc on your weight and metabolism, and now there's evidence that added sugar in beverages does much more harm than ever imagined. That additional sugar usually comes in the form of high-fructose corn syrup, which is nothing more than a high-calorie, nutrient-free setup for chronic disease.

ANYTHING BUT SWEET

Let's start with some of those innocent looking sugar sweetened beverages. Check out the ones I call out on the list of high SI drinks, and notice that if you're going to remove hidden sugar from your diet, you'll need to have more than soda in your crosshairs.

Fruit juices, instant breakfast mixes, and even most vitamin-supplemented waters all have added sugar, too, and I bet the odds are good you're drinking one or more beverages on that list most days, if not every day.

You may be justifying these drinks away or, worse yet, barely aware you're slurping in empty calories and setting yourself up for chronic disease. The harsh truth? You can't afford to give this habit a pass. To your body, there's no difference between a Gatorade and a full-sugar soda (though diet sodas are actually worse, as I'll explain in Chapter 7). Enhanced waters and fruit juices can be just as bad, and forget about any sweet drink you need to make with a scoop. Of course, drinking one of those canned "weight-loss" shakes to lose weight is, well, just ironic (check the sugar content—it's shocking!).

But the news is especially bad if you drink carbonated sodas infused with high-fructose corn syrup. Sugary sodas have been linked to a 78% increased risk of endometrial cancer. A study published in *Cancer Epidemiology, Biomarkers and Prevention* looked at data from more than 23,000 postmenopausal women who were followed for 24 years, from 1986 to 2010. These women might have had a lot of other unhealthy habits, too, but there's mounting evidence that just drinking sugary drinks is enough to put you at risk for serious health conditions, especially because of the fallout from the pounds it packs on.

Obesity is its own problem, but it also creates risk factors for more serious disease. It increases estrogen and insulin levels, and higher levels of those hormones are risk factors for—guess what?—endometrial cancer. See how that goes? Study after study shows the link between the added sugar in drinks and the swing they take at your health. They hook you, then take you down ounce by ounce, with no obvious signs, until suddenly you don't even recognize the chunky, exhausted, aging person in the mirror.

Sugar-sweetened beverages have been connected to an increased risk for obesity and diabetes, which are also linked to lower cognitive performance and cognitive decline. They're also connected to heart disease and metabolic disorders. Seriously! What this essentially means is that if you keep drinking sugar-sweetened soda, you're damaging your body in countless ways.

CAFFEINE

If you're a coffee drinker, you might be reaping some serious rewards for your habit, even beyond its help popping your eyes open in the morning. That is, as long as you're not pouring in sugar and cream and serving that cup of joe up with a muffin.

Coffee beans and green tea are packed with beneficial antioxidants, so there's more to that cup than meets the eye. Green tea has been used medicinally for thousands of years, and both it and coffee have many health benefits attached to the plant chemicals still in them when they're brewed. Caffeine sparks an increase in adrenaline, which triggers the release of fatty acids from your fat storage (something called lipolysis). So the buzz and energy you get from caffeine, or that you used to get before you needed it just to feel normal, is due both to the shot of adrenaline and these fatty acids floating around serving up energy to burn.

So it's no surprise that most research points to evidence that our beloved, humble coffee is linked to lower weight. But what's really interesting is that studies show in the long run caffeine actually improves your insulin sensitivity and lowers your risk for diabetes. And it can improve liver function. Coffee can also reduce your hunger, even if it's decaffeinated, according to a study in the *Journal of the American College of Nutrition*. Coffee's not a complete disease-fighting slouch, either. Last July, the American Institute for Cancer Research and the World Cancer Research Fund International announced findings that the antioxidants in coffee and its role in regulating insulin may make it protective against endometrial cancer.

If you're a green tea drinker, you're an even bigger winner. Green tea may actually hydrate as well as water (the idea that caffeine causes dehydration is a myth). Plus, it's full of heart-protective and free radical–fighting polyphenols. Green tea lowers your risk for developing chronic diseases ranging from cardiovascular disease to cancer. It's rich in flavonoids, including the catechin epigallocatechin gallate, which is thought to be key to green tea's anticancer and antioxidant powers.

Too much caffeine can work against you, though, and you know what I'm talking about if you've ever thrown back just one cup too many, or downed that Americano too late in the day. Or you may just be a slow caffeine metabolizer, which makes you more sensitive to caffeine than most. It can make you wired, anxious, and irritable. So stick to a cup or two a day (organic, and without mycotoxins, if possible), get the benefits you deserve, and sleep well.

ALCOHOL

If you're not a drinker, you can skip ahead. And if you don't drink now, I'm not encouraging you to start. But for those of you who like to uncork now and then, I'm going to make you just as happy as that glass of wine does—the Sugar Impact Diet will not take away your wine (personally, I would never do a diet or create one that took away mine for the long term!).

Alcohol isn't sugar, but its fate is nearly the same. Fermentation of fruit and grains creates alcohol. During the fermentation process, enzymes gobble up the sugars. Wine, beer, and hard alcohol generally don't have residual sugars, though some of the cheaper wines or sweeter wines do (it's why quality matters). Of course, if you're using a mixer like tonic water or cola, or an alcoholic blend that has added sugar, you're getting both alcohol and sugar.

Although alcohol is metabolized differently than sugar, the end result is very similar to that of fructose metabolism. Most of that glass of wine or shot of tequila (roughly 80%) skirts insulin response and takes the HOV lane to your liver. Your liver then converts it to acetaldehyde (a close relative of formaldehyde, and a poison). Some of the alcohol becomes glucose, but a lot of it becomes free fatty acids, triglycerides, and VLDL—the end products of fructose metabolism.

It turns out that a little alcohol—5 ounces of red wine, 1 ounce of hard alcohol—may be cardioprotective and help with weight loss. Evidence suggests that reasonable drinking of any kind of alcohol can raise your good cholesterol, the large fluffy HDL particles. If wine isn't your thing, your second best option is tequila. Unlike vodka and other hard liquors, it's not made from grains (see Chapter 4).

But, as with everything, it's all about the dose. Too much can lead to fatty liver, poor eating habits, nutrient deficiencies, and inflammation. For the transition weeks in Cycle 2 (yes, I'm asking you to abstain—but only for 2 weeks!), we're giving the liver a much-needed break, and removing alcohol is part of that strategy. Why?

When you drink alcohol, you'll sideline fat-burning. Alcohol cuts to the front of the metabolic line as soon as it arrives. Your body puts everything else on hold, including fat metabolism, to metabolize alcohol.

A word of warning to the ladies—you get intoxicated more quickly than men (even of the same weight) because you have less of the enzyme alcohol dehydrogenase in your stomachs than men do, so you can't break the alcohol down as fast. If you're menopausal, you'll also become more intoxicated on smaller doses of alcohol than you did when you were younger.

And another brief caution: alcohol seems to stimulate appetite, not suppress it, so if you thought you were going to get away with swapping out alcohol calories for dinner, think again. It doesn't affect satiety like food calories do, and it can actually increase hunger and mindless grazing. Basically, that means when you've had a few, you decide you're starving and you don't have the willpower to keep yourself from plowing through the salty snacks in the pantry (because we both know you're not going to binge on crudités, right?). You wake up feeling lousy for all kinds of reasons, not the least of which is the remorse and guilt that come with falling off the diet wagon.

What About Cooking with Wine?

When you're moving from high-SI beverages to medium-SI options, as you will be in Cycle 1, you'll be okay to cook with some dry red and white wines. But when you hit Cycle 2, and you're not having any alcohol, leave it out of recipes altogether. Wine doesn't completely evaporate during cooking (I know, surprise!) so it's another place sugar can sneak into what you're eating without you even realizing it. But don't panic—it will be there for you when you get back, when you reintroduce it in Cycle 3.

GO GREEN

Juices can be dicey; you have to be really careful about sneaky sugar. The best vegetable juices and green drinks are *straight* green, meaning, made only from vegetables. Otherwise, you have to be sure they're not tweaked with added fruit and bottled as "healthy" juices. Check the label (especially for apples, carrots, or beets), or, better yet, make your own.

Even if you do, don't go thinking you'll drink them all day, every day. Sure, they're low in sugar and carbs, but they can still drive up your blood sugar! Ideally, drink one with your meal, but if you're having it as a snack, consider adding a tablespoon of chia seeds for some extra fiber and protein to temper your blood sugar response.

WATER: THE CLEAR WINNER

Of course you can never go far without hearing the consistent chorus about getting eight glasses of water in a day, and I'd have you drink even more if I ruled the world. If you want to burn fat, build muscle, and have glowing skin, water is your answer. Let me give you seven reasons that drinking enough water is *that* important:

1. **Water helps you eat less during your meals.** A study in the journal *Obesity (Silver Spring)* showed that when people drank 8 ounces of water before each reduced-calorie meal, they had greater fat loss compared to people who didn't drink water before they ate. Another study presented at the American Chemical Society's annual conference showed that 2 glasses of water before every meal helped people lose an average of 15.5 pounds (5 pounds more than the non-water drinkers) over 3 months. The one time I *don't* want you drinking water is *during* meals, because it can dilute the stomach enzymes that break down protein. But before and after your meal, drink up!

2. **Water can make your skin glow.** I've met women who spend hundreds of dollars at a time on top-shelf skin care to hydrate their skin, when they should really be reaching for some H_2O. Because skin is your body's largest organ, it's also your most significant *detoxification* agent. Perspiration and evaporation are mechanisms designed to cleanse your skin and remove waste. Without adequate water, that waste builds up, leading to breakouts, acne, and other problems. Poor hydration also means your body can make less new collagen, and the existing collagen becomes brittle.

3. Water helps muscle maintenance and recovery. Muscle tissue is about 75% water, which explains why even 3% dehydration can reduce muscle strength up to 15%. Dehydration also shrinks muscle cells and leads to protein breakdown. Optimal hydration replenishes electrolytes and reduces exercise-related inflammation.

> *Even 3% dehydration can reduce muscle strength up to 15%.*

4. If you're not well hydrated, you're not detoxifying. Even if you're eating organically, dehydration means your body can't detoxify with maximum efficiency. Water flushes waste from your cells, but when you're dehydrated, your cells draw water from your blood, stressing your heart and preventing your kidneys from purifying blood. Your liver and other organs also feel the pressure. Toxic buildup leads to constipation, literally forcing your body to cling to the waste it needs to eliminate.

5. Dehydration can raise stress hormones. Some experts believe dehydration is the number one cause of stress. Even mild dehydration of 1–2% can raise levels of the stress hormone cortisol. And what's cortisol good at? Storing fat around your middle and breaking down muscle.

6. Dehydration can create fatigue. When you don't drink enough water, nothing good happens. Your metabolism screeches to a halt, your fluid balance is upended, and your blood volume drops. Your heart struggles to deliver nutrients and oxygen to your tissues. You're hit with headaches, brain fog, and fatigue. Ironically, fatigue will probably mean you reach for a different liquid altogether—keep the coffee coming, right?

7. Water can reduce cravings. Thirst can come disguised as hunger, and you're in a bad way when you can't tell the difference between just needing some water or that Krispy Kreme donut.

Hint: try the water first. And if cravings are gnawing at you before bed, see if water beats them back. According to a study at the University of Washington, drinking 8 ounces of water at bedtime can shut down your evening hunger pangs. Sweet dreams.

See page 183 in Chapter 8 for more helpful information on water, including how much of it to drink and when.

YOUR SUGAR IMPACT SWAPS: DRINKS

You'll make the biggest impact on fast fat loss, higher energy, and glowing skin when you stop drinking your calories. Sugar-sweetened drinks are one of the biggest barriers between you and the you you're about to become. Ditch high-SI drinks, especially sugar-sweetened sodas, for *anything* on the low SI list. And remember, water is a great swap for any beverage!

Swap Your...	For...
Beer	Gluten-free beer
Carrot juice	Green juice
Energy drinks	Organic coffee or green tea
Gatorade	Unsweetened coconut water
Hot chocolate	Warm coconut milk and chocolate protein powder
Jamba Juice smoothie	Sugar Impact Shake
Latte	Espresso with coconut creamer
Regular/diet soda	Sparkling water
Sweet tea	Brewed tea with lemon
Sweet wine	Pinot noir
Vitaminwater	Hint water

YOUR SUGAR IMPACT SCALE: DRINKS

Sneaky sugar in sweet beverages has a huge hidden impact—it's one of the biggest highjackers of your waistline and health. When you drop high-SI beverages from your daily routine, you'll fast-track fat loss and support your move from sugar burner to fat burner. Stay hydrated, my friends.

LOW SUGAR IMPACT

All teas
Green drinks (greens only—no fruit, carrot, or beet added)*
Green tea (no sugar added)
Hint water
Organic coffee and decaf coffee

Sparkling mineral water
Teeccino
Unsweetened coconut water
Unsweetened fruit essence teas
Water

* Do not drink on their own—add fiber.

MEDIUM SUGAR IMPACT

Dry red wine
Dry white wine
Gin
Gluten-free beer
Kombucha tea (no sugar added)

Tequila
Tomato juice
V8 (not with fruit juice)
Vodka

HIGH SUGAR IMPACT

Beer
Brandy
Capri Sun
Carnation Instant Breakfast
Carrot juice
Champagne
Commercial "smoothies"
Crystal Light
Diet soda
"Enhanced" waters (with sweeteners)
Fruit juices
Fuze
Gatorade
Kool-Aid

Mixed drinks
Nestlé's Quik
Port
PowerAde
Rockstar energy drink
Rum
Slim-Fast
Sobe
Soda
Sweet tea
Sweetened coconut water
Vitaminwater and most vitamin-supplemented waters
Wines—sweet, dessert

SAYONARA SUGARY DRESSINGS, SAUCES, AND CONDIMENTS

If there's one thing I wish, it's that I was standing next to each and every one of you when you took your Sneaky Sugar Inventory. Before that, I bet you might have looked me square in the eye and sworn, with impressive conviction, that you weren't eating any sugar.

So if you now find yourself taking a deep breath about taking sugar banishment to the next level, not to worry. We're going to ease into this nice and slowly, removing sneaky sugar and swapping sweet dressings, sauces, and condiments for near-even taste trades, but with huge improvements in SI. You're going to hand over the sugary toppings and replace them—from high to medium to low SI—with healthy oils and real vinegars. You'll trade sauces and ketchup for mustards and salsas. Odds are, you'll like your swaps so much that you'll never look back. They'll bring fireworks of rich, layered flavors to your food—and they'll be supporting you, not sabotaging you! Let's show them some love!

SWIMMING IN SUGAR

This category is about to expose you to the land mines of sugar lurking in your fridge and pantry, just waiting to plump you up and wreak havoc on your blood sugar. Keep spooning them in and before you know it, dollop by dollop, they'll have laid the groundwork for insulin resistance and chronic disease. But the good news is you can dodge them—and all their hidden sugar and the harm they might do—when you simply know where they are. It's time to liberate yourself from the grip of goop with hidden ingredients!

You may already be on to the fact that barbecue sauces and ketchup are loaded with sugar. But this is not just about the obviously sweet sauces—you have to be vigilantly en garde with *any* kind of sauce or spread. Regard them all as suspect. You'd be amazed at the amount of sugar in everything from balsamic vinegar to sundried tomatoes. (Yes, even in sundried tomatoes! I know! It was a complete eye-opener for me, too.) And let's be honest—anything glazed is just code for "shined with sugar."

Sugar isn't the only thing slipping into these pre-packaged dressings and toppings hoping to go unnoticed. Salt is dumped in with a heavy hand, as are soy and gluten. If you're sensitive to either of them, be sure you're reading labels; if you don't, you may find out they're in there the hard way. But remember, this is not about giving up the sauces (or any food) you love. It's about making smart exchanges. There are great alternatives to every dressing and condiment you're using, I promise. I'm also willing to bet they'll improve the flavor and nutritional value of your food.

Here's a great example. If you're sensitive to soy, trade soy sauce for coconut aminos. If you don't have a soy issue, get rid of gluten-y, salty soy sauce anyway and, instead, use liquid aminos or wheat-free tamari. Yum! In fact, as far as swaps go, I like coconut aminos even better than soy sauce, and I've discovered red wine vinegar is a huge improvement in flavor over balsamic. I've tossed sugar-sweetened marinara and will never go back now that I have mad love for checca sauce, which is just chopped tomatoes, olive oil, and basil (see the recipe on page 258).

Swaps really are the secret sauce (pun intended) to success on the Sugar Impact Diet, and I'm going to take all the work out of finding them for you so you have healthier and tastier options at the ready. But swaps are so much fun, you'll be coming up with your own in no time, then passing them on to the next wave of SI players.

VINEGARS: PUCKER UP!

Vinegar is a sour-tasting liquid used as a condiment and for pickling, not to mention its function as a natural cure-all and cleaning agent. It also has a built-in chef's bonus—an indefinite shelf life! It's made by turning sugars into alcohol, and that alcohol into acetic acid. The alcohol used is typically wine, cider, or beer, but any fermentable carb, including fruits, can be used as a source. It's the acetic acid it becomes, though, that's the organic force to be reckoned with.

Vinegar has been used medicinally—and as a seasoning and preservative—for thousands of years. But until recently, most of its use in treating everything from cuts to tummyaches was scientifically suspect. Now? There's a lot of recent evidence to suggest it really is useful as a health aid, especially in lowering blood sugar levels.

Carol Johnston, Ph.D., head of the nutrition department at Arizona State University in Tempe, has done studies showing that vinegar decreases both fasting blood sugar and post prandial blood sugar, and has suggested it can help people with type 2 diabetes manage their disease. And other studies, including another by Johnston, show there's reason to believe vinegar improves insulin sensitivity to a high-carb meal in people who have insulin resistance or type 2 diabetes.

So there doesn't seem to be much harm in having a couple of teaspoons spritzed on top of your salads. Plus, vinegar is a natural, flavorful tenderizer, so you can also use it to marinate your clean, lean protein—whether it's grass-fed beef, free-range organic chicken, or wild-caught, cold-water fish. If you have issues with Candida (see the Resources online at http://sugarimpact.com/resources for how to find out), avoid all vinegars except unfiltered apple cider vinegar—it may actually be helpful in fighting a Candida overgrowth by serving as a prebiotic and helping restore beneficial microflora balance.

GOODBYE, BALSAMIC

Even for all vinegar's real or imagined magical powers, there are exceptions to the rule. Enter balsamic vinegar. Yes, the very one we love and use the most, the most flavorful, and the one we thought was healthiest of all. I'm sorry to be the one to break it to you.

Balsamic vinegar comes in two varieties, the real deal and the get-it-on-the-shelf-fast kind. Authentic, traditional balsamic vinegar has been made in Italy for hundreds of years. It's expensive and prized by gourmet chefs and foodies. It takes years to come to market and undergoes rigorous testing before it does. Made from white grape juice, which is boiled to create a concentrated syrup, it's fermented and then aged in wooden casks for a minimum of 12 years. The aging process removes water, making balsamic vinegar thicker than regular vinegar and further concentrating the grape sugar. Since it has more sugar, it has more calories, too (even though, like apple cider vinegar, it does have antioxidants).

But, of course, big food companies aren't going to endure a 12-year production process to get a product in stores. So they accelerate its journey to the shelf with highly processed manufacturing, supplying you with something called "condiment balsamic vinegar," modeled after the good stuff. There are variations in the process and the time it takes, but there's no requirement that it be aged 12 years; sometimes it's aged as little as 2 months. This vinegar we know as balsamic is usually made from white wine vinegar and has caramel coloring (for color *and* added sweetness) and thickeners like cornstarch and gum, all of which add calories.

The condiment balsamic vinegar is the stuff we get in salad dressings, sauces, dips, and marinades. It can have as many as four times the number of calories in a cup as regular cider vinegar! So proceed with caution, whether you're using balsamic vinegar or its kissing cousin balsamic vinaigrette, which, as a salad dressing, can have added sugar, oil, and seasonings.

TOMATOES—NOT JUST FOR RATING MOVIES

Tomatoes seem like they're more at home in the veggie bin, though technically they're a fruit. But whether you say to-may-toe or to-mah-toe, they have all the antioxidant power we attribute to the planet's healthiest foods.

The health outlook for tomatoes gets pretty bleak, though, when they're puréed and packaged with sugar. If there's a kitchen in your house, odds are there's marinara sauce on the shelf. It's as much a staple as salt and pepper—pasta is always there for you as a quick, feel-good go-to when you need to serve up something filling, fast. But store-bought spaghetti sauce, even the ones with labels that look like they came right off the boat from Italy, are often vessels for added sugar and other preservatives.

People often excuse adding sugar in marinara as necessary to cut the acidity of the tomatoes, though it's possible to choose less-acidic tomato varieties. It's beside the point in large-scale manufacturing, anyway; usually in commercial production, sugar—even high-fructose corn syrup—is poured in simply to help hide cheap ingredients and increase shelf life. The added sugar (and usually salt) enhances taste in the absence of good tomatoes and herbs, and there's often artificial coloring and thickeners (again, high-fructose corn syrup!) to boot.

So to avoid dumping a dessert sauce on a meal already pretty high in carbs, skip pasta sauce that lists sugar—of any kind—as an ingredient. I hope it goes without saying that includes those with high-fructose corn syrup. White and vodka sauces should throw up obvious red flags, too—they often have even more sugar and calories because they contain cream and cheese. But others are sneakier; they slip in sugar as lactose in low-fat cheese.

Also, be sure to check out the amount of sugar per serving. Usually a serving of pasta sauce is a half a cup, way less than you'd ever ladle on your noodles. Some sauces contain 12 grams of sugar—or almost 2.5 teaspoons—in that half a cup. Before you put that jar in your cart, ask yourself whether you'd be willing to swap the sauce for a handful of sugar cubes on your rigatoni. Eek!

I suppose you could argue that you have a fighting chance with jars of marinara and other sauces—at least you can read their labels before you buy them. You actually have to hunt online to find the ingredients used in the sauces on big brand pizzas. And when you find them, you'll never be able to unknow what's in them. You've been warned!

NOW YOU'RE COOKIN'

Instead, make your own! It's so fast and easy! Think of the warm, slow simmer of tomatoes on your stove, filling your kitchen with a delicious aroma. You're stirring in some love...okay, maybe I'm getting carried away. But you get the gist—homemade always tastes better, and it gives you control over what's in your food. (See page 275 for my favorite sauce recipe.)

As a fruit, tomatoes already have a small amount of sugar in them, and they're exploding with natural flavor. So when you make your own sauces—from alla checca to marinara—you don't need to add any sugar. Start with meaty, fresh organic (or home-grown) tomatoes with low acidity. You can also use diced tomatoes or pureed tomatoes with no added sugar; just make sure you're choosing ingredients in a glass jar or a BPA-free can.

There's no single way to make marinara sauce—everyone's claim to the best is based on tradition and taste. Beyond tomatoes, the ingredients you can add run the gamut. They can be as colorful or conservative as you like—extra virgin olive oil, onions, carrots, garlic, herbs, parsley, anchovies, sea salt, freshly ground black pepper...even red wine (after Cycle 2). So experiment and enjoy!

SLIPPERY SAUCES

People love to slather. Gooey sauces and condiments are squirted, squeezed, and swiped on almost anything edible in an effort to add flavor, and, usually, some sweetness. Sugar is an addiction, after all, and that means we can contrive ways to make it go with anything, anytime, anywhere.

Ketchup and barbecue sauce are faves all over the world, and their popularity (and contribution to waistlines) is only growing. Yes, there are tomatoes in ketchup. And some vinegar and a few other tasty good seasonings and spices. But conversation about their nutrient content ends there. Commercial ketchup is dosed with sodium and sugar, usually high-fructose corn syrup. There's typically 4 grams of sugar in a single tablespoon of ketchup! That's a teaspoon!

Barbecue and steak sauces are other tomato-based flavorings notorious for sneaky sweeteners. They come in many more shapes and sizes than ketchup, and some US-based regional preferences have more sugar than others. The source of added sugar in them ranges from brown sugar to molasses and honey, and 2 tablespoons contain around 13 grams of sugar. Even quick and easy homemade recipes often casually call for ketchup as a base, so right out of the gate, you've got added sugar in your sauce.

I know we're mostly talking sugar here, but beware the high salt in gluey, brush-on pastes, too. We get most of our daily salt from processed foods. (Did you know sundried tomatoes are also really high in salt? Strike two!) The current FDA recommendation for salt is to get no more than 2,300 milligrams a day, with the added note that certain groups should have no more than 1,500 milligrams a day. When 1 tablespoon of ketchup has over 150 milligrams of salt (and almost 3 grams of sugar, and over 4 grams of total carbs), you have to wonder if that sweet sauce is worth it. You're not really wondering, are you?

Research on salt's impact on blood pressure is mixed, but I, for one, am not risking the potential health smackdown from the sugar-salt combo in sauce packets. And I don't want you or any other Impact player to, either. There are way too many delicious and interesting ways to flavor your food and support your health in the bargain. That world is just about to open up to you, as soon as you kick your sugar habit and reset your sensitivity to it. (Rest easy, it's only going to take 2 weeks!)

Need a little mouthwatering encouragement? Homemade salsa and alla checca are fresh, amazingly flavorful alternatives to marinara and tomato-based sauces. In Cycle 3 of the Sugar Impact Diet, you can also bring back marinara sauce and some dressings, even those with a little bit of sugar. Remember, this is a low-SI diet, not a no-sugar diet!

HOMEMADE VERSUS STORE-BOUGHT DRESSINGS

Flip over any bottle of commercial salad dressing, including those hawked with healthy labels, and a-ooga! Wow, what a surprise. It's like an anti–weight loss party—added sugars, high sodium, less-than-stellar oils like soybean oil, and sometimes even hydrogenated oils—or more accurately, trans fats. Lots of dressings are high in sugar, including vinaigrettes and creamy ones like French and Thousand Island.

You may feel like you're wearing a healthy halo when you're eating a nutrient-dense salad, but if you're dousing it with a sugar-laden salad dressing, you may have solved one of the weight-loss resistance mysteries that's been plaguing you for years. I'm not saying you might as well have been pouring fudge over your veggies but—well, okay, that's exactly what I'm saying.

Most full-fat dressings have 2 grams of carbohydrate per serving (a serving is usually 2 tablespoons), but the fat-free versions contain 11 grams or more. That's over a teaspoon of sugar for each tablespoon of dressing! Run!

My advice? Keep it simple—mix a base of some high-quality extra virgin olive oil with a dash of lemon juice, a pinch of salt, and some seasoning to taste. Voila! Or experiment with some red wine vinegar and Dijon mustard combinations. If you're feeling creative, you can try tahini, a creamy spread made from sesame seeds. How about olive tapenade in place of olive oil, or some guacamole? As long as you're working with low-SI ingredients, mixed to suit your taste, it's hard to go wrong.

NO THANK YOU, JAM

Many a morning ritual begins with some sort of fruity spread being dragged, bleary eyed, across a piece of burnt toast or a muffin. Jams, jellies, and marmalades propped on breakfast tables across the country all bask in the fruit-association glow, but they don't get the pass whole fruit does as a healthy breakfast choice. Why not, you ask? I'll give you one guess!

Whether they're store-bought or homemade, how many jams do you know that are made only from fruit, and fruit alone? Even if they are, jams are a condensed sugar hit—like juice with a lot less liquid.

So steer clear of jams and jellies, even homemade. Fruit should be sweet enough to give you your morning fix—and once your taste buds are reset to pick up the rich, subtle sweetness fruit offers, it will be.

MY IMPACT!

Susan Stephens
Starting weight: 124 lbs.
Current weight: 114 lbs.
Total lost: 10 lbs.

I lost 30 pounds on the Virgin
Diet this past year, but I was still
struggling with sugar and gluten.
I could never just have three bites
of either—one or two bites would trigger a feeding frenzy. I have
always had a sweet tooth, and sugar was my drug of choice when
I was overstressed.

I have IBS, so I would get severe gas and pain in my abdomen
after overindulging. The gas at work was very embarrassing after
eating lunch. My gut was not healing even after using the gut-
support protocol.

Then I tried the Sugar Impact Diet, and everything changed.
I did not gain my normal 10 pounds over the holidays. I lost 10
pounds! My total weight loss for this year is 40 pounds, including
the weight I lost on the Virgin Diet. I lost inches from my waist.
My fasting blood sugar went from 97 to 80. The gut-support
supplements are working better. I am getting a better night's sleep.
I am more aware of the hidden sugars and am diligent in keeping
them out.

I am looking forward this next year to learning to cook
delicious and healthy meals that my diabetic husband will
enjoy, too. Overcoming my addiction to sugar has made me
more focused at work and less in a fog, which has increased
my performance. I feel more confident that I can set goals and
complete them. Thank you, JJ Virgin, for your diligence in
helping us all become healthier.

7

SEE YA, SWEETENERS
AND ADDED SUGAR

Aristotle said, "Change in all things is sweet." He was a pretty bright guy. Just wait 'til you see how sweet this change is about to be for you! Ditching the high-Sugar Impact (SI) sweeteners can feel like the final frontier in kicking your sugar cravings to the curb. They've got their hooks in you deep because they're actually causing you to crave more and more sweet, while your brain has you convinced that they're the perfect, no- or low-calorie antidote to the evils of bright, white sugar.

If you can't let go of the sweeteners that are fueling your sugar addiction and you're feeling defeated, hardly able to recognize yourself with those extra pounds and flagging energy, do not give up! You've found support. This fight isn't over, and you're about to be the comeback kid!

Let's start with a point of weakness: cravings. It's possible you're looking at them all wrong. Cravings are just information. They're your body's way of telling you that something may be off, that you're not reacting to something well or that you're out of balance. The next time you get cravings, rather than rush to self-soothe, try a few Sugar-Attack Survival Strategies in Chapter 8 (see page 182). They're designed to come to the rescue at just those moments.

Getting your cravings under control is a key piece of the puzzle in regaining control of your appetite and finding a new you in the mirror. When you slide down the ladder of high- to medium- to low-SI sweeteners (and sweet treats with added sugar), you'll make huge strides in breaking free of your sugar cravings because sweeteners have just been stoking the fire of your sugar addiction all along.

This new way forward, free of cravings for sweet, will be cleared for you when you reclaim your sugar sensitivity and reset your taste buds to appreciate the natural sweetness of things like vanilla and cinnamon. Believe it or not, you'll notice that some things are actually too sweet (yes, it's possible!).

Even if you're not a sugar adder, it will help you familiarize yourself with natural and artificial sugars, to learn which are safe, and to know how they're identified on a label. But if you have a genetic sweet tooth, you need to work with it, not against it. That's what this chapter is designed to help you do. As always, this transition involves swaps to hold your hand along the way. You're going to be trading natural and artificial sweeteners for sweet herbs and sugar alcohols. Agave and Splenda are out; stevia and erythritol are in. And you're going to love them.

This is a lifestyle change *for life,* and it will give back in spades. Weight will go. Energy and focus will come. Stick with me— you'll see.

ARTIFICIAL SWEETENERS: THE WOLF IN SHEEP'S CLOTHING

Research has shown that the artificial sweetener acesulfame potassium (very common in many "diet" foods and drinks) can trigger an insulin release much like sugar can, leading to cravings and stalling fat loss. In fact, your insulin shoots up as soon as you taste the artificial sweetener saccharin...it thinks food is coming.

In another study, 100 women ate a diet heavy in sugar, dairy products, and artificial sweeteners. From urine samples, researchers determined that eating those foods elevated their glucose, arabinose, and ribose—all of which feed Candida Albicans. When the women eliminated sugar, dairy, and artificial sweeteners, they reduced the frequency and severity of their Candida. Surprising, right?

Artificial sweeteners also cause glycation, just as sugar does. The process is like the browning that happens in high-heat cooking— only it goes on inside you. During glycation, sugar binds to proteins, like those in your skin and arteries, making them stiffer. They also spew free-radical inducing advanced glycation end products, or AGEs, into your system. Yep, that sure will AGE you!

Now, you might be thinking, well, even though they do all the things sugar does, at least I get the *no calories* win. Not so much—they might actually be *worse* than real sugar in that regard. Even though they don't have calories, they generate responses in your body that set up the expectation of calories, so they can trigger cravings and make you eat more (and not more wild fish and asparagus, either!). This phenomenon is called calorie dysregulation; your body loses its ability to calibrate the degree of sweetness in food with the amount of calories you're consuming, which sets you up to overeat. And, as you're well aware, when you eat sweet you want more sweet.

Studies also show that eating sweet substances without calories sets you up to fail, because your body misses all the cues it's looking for to stop eating. When that relationship between taste and calories falls apart, it may contribute to overeating and weight gain. So artificial sweeteners are far from a free ride—they can seriously stall fast fat loss, the very reason you were eating them in the first place.

Artificial sweeteners can seriously stall fat loss.

And study after study shows that diet sodas increase diabetes risk. In one study published in *The American Journal of Clinical Nutrition*, women who drank just one diet soda a day had a 33% increased risk of type 2 diabetes. The diet soda drinkers also consumed twice as much soda as the sugar-soda drinkers.

Here's something else, and it's more than a little scary: did you know that artificial sweeteners might be neurotoxic? If you didn't, I hope you'll never forget it now. Aspartame gets called out of class for the most recognition on this one. Even though most of the evidence is anecdotal (though more studies are validating it), aspartame is also reported to create a laundry list of symptoms, including headaches, dizziness, poor balance, vomiting or nausea, change in vision, memory loss, fatigue, and other neurological issues like brain fog or lack of concentration. Aspartame is considered an excitotoxin, which means what it says: it's an FDA-approved way to excite your brain to toxic levels. It causes your brain cells to become overstimulated and fire uncontrollably, which leads to cell death.

I think it's fair to summarize it this way: artificial sweeteners can make you fat, put you at risk for metabolic syndrome, type 2 diabetes, and cardiovascular disease, and some may kill your brain cells in the process. Plus, they're so much sweeter than regular sugar, the more you eat them, the sweeter tastes you crave. Not much more to discuss, is there? Just give them up, okay?

NATURAL SWEETENERS

If you've been convinced the world will stop spinning without sweets, you may hold the view that natural sugar is the best way to go. The trend to move away from artificial sweeteners is certainly a step in the right direction. But as for feeling so much better about yourself for emptying that little brown packet of "natural" sugar into your coffee, or using molasses in your cookies, well, nice try.

I get more questions about sugar and sweeteners than anything else. Everyone is desperate to know how they can lose weight fast, get their energy back, and look great—and still hang onto a little sugar (just a little!). Is honey okay? Fruit juice concentrate? Can I have agave—it's natural, right?

So here's the headline—sugar is sugar. It doesn't matter if it comes from bees or sugarcane—it still breaks down in your body as sugar. Sweeteners, natural or not, are processed carbs. That's not hard to figure out when we're talking about refined white sugar or powdered sugar, but molasses, honey, and brown sugar can be heavily processed, too. Coconut sugar is a step up in the sugar echelon from high-fructose corn syrup. But it's all sugar, period.

Sugar is sugar.

IS IT HONEY DO? OR HONEY DON'T?

True, raw natural honey is packed with phytonutrients, and black-strap molasses is rich in some minerals like iron, potassium, and calcium, but a "natural" label in the sweetener category doesn't bestow an automatic gold star. To be sure, it's better than the alternative, but there are varying degrees of "good" among the natural-branded sweeteners, and there are only a few that will pass my test, even as you transition to Cycle 2. And sugar, whether you call it natural or not, spikes your blood sugar and sends you on a mood ride you know all too well, while in high doses it takes you down a path to weight gain, insulin resistance, and disease.

That's why processed honey and molasses, along with maple syrup, are given a high-SI rating. They're really high in calories and dense with sugar. Besides, most honey is heavily processed, and processing strips the nutrients out of it. Locally grown organic raw honey is full of vitamins and minerals and has some homeopathic benefits for wounds and allergies. If you have immune responses to bits of mold and dust, organic honey can strengthen your immune system and help you handle those things better. But you only need about a half teaspoon a day to do the job.

SWEET NOTHING

And, of course, there's agave. Agave is often lumped in with honey and molasses when people refer to natural sweeteners. It's taken from the agave plant, true enough, but the natural stops there. It's not only an imposter, it's a major high-SI culprit. Don't feel bad if you bought into the hype—there's been a lot of public duping about agave.

The truth is, many agave nectars contain 70–90% fructose—more than in high-fructose corn syrup. Most of the nutrients in this fructose syrup are destroyed during processing, so there's not much left to get excited about. It has a low glycemic index, which means it doesn't spike blood sugar as much as some other sugar, but you know by now that's not always a good thing. The high amount of fructose in agave goes right to fat metabolism central—your liver—where it can raise your triglyceride levels, store them as fat (hello, belly!), and trigger inflammation.

FRUIT JUICE CONCENTRATE

Another common misconception is that fruit juice concentrate is a great natural sweetener because it's nothing more than fruit, concentrated. Now that you're an expert in all things fruit, you know fruit in any form is *not* the all-you-can-eat food we all want it to be. Making fruit juice concentrate involves little more than removing the liquid from natural fruit juice.

What the process really concentrates is the sugar and the

sweetness of the fruit. When you compare the same volumes of freshly squeezed fruit juice and concentrated juice, the concentrate packs a lot more sugar and calories than juice itself, pound for pound. In full-volume juice, nutrients and sugars are diluted to a fraction of what they are in a sample from concentrate. And you know that when food is "unwrapped" from its fiber, and fruit juice most certainly is, it's left without its protective phytonutrients, vitamins, and minerals, and its SI is exponentially increased. More processing just exacerbates the issue.

Don't be fooled: this was never really about giving us a natural sweetener; it helps manufacturers save money and space for shipping, and it extends shelf life. To be made into a sweetener for mass production, fruit juice concentrate is stripped of its vitamins and minerals until it's reduced to a sugar syrup, so it can be used just like corn syrup. It also has the same effect on your blood sugar. The clincher is that manufacturers aren't required to identify this as added sugar, so you'll find it in "healthy" products, listed as fruit juice concentrate along with the "no added sugar" claim.

NATURAL BEAUTY

I promised that I wouldn't leave you without any solutions, and that's true: there are plenty of low-SI sweeteners out there for you to choose from. I've done the homework so that you don't have to! Here's the skinny on your best SI options: monk fruit, stevia, the sugar alcohols erythritol and xylitol, chicory, and inulin.

MONK FRUIT

Monk fruit is a lemon-sized fruit with an extract 300 times sweeter than sugar. It's also known as Lo Han Guo and is commonly marketed as "Lo Han sweetener." It's been used for centuries as a sweetener and in herbal medicine. In China, monk fruit sweetener has been used for nearly a thousand years to treat obesity and diabetes. Studies show monk fruit is rich in antioxidants and offers anti-inflammatory benefits.

I'm seeing more manufacturers use monk fruit as a sweetener these days. So Delicious Dairy Free coconut milk ice cream has no added sugar and comes sweetened with monk fruit (and a whopping 10 grams of fiber per serving). A delicious low-SI win!

The company that makes Splenda has marketed its version of monk fruit sweetener as Nectresse. Although they claim it has "zero calories," they've added erythritol (which is good; more on this soon) but also sugar and molasses (bad) to their monk fruit powder. Thankfully, there's a minuscule amount of sugar and molasses, so little they don't even register as calories. But if you can find pure monk fruit, or monk fruit blended only with stevia, xylitol, or erythritol, they're a far better choice.

STEVIA

Stevia is an herb that grows in North and South America that's also 300 times sweeter than sugar. Stevia is available in liquid and powder forms, but all of them are extracted from the leaves of the stevia plant. Some people like it, but others complain it has a licorice or bitter aftertaste. It has no calories and is a low-SI natural choice, but beware of calorie dysregulation. Oh, and it's not so hot for baking.

Unlike the artificial stuff, it has no adverse effects on blood sugar, though. One study on human volunteers even found it can increase glucose tolerance, which makes stevia an ideal sweetener for people with insulin resistance and diabetes, though most similar studies have been conducted in rats. One randomized, double-blind, placebo-controlled trial in Chinese men and women also showed stevia can reduce mild hypertension.

SUGAR ALCOHOLS

I'm a big fan of sugar alcohols as natural sweeteners. They got their name because their biochemical structure resembles a hybrid of a sugar and an alcohol. They're naturally occurring in foods like fruits, and they're used as sweeteners in treats like chocolate, candies, chewing gum, and jams. They're also used as bulking agents, and they have some, but only a few, calories.

I like sugar alcohols precisely *because* they contain *some* calories, though even those are incompletely absorbed by the body. Remember, the problem with no-calorie sweeteners like stevia is that they throw off your body's ability to associate sweetness with calories.

Some common sugar alcohols are sorbitol, mannitol, maltitol, erythritol, and xylitol. Of these, my favorites are erythritol and xylitol, because they can actually have some health benefits. Xylitol is thought to be antibacterial and has an impressive history of reducing cavities and ear infections. Other studies show xylitol can reduce risk for osteoporosis and control oral infections of Candida.

Erythritol doesn't seem to create the gastric distress other sugar alcohols can, although as with any sugar alcohol, a little bit goes a long way. Studies show that erythritol is tooth-friendly and doesn't contribute to dental problems. It also makes an ideal sweetener for people with diabetes. One study showed it had no adverse effects on blood glucose levels. I recommend that you look for 100% erythritol or an erythritol-stevia blend.

CHICORY AND INULIN

Chicory is a woody perennial plant used to bring out flavor in everything from salads (its leaves) to coffee (its roots). It adds sweetness and sourness, and can intensify chocolate flavors, which is just one of the many reasons to love it.

Chicory root syrup is a natural sweetener made from the root of the chicory plant. Chicory root is one of the highest natural sources of inulin, which is used to replace sugar, fat, and flour in processed foods. Chicory syrup has a mildly sweet taste, but it's not absorbed by the intestines, so it doesn't affect blood sugar levels.

It's been suggested that it has other health benefits, too, like supporting liver function by pulling toxins out of the body and helping break down fat. Chicory root is also considered a natural prebiotic that feeds the good bacteria in your gut. Both chicory syrup and inulin have a low SI and get the green light, even in Cycle 2.

YOU'RE SWEET ENOUGH

Best of all, when you do reset your sugar sensitivity, you'll be moving toward full appreciation of the gentle sweetness in whole natural foods and natural sweeteners like cinnamon and vanilla. They can give your tea or organic coffee a kick and wonderful flavor without any downside.

The goal is to move slowly away from addiction to sweet, and to focus on savory flavors such as sea salt, basil, rosemary, and other yummy spices. I want you to reclaim your sensitivity to sweet—and your taste buds. They're yours, take them back!

You'll also be eating good sources of clean, lean protein, and they'll help reduce your cravings and support your move away from sweet foods, too. So don't go crazy with legal sweeteners. I'll be watching!

Sugar and Spice

Cinnamon can reduce blood glucose levels because it slows stomach emptying, making you feel full faster. And the good news is it doesn't take much—1½ teaspoons a day seems to do the trick. Just make sure it's fresh cinnamon, as its polyphenols and active ingredients degrade over time.

As for vanilla, a study at St George's Hospital in London found that vanilla-scented patches on the backs of people's hands helped reduce their cravings. In a 2004 study in *Alternative Medicine Review*, vanilla bean extract showed promise in blocking carbohydrate absorption, and it's always been a favorite when it comes to boosting endorphins. A 1994 study of 57 patients at Memorial Sloan-Kettering who underwent magnetic resonance imaging testing found that a sweet vanilla scent significantly reduced their anxiety during the procedure.

DARK CHOCOLATE IS NOT MILK CHOCOLATE WITH THE LIGHTS OFF

You're going to love me for this: I want you to eat chocolate every day. Even in Cycle 2, as long as it's 100% dark chocolate with no added sugar. Yes, feel free to do the happy dance! Dark chocolate is another sweet way to satisfy your cravings and support your blood sugar.

To save you the hunt and the trouble of trying lots of brands that don't measure up, I'm going to give a shout-out to two brands I've found that are making 100% dark chocolate with no sugar. It's been tough searching and taste testing for you (cough), but at long last I can suggest these amazing options. If you're in the United States, check out ChocolaTree Organic Oasis, and if you're in Canada, you have Aracana Soba chocolate (see Resources at http://sugarimpact.com/resources). Both of these have no sugar whatsoever, and eating them is sort of like eating raw cacao, which I do every day. I really love raw cacao nibs, and I throw them on top of my shakes. They're packed with fiber, and they've got just a little natural sweetness. It's such a great way to check that box when a craving just won't give you any peace. You're welcome!

Sweet Strategies

If you find that one sweet treat a day isn't getting you by, refer to Withdrawal Strategies and Sugar-Attack Survival Strategies in Chapter 8 as you move through the cycles. It will get easier as you move off the high-SI treats.

BECOME A SUGAR SHERLOCK: READING LABELS

Sugar is a master of disguise, and labels have been designed to win a high-stakes war for your precious dollars, not look out for your health. Key into what these labels really mean, and you'll be less likely to be deceived into buying a sugar- or sweetener-heavy food that will stall fat loss instead of kicking it into high gear.

LITE—RIGHT!

The FDA guidelines for using "Lite" (or "Light") is that the product has one-third fewer calories, 50% less fat, or 50% less sodium than the original version. The hidden land mine to look for is what's compensating for the light ingredient—the food still has to taste good, and that means it could be heavy in another unwelcome ingredient.

NO ADDED SUGAR AND SUGAR-FREE

When I see "no added sugar" and "sugar-free" labels, I look around to see if somebody's winking at me. Technically, this label means the food has fewer than 0.5 grams of sugar or fat per serving. But even if there's no added sugar in a packaged product, it doesn't mean it doesn't *have* sugar or that it's low in sugar. First, that processed treat made of flour is really sugar—just give it a few bites and see. Plus, it can still be sweetened with fruit juice concentrate or full of artificial sweeteners. If that's the case, you'll probably eat more, since you're at twice the disadvantage—your body isn't registering sweetness, and you don't want to stop pretending those cookies are calorie-free.

This will fire you up, too—manufacturers only have to list the calories of an ingredient if it is a half-gram or more, so if it has 0.4 grams of sugar, they can leave the sugar off the label! Sometimes portion sizes are scaled down in order to make a product look better than it really is. So "no added sugar" foods are far from being all-you-can-eat, worry- and guilt-free fests.

REDUCED SUGAR

The by-the-book definition of a reduced sugar label is that the food has at least 25% less sugar than the original item. It doesn't mean it has to have fewer calories. The low-sugar label, on the other hand, is completely unregulated and can mean anything a manufacturer decides it means. My thoughts exactly.

ALL NATURAL

Danger ahead! This is another "anything goes" label. The FDA doesn't have a definition for "natural" (there's a joke in there somewhere) but it does have a decades-long policy that says it won't object to a food being labeled "natural" as long as the product "does not contain added color, artificial flavors, or synthetic substances." Good to know!

YOUR SUGAR IMPACT SWAPS: SWEETENERS AND ADDED SUGAR

After reading a chapter about making better sweetener choices, you may have a pretty good idea of where to go from here. But I always like to give you a cheat sheet just to make sure you're crystal clear on which swaps will help kick your sugar addiction the fastest. I mean, there's no point in dragging this out, is there?!

Swap Your...	For...
55% dark chocolate	85% dark chocolate
Agave	Erythritol
Maple syrup	Chicory syrup
Milk chocolate	Dark chocolate
NutraSweet	Monk fruit
Processed brown sugar	Raw brown sugar
Processed honey	Raw organic local honey
Processed molasses	Blackstrap molasses
Splenda	Stevia and xylitol
Sugar	Stevia

YOUR SUGAR IMPACT SCALE: SWEETENERS AND ADDED SUGAR

Sweeteners and added sugars keep your body in sweet-seeking mode, so lowering your SI in this category will be a huge leap forward in your ability to kick your cravings and satisfy your sweet tooth with the real deal in whole, natural foods.

LOW SUGAR IMPACT	
100% dark chocolate	Monk fruit
85% dark chocolate*	Raw cacao (powder and nibs)
Chicory	Stevia
Erythritol	Xylitol
Inulin	

Stay off in Cycle 2 unless made with low-SI sweetener.

MEDIUM SUGAR IMPACT

70% or higher dark chocolate
Blackstrap molasses
Cane syrup (non-GMO)
Coconut palm sugar
Coconut sugar
Glucose (aka dextrose; non-GMO)

Local organic raw honey
Mannitol
Raw brown sugar (nonprocessed)
Rice syrup
Sorbitol

HIGH SUGAR IMPACT

<70% dark chocolate
Acesulfame-K
Agave
Aspartame
Candy
Caramel sauce
Chocolate syrup
Corn syrup
Crystalline fructose
Cyclamates
Fruit juice concentrate
High fructose corn syrup

Honey (processed)
Licorice
Maltodextrin
Maple syrup
Marshmallows
Milk chocolate
Molasses
Neotame
Processed brown sugar
Saccharin
Splenda
Sucralose

As the last of the seven high–SI foods, sweeteners and added sugar may have been the most surprising. When you lower your SI here, you break the habit of making your foods overly sweet, and really throw your addiction a knockout punch. It's a giant leap toward getting more satisfaction from what you eat and ensuring spectacular, long-lasting results from the Sugar Impact Diet.

PART III

2 WEEKS TO FAST AND LASTING FAT LOSS

8

CYCLE 1: TAPER

The Sugar Impact Diet will end your sugar cravings, help you regain control of your appetite, create steady elevated energy, and sharpen your focus. But to make the move, you have to become a sugar sleuth. This isn't just about exposing hidden sugar in processed junk food. It's about where the sugar hides in all your food, because all sugar will have an impact on you, and you want to be in control of that impact. By the time you shift from high-SI foods to mediums and then down to lows, you'll have lost weight fast and reclaimed your sugar sensitivity without feeling a thing. Except better.

So here we go! I am beyond excited to welcome you to Cycle 1—the taper cycle. During this 1-week cycle, you're going to begin to let go of your dependence on sugar. It's just the beginning, just a slow push back from the table. And get ready, because you'll feel so good, so fast!

Unlike other diets, you're being set up to succeed—nothing is left to chance. I've provided you with clear "eat this, not that" categories, but you'll also learn how to make choices that keep you on course, if you're someone who prefers a little freedom. Either way, you'll have tons of support! The grip sugar has on you is going to disappear fast. Your sensitivity to sugar could reset in as little as a few days, your energy will come roaring back, your moods will stabilize, and you'll kiss the extra weight goodbye.

Cycle 1—Taper
■ Swap high-SI foods for medium-SI foods
■ Begin to shift from sugar-burning to fat-burning
■ Eat by the Sugar Impact Plate
■ Eat by the Sugar Impact Clock
■ Use Sugar-Attack Strategies if you need extra help

SET YOUR GOALS

The most important gift you can give yourself before your Sugar Impact (SI) journey gets under way is to take a quiet moment, look inside, and ask yourself what you really hope will come of it. What are your goals? Three weeks and 2 cycles from now, what do you hope to have achieved? How do you want to feel? Do you want to lose weight? Have higher energy? Improve your focus? Get rid of bloating? All of those things?

Identify the simple things that you want to see change quickly, because that's exactly the way it's going to go for you. And fast change is the best change, especially when it comes to pounds. Research shows that people who take weight off fast lose more and keep it off. That could be you!

Your goals should be realistic, measurable, and trackable. Those are the keys to lasting change. In the next couple of weeks, you're going to prove to yourself what's really possible. I've created a simple goal–setting worksheet that you can download at http://sugarimpact.com/resources.

SUGAR IMPACT TOOLS

I've reviewed all the other diets, and I know what works. I'm going to give you every tool you need to succeed. I want that for you just as much as you do!

There's some housekeeping to take care of before you get under way, which we'll explore below. You can only change what you can measure, and I want you to really get how far you're about to go. You won't have any idea where you've ended up if you don't know where you started.

> You can only change what you can measure.

SNEAKY SUGAR INVENTORY

By now you should have done your Sneaky Sugar Inventory (see pages 26–30 or download it online at http://sugarimpact.com/resources) to help you identify how much sugar you're actually eating. Don't you just love surprises? Even I had a Whoa! moment after I went through that list. It's evidence of where sugar is hiding in your diet, and it will serve as your baseline. You'll get a much more pleasant surprise when you take the inventory again after Cycle 3.

Once you take a hard look at all the sneaky sugar-laden food you've circled, you're going to have to face your kitchen and get the enemy out of the house. Before day one of the Sugar Impact Diet, toss any food that tempts you or that you find irresistible. You know

> Get the enemy out of the house.

your own triggers—just admit that you're going to rip it, cut it, or twist it open in a weak moment if you know it's under your roof. Personally, I can't bring popcorn into my house...there's no such thing as a "little bit" of it for me—the bag becomes my serving, and when that's gone I have to fight myself not to drive back to the store for another. I know you can relate!

You can't rely on willpower. Do not keep something you're addicted to nearby while you're trying to quit. No one is superhuman. Cold sweats and clawing at the walls do not win any extra points, only getting yourself to the finish line does. So set yourself up for the win.

Next, make a run to the grocery store to stock up on low-and medium-SI rations (shopping lists are provided on my website at http://sugarimpact.com/resources). That shopping trip is so much fun! I hope you'll feel puffed up with pride when you look into your cart at checkout. Health is a process, it's a journey, and you've begun.

SUGAR IMPACT QUIZ

You should have also taken the Sugar Impact Quiz (see page 21 or download it online at http://sugarimpact.com/resources)—it goes hand in hand with the Sneaky Sugar Inventory. They're connecting-the-dots companions. With them side by side, you'll see where sugar is hitching a ride into your diet and the impact it's having on you.

Your body had a slew of warning signs that you're heading down a dangerous path. It's just like the little car light that goes on when you've got low fuel or you need air in your tire. Your body is blinking and dinging and flashing like crazy, trying to get your attention to tell you you're about to crash. I designed the Sugar Impact Quiz to expose these signs and their cause: sugar.

When you take a close look, you can see that sugar is really at the forefront of almost every disease. It suppresses your immune system and sets off an inflammatory response, and we know inflammation is the precursor to most chronic diseases. Disease doesn't happen overnight. It happens over time, often because of poor lifestyle choices.

After you take the Sugar Impact Quiz, you'll have a very clear picture of how your body is trying to tell you that sugar is leading you down that path. There are seven common symptoms of sugar sensitivity—low energy, cravings, gas and bloating, unhealthy weight or weight gain, uncontrollable appetite, moodiness, and an expanding waistline, and you're going to track each of them during your journey.

As you now know, the Sugar Impact Quiz is also a serious eye-opener. Don't be discouraged by what you see. What you measure, you can improve. Up until now you might've been willing to brush off your bloat or power through your fatigue, thinking this is just what happens when you get older or when you're stressed. Well, it isn't, and when you take them all together, rate them and realize what you're dealing with every day just because of the foods you're eating and the beverages you're drinking, you're going to resolve to beat this thing.

What you measure, you can improve.

The symptoms on the Sugar Impact Quiz will also be used as a benchmark as you move from one cycle to the next. There's room for improvement for everyone, so if you start with a good score of 2 or less per symptom, and less than 12 overall, you'll still see a benefit, and the commitment to this new low-SI lifestyle means you're warding off weight gain and disease down the road.

If you score 20 or more, or a 4+ in any two categories, you may have to extend Cycle 1 by a week or more to ease your transition (and consider using one or more of the Speed-Healing Techniques in Chapter 13 on page 223). Take that time if you need it. It's much more important that you don't move on before you're ready, or you'll set yourself up to fail. Do what you need to do to get yourself to your goals—you're not in competition with anyone. This is for you!

SAY CHEESE

Yes, the dreaded *before* picture. Don't fret and don't hide behind a planter, or your cousin. You'll be documenting a very big moment—you're on your way! Out with the old, in with the new. You'll thank me later.

WEIGH AND MEASURE

Just as much fun as the picture! But denial and snubbing your scale aren't tools for change—measurement is. Take your weight and measure your waist and hips. Write your results down and keep track of them each time you check in with these numbers throughout the program. There is also a tracking sheet available online at http://sugarimpact.com/resources if you want or need it. I can't wait for you to see them come down (and fast!). So exciting!

JOURNAL PAGES

Your daily journal will be the single most important tool in your arsenal. It's essential that you write down everything you eat! So keep your own pages or use the journal I have online—you can download it at http://sugarimpact.com/resources. Your commitment to this (or lack thereof) will make or break your success. As simple as it sounds, writing down what you eat is instrumental. A 2008 study of nearly 1,700 participants published in the *American Journal of Preventive Medicine* found that it was the number one factor in predicting weight-loss success. People in the study, who were also asked to follow a diet rich in fruits and vegetables and exercise at least 30 minutes a day, lost twice as much weight if they kept daily food records compared to people who kept none. So this is non-negotiable, and you'll actually find that that journaling becomes a welcome new habit.

You'll see that your journal paints a fascinating picture pretty quickly. If you tried to play a speed round of what you had for meals over the last week and a half, how do you think you'd do? Not a chance of remembering, right? That's how we get ourselves in trouble—we don't see the big picture, and how meal after meal, day after day, the sneaky sugar adds up.

But glance at that little journal, and there's no missing that you haven't eaten enough today (that's why I don't have any energy!), you went too long between meals (that's why I have a headache!), or you didn't drink enough water and you were hungrier than ever.

Food is information. Connect the dots between what you're eating and how you feel. Your fork is the

Connect the dots between what you're eating and how you feel.

most powerful way to impact your weight, your mood, your energy, your joint pain, and the rate you age. Tune in! It's really easy to do when you have a journal.

SHOUT IT FROM THE MOUNTAINTOP

Publicly proclaim your intention and circle the wagons. Stay away from anyone or anything that will sabotage your efforts. Steer clear of sugar pushers and situations you know you can't handle (holiday cookie parties and school bake sales come to mind). There are just some situations where sugar is impossible to avoid, and you don't need to make this hard on yourself.

Find an accountability partner, recruit a friend or coach to help, or join a support group. Surround yourself with love and lots of cheerleaders. You'll want to do some high-fiving in a couple of weeks!

Losing Weight and Feeling Great: The 4Ts

Once you Test, you'll be ready to begin your three-cycle journey to a low-SI life: you'll Taper, Transition, and—once you reach
Cycle 3—be Transformed! It's that easy!

WELCOME TO CYCLE 1

The Sugar Impact Diet is built around the Sugar Impact Scales,
which were introduced in Chapter 2 and covered individually in
Chapters 4 through 7. The scales are based on the impact a food
has on your body. They consider a food's fructose content, glycemic load, nutrient density, and fiber, as well as serving size. In
Cycle 1, you'll use the Sugar Impact Scales to swap high SIs for
medium SIs in each of the seven food categories: grains, roots,
packaged fruit, low/no-fat dairy and diet foods, drinks, dressings
and sweeteners, and added sugar. You'll be slowly tapering from a
high-SI diet to a medium-SI diet. The key here is to transition over
time, so you don't experience sugar withdrawal in Cycle 2.

It's critical that you don't go cold turkey and try to eliminate
sugar completely and immediately. That's a recipe for disaster, even
for me. When I took my Sneaky Sugar Inventory and realized that
Trojan horses like balsamic vinegar and sun-dried tomatoes were
sneaking extra sugar into my diet, I couldn't believe it. It meant
that I couldn't dive right into Cycle 2, either.

So take this one step at a time, and don't hop over medium-SI
foods; Cycle 2 will take you low. When you taper and trade your
way down, you'll hardly notice the huge shift your body is making
into fat-burning mode.

THE SUGAR IMPACT PLATE

Let's get into the Sugar Impact Plate in more detail. It's a tool with giant training wheels to keep you steady and strong. The beauty of the plate is that there's no guesswork, no trial and error, no deprivation or starvation. Just a straightforward, healthy, happy way of eating—until suddenly, you're 10 pounds lighter and much healthier thanks to your low-SI lifestyle.

PORTIONS

The plate portions are not arbitrary. I want you to strive for them at each meal. They're the right balance you need to keep the SI of the food low and to prevent as much sugar as possible from being stored as fat. You want to burn, baby burn. So pay careful attention to portion sizes to ensure you're eating the right amount of food in each of the four categories in your meals and your one optional snack.

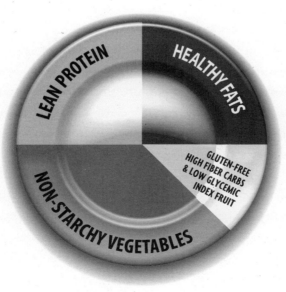

The Sugar Impact Plate

The Sugar Impact Plate is designed specifically to keep your blood sugar balanced. It's part of a master plan to crowd out sugar, reduce its impact on your weight and health, and help you reclaim your appetite awareness (so be sure you include notes in your daily journal about your level of hunger as you go through each Cycle).

Here's a breakdown of the plate and what each meal should include.

Clean, Lean Protein

1 serving of clean, lean protein:

- Animal proteins: fish, beef and pork, seafood, turkey, chicken, game
- Approved protein powders (see Resources online at http:// sugarimpact.com/resources.)

Protein Serving Size

- Women should eat 4–6 ounces at each meal; larger or more athletic women may need 6-8 ounces
- Men should eat 6–8 ounces; larger or very athletic men, up to 10 ounces
- Remember—those ounces are not necessarily pure protein, depending on your protein source. Most animal protein includes protein and fat. So the leaner the cut of meat, the fewer ounces necessary.

Healthy Fats

2–4 servings of healthy fats per meal (1–2 for snacks)

- Serving size: 1 tablespoon olive oil, ½ small avocado, 4 ounces cold-water fish or grass-fed beef, 5–10 nuts, 1 tablespoon nut butter, 5 olives

- Be sure to count fat from protein. Grass-fed beef and fatty fish count as a fat serving.

Non-Starchy Vegetables

2+ servings of non-starchy vegetables per meal

- Serving size: ½ cup cooked or 1 cup raw
- More is better! Ideal is 10+ servings a day
- You can always increase the portion size of your non-starchy vegetables

Slow, Low Carbs

1–2 servings of slow, low carbs per meal or snack

- Serving size: ½ cup cooked beans, quinoa, wild rice, or legumes, or 1 cup fruit or tomatoes
- 2–3 servings if larger male or more active female

Dishonorable Mentions

Don't succumb to the temptation to stack that protein quarter panel with processed lunch meats! I know they bat their eyes at you as a quick and easy solution, but those ready-to-eat loaves are plumped up with more surprises than a kid's cereal. They can have fillers, extenders, and additives like soy and corn. And too often, they're also souped up with high-fructose corn syrup, gluten, and MSG, which is an excitotoxin.

THE MEAT-FREE PLATE

For you vegans and vegetarians out there, the challenge is getting enough protein without overdosing on carbs or fat. Ideally you'll get the protein you need by combining nuts and seeds with grains and legumes. See how they're incorporated in the plate below. Vegan protein powder is also an easy way to get optimal protein at one of your meals.

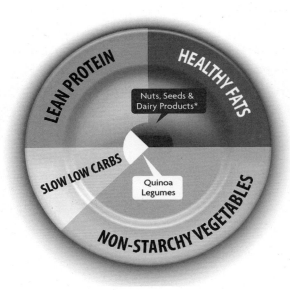

The Sugar Impact Plate for Vegans

When it comes to protein, you should strive for:

20–30 grams of protein per meal
10–20 grams per snack

This will vary depending on your size and gender, and whether you're doing heavy training or recovering from an injury, surgery, or under high stress.

HOW VEGAN PROTEINS MEASURE UP

Here are some average grams of protein, along with corresponding carb counts.*

Almonds—1 ounce
6 grams protein
6 grams carbs (5 grams fiber)
15 grams fat

Chia—1 ounce
9 grams fat
12 grams carbohydrates (11 grams of fiber)
4 grams protein

Quinoa—1 cup
4 grams fat
39 carbohydrates (5 grams fiber)
8 grams protein

Black Beans—1 cup
1 gram fat
41 grams carbohydrates (15 grams fiber)
15 grams protein

Lentils—1 cup
1 gram fat
40 grams carbs (16 grams fiber)
18 grams protein

*Vegan All in One Protein Powder**
2 scoops
5 grams fat
14 carbohydrates (6 grams fiber)
22 grams of protein

*(Counts vary by manufacturer; look for a powder with these average proportions.)

PROTEIN BOOSTS

Here are a few simple things you can do to crank the protein:

- Toss some pepitas into your quinoa
- Make "power oatmeal" by adding in protein powder
- Add lentils and almonds to your salad
- Snack on hummus with crudités
- Have lentil soup and celery sticks with almond butter

Remember: count nuts and seeds as fat and protein, and quinoa and legumes as slow, low carbs and protein.

One Size Doesn't Fit All

You may need to tailor these general guidelines to fit your goals or lifestyle. Here are some tips:

- If you're very athletic, have significant weight to lose, or are recovering from surgery or injury, you may need to increase your protein intake by 10–20%.
- If you're very athletic or are trying to gain weight, you may need to increase servings in each plate category by one or stay at the higher end of the recommendations.
- If you're focused on weight loss, stay on the lower end of the slow, low carb and fat categories.

YOU SHOULDN'T BE HUNGRY

As you taper in Cycle 1 and transition in Cycle 2, you'll be adding food. That's not a typo. I want you to eat more, so you'll never be hungry. I like to add food before I take any away because I want to support your success, not contribute to your suffering. Snatching away your high-carb foods without giving you any crutches would just be mean! So here's how I aim to help, step by step. Paste this to your fridge or your forehead, whichever will make it a constant presence to guide good choices and help keep you on track, especially if you've been overdoing the slow, low carbs:

1. Follow the recommended portion sizes—eat by the Sugar Impact Plate
2. Increase non-starchy veggies to at least 5 servings per day; ideal is 10+
3. Trade your high-SI foods for medium-SI foods
4. Replace one meal a day with a Sugar Impact Shake
5. Limit fruit to 2 servings per day maximum
6. Eat by the Sugar Impact Clock (see page 173)—eat every 4–6 hours; eat 3 meals and one optional snack per day
7. Drink up—water, that is; get your 8 glasses in between meals

Notice, too, that item 4 is to "replace one meal a day with a Sugar Impact Shake." This one simple little trick makes all the difference in jump-starting your metabolism for fast fat loss, and for setting the stage for a successful transition to a low-SI diet. And it's so easy!

Most people have dessert for breakfast, usually without the pleasure of knowing it. And it wreaks havoc on their metabolism the whole day. If you start your day with sugar, you've set your body's expectation for the day, and that's what you'll crave—and eat—all day long. But with a shake, you give your body a low-SI treat that delivers the protein you need to fuel a fat-burning metabolism and fight cravings until it's time for your next meal.

Cycle 1 gets your conversion from sugar burner to fat burner under way with intentionally measured tapering and the introduction of swaps. These will not necessarily be exact trades—you'll swap from high-SI to medium-SI foods in this cycle, but you may also trade high-SI foods for protein, fat, and fiber! Fat and fiber help you feel full more quickly—and longer—because they slow stomach emptying and engage your satiety hormones. They also keep your addiction-inducing reward system from firing off the charts, as it does in response to sugar.

As I mentioned on page 48, if you suspect you have a food intolerance or sensitivity to dairy or eggs (or any other food), avoid them and pick a different protein option. That includes dairy *products* like cottage cheese and yogurt.

Cycle 1: Foods for the Plate

Protein

Choose free-range, cage-free, grass-fed, wild, and no-hormone-added sources whenever possible.

- Lean chicken and turkey
- Lean, grass-fed red meats
- Cold-water wild-caught fish and shellfish—wild salmon, Alaskan halibut, sole, scallops, sardines
- Game
- Lamb
- De-fatted beef, pea, rice, chia, cranberry and/or chlorella protein powders
- Pastured pork
- Bison
- Pastured eggs
- Organic dairy, including cottage cheese, goat or sheep cheese, ricotta cheese, and Greek-style yogurt (grass-fed and raw whenever possible)

Healthy Fats

These include oils, butters, nuts, and seeds—and remember to count the fat from fish and meats.

- Dehydrated or low-roasted nuts (not peanuts)
- Grass-fed ghee and butter
- Avocado and avocado oil
- Fresh ground flaxseed meal
- Olive oil, olives
- Coconut milk or oil
- Chia seeds

- Hemp seeds
- Coconut wraps
- Malaysian palm fruit oil
- Tahini
- Sunflower seed butter
- Coconut flour
- Almond flour

Non-Starchy Vegetables

- Artichokes
- Arugula
- Asparagus
- Bamboo shoots
- Bean sprouts
- Beet greens
- Bell peppers (red, yellow, green)
- Broccoli
- Brussels sprouts
- Cabbage
- Carrots
- Cassava
- Cauliflower
- Celery
- Chicory
- Chives
- Collard greens
- Coriander
- Cucumber
- Dandelion greens

- Eggplant
- Endive
- Fennel
- Garlic
- Green beans
- Jalapeno peppers
- Jicama
- Kale
- Kohlrabi
- Leeks
- Lettuce
- Mushrooms
- Mustard greens
- Okra
- Onions
- Parsley
- Radicchio
- Radishes
- Shallots
- Spaghetti squash
- Spinach

- Summer squash
- Swiss chard
- Turnip greens

- Watercress
- Zucchini

Slow, Low Carbs

Grains, winter squashes, legumes, and fruit

- Squash (acorn, butternut, winter, kabocha)
- Lima beans
- Pumpkin
- Turnip
- Legumes
- Black beans
- Adzuki beans
- Chickpeas (garbanzo)
- Cowpeas
- French beans
- Great Northern beans
- Kidney beans
- Lentils
- Mung beans
- Navy beans
- Pinto beans
- Split peas
- White beans
- Wild Rice
- Groats

- Oatmeal (steel-cut or rolled)
- Quinoa
- Persimmon
- Star fruit
- Peaches
- Nectarines
- Passion fruit
- Guava
- Berries (blackberries, blueberries, boysenberries, elderberries, gooseberries, loganberries, raspberries, strawberries, acai)
- Tomatoes
- Grapefruit
- Oranges
- Lemons
- Limes
- Cranberries
- 85–100% dark chocolate (count as 1 carb and 1 fat serving)

Good Gut Feelings

Cycle 1 will probably introduce more beans and legumes into your diet than you're used to, and Cycle 2 will introduce even more. Condition your gastrointestinal tract in the first cycle by eating 1 tablespoon of beans every day so you don't slam into a gastrointestinal nightmare next week. You're welcome! If you're still struggling, try adding a little Beano as well or one of these other tips to fight gas naturally from my pal Donna Gates, nutrition expert at Body Ecology:

- Re-inoculate and restore your inner ecosystem. Gas is produced by the microbes—the good, the bad, and the neutral bacteria—that live deep down in your gut. When you balance the ecosystem of your intestines by re-inoculating it with good bugs, you get rid of digestive issues like gas. To do that, eat probiotic-rich foods or consider taking a probiotic supplement.

- Ferment your veggies. Many plant foods, such as cruciferous vegetables, onions, garlic, and legumes, contain simple sugars that easily ferment in your gut and feed the microbes living there, causing gas. To safeguard against this, ferment them ahead of time. Fermenting your foods pre-digests them and reduces your risk of gas.

- Cook your food. Cooking helps kill dangerous microbes hanging out on food, and it breaks down vegetable fiber, leaving less for intestinal microbes to munch on. Make the switch from raw salads to lightly steamed or sautéed veggies. Also consider browning onion and garlic in a little coconut oil before you eat them or add them as an ingredient to other recipes.

THE SUGAR IMPACT CLOCK

If you're a snacker and can't go too long between meals, that's a sure sign you're a sugar burner. Your habit means you're probably used to eating every 2–3 hours. There are schools of thought that will tell you that's a good thing for your metabolism, but I don't go to those schools for all the reasons I explained on pages 62–63!

On the Sugar Impact Diet, you'll eat by the Sugar Impact Clock. You'll begin to slowly stretch your time between meals and snacks and shift your eating routine to a solid three meals and one optional snack a day. Adding fiber, fat, and protein to your meals will help keep you full longer, as will having more water between meals. And getting off sugary, salty manufactured snacks and replacing them with healthy, whole, low-SI snacks will have a dramatic effect on your energy, blood sugar levels, and fat-burning. Bye-bye fatigue, headaches, and mood swings!

You can also help yourself de-snack by brushing or flossing your teeth when you're done eating. You'll first work on getting yourself to 3 hours between stops for food, then 4. If you've trained yourself to eat every 2–3 hours, it may take you 2 weeks to make this shift, especially if you scored higher than 20 on the Sugar Impact Quiz. But honestly, I've seen this issue get fixed in a matter of days. So don't despair, it will happen for you.

If you get up at 7 a.m., here's what your eating schedule might look like:

1. 8 a.m.: Breakfast
2. 12 p.m.: Lunch
3. 3 p.m.: Optional snack
4. 7 p.m.: Dinner

Don't Chew It!

Whatever you do, quit the gum! Gum can actually make you hungrier, and that minty taste it leaves in your mouth doesn't make you want to reach for carrots. You'll be diving for the salty snacks. The sweeteners used in most gum can also create some digestive unrest, so there's more than enough reason to spit it out.

Crunch, Crunch, Crunch

At Home

Here are some easy snacks to enjoy at home:

- Hummus and veggies
- Tapenade on endive
- The Sugar Impact Shake—try different flavors! Yum!
- Turkey rollup with guacamole
- Black bean soup
- Celery with almond butter
- Goat cheese and tomatoes (if no goat-dairy sensitivity)

On the Go

Find new treats and carry them with you! Always have an emergency stash on hand to prevent the crash and burn that comes with cravings and chaos on the run.

- Turkey, beef, or wild salmon jerky (no added sugar)
- Aseptic-packed wild salmon
- Slow-roasted nuts (put in a baggie with raw cacao and coconut)
- Virgin Diet Bar or other approved bars (see Resources at http://sugarimpact.com/resources)
- Pastured hard-boiled egg (ensure that shell isn't cracked so it won't spoil)

BREAKFAST

The clock starts with breakfast. I want you to eat within an hour of waking up. I'm not a fan of skipping breakfast. Your body has to eat, and it needs fuel. When you're not eating, your body is eating you, and it's not snacking on your belly fat. It's snacking on your muscle. The last thing you want to do is break down muscle, because muscle is essential for maintaining insulin sensitivity.

Breakfast sets your metabolic tone for the day. A lot of mindless mistakes are made first thing in the morning, and sugar comes rushing in through cereals and muffins (with juice!). Once you've set your blood sugar in pinball motion, it's a roller coaster you never get off.

A big, protein-rich, high-fiber, low-SI breakfast is the best way to prepare you to take on the world. A recent study published in *Obesity* followed two groups of overweight and obese women with metabolic syndrome for 12 weeks: one group ate high-calorie breakfasts and low-calorie dinners, while the other did exactly the opposite. The researchers concluded that a higher-calorie breakfast can be beneficial for fat loss and help you eat less overall.

My go-to breakfast at home and on the road is my Sugar Impact Shake. It serves up everything that's good—it's packed full of flavor and nutrients, it's filling, and it tastes great! Check out the basic recipe (on page 177) and then tweak to your taste. I want you to look forward to breakfast!

What to Look for in a Shake Mix

Replace a meal a day with a healthy shake to support fat loss, optimal nutrition, and ideal body composition. Check out my shake recipes beginning on page 239. You can also buy great shake mixes—see the Resources on my website at http://sugarimpact.com/resources for more information. Here are some guidelines:

- Protein sources. I recommend a blend of vegan proteins: preferred sources are pea, chia, cranberry, chlorella, or rice. The new kid on the block is beef protein (look for de-fatted with no antibiotics or hormones added). Avoid soy, egg, or milk protein powders.

- Go natural. Look for GMO-free and hormone-free (no recombinant bovine growth hormone, or rGBH).

- Go low SI. Look for 4–5 grams of sugar per serving, max. Stick with a very small amount of natural sweetener or sugar alcohol (i.e., stevia, xylitol, erythritol, rice syrup, evaporated cane juice syrup, dextrose). Avoid artificial colors or sweeteners and high-SI sweeteners such as fructose, agave, aspartame, and sucralose.

The Sugar Impact Shake Recipe

1 serving shake mix (see note)

8–10 ounces coconut, almond, or cashew milk (I like So Delicious Dairy Free Unsweetened)

1 serving fiber blend supplement (see Resources online at http://sugarimpact.com/resources)

1–2 tablespoons freshly ground flax, chia, hemp, or nut (not peanut) butter

Ice to desired thickness

Note: Follow package instructions regarding serving size, but this should give you approximately 20 grams of protein; this can be the Virgin Diet All-in-One-Shake or a shake mix of your choosing (see Resources online at http://sugarimpact.com/resources).

Optional Add-Ins:

Espresso powder

Lemon, lime, or orange zest

Spices including cinnamon, nutmeg, cayenne pepper

No-sugar-added extracts, including vanilla, almond, orange

Raw cacao nibs or powder

Kale, spinach

Avocado

Raw coconut cream

Low- or medium-SI fruit (in Cycles 1 and 3)

LUNCH AND DINNER

Eating by the Sugar Impact Plate ensures you're always getting some clean, lean protein and healthy fats at every meal. In Cycle 1, you'll have medium- and low-SI slow, low carbs.

When you eat with the balance the Plate gives, you should be able to go 4–6 hours before you need to eat again. If you can't, stop and remember that food is information. Go back to your journal and review your choices. Did you get enough clean, lean protein and healthy fats? Did you choose the right slow, low carbs from the medium- and low-SI columns only? Or did you cheat and now are paying the price?

We talked about fructose's impact on your appetite-control hormones. Clean, lean protein and the fiber from slow, low carbs work together in precisely the opposite way; they engage insulin to suppress ghrelin, the hormone produced by the stomach to tell your body you're hungry. You want to keep ghrelin low. Fat supports the effort to control your appetite from the small intestine, where it triggers the release of certain neuropeptides to tell your brain you're full.

So, when you eat by the Sugar Impact Plate, clean protein, healthy fats, and slow, low carbs send the message to your body to keep blood sugar stable and insulin low. That in turn gives you steady, sustained energy so you're not hungry for hours, and you can think clearly and allow your body to heal. That's a very different message than the fat-storing message from fructose, huh?

Sugar Impact While You Get Your Zs

Food never stops giving your body information, and that includes when you sleep. That doesn't mean you can't control that conversation during the night—you can, by eating a couple of hours before you go to bed.

When you go to bed full, you're not moving your diet or your healing in the right direction. First, it's not comfortable to try to sleep with a full stomach. But going to bed on a full stomach can create some other complications, which brings us back to ghrelin. Once you've eaten, assuming you've eaten well, you're suppressing ghrelin (remember?). Well, the one time you want ghrelin to be high is during the night. Ghrelin triggers the release of growth hormone when we sleep. Growth hormone helps your body heal and recover and make muscle and bone, so ghrelin is the last thing you want to shut down during sleep.

STAY AHEAD OF SUGAR WITHDRAWAL

Sugar is a drug, and getting off a drug is never easy. But the fact is, you're putting yourself through withdrawal hell, little by little, every day. Each time your blood sugar crashes, you're taken over by cravings, you're irritable, you have headaches, and you're shaky and hungry. There's no way you can get over that. Your body is set up to survive. The symptoms of withdrawal are biologically designed to be diabolical, so you'll go right back to the drug to which you're addicted to make them stop.

So resolve to be done with your addiction once and for all, and do this right. Take the time to move through medium-SI foods. It's only a week! At most, two. You shouldn't be feeling any of those symptoms of withdrawal if you're tapering. If you experience fatigue, headaches, irritability, or cravings and hunger, slow down—this isn't a race! And use every resource, strategy, and support system at your disposal. Have them in place right from the start, and don't be shy about pulling out the stops with every one of them to get you through moments of weakness.

HUNGER AND CRAVINGS

Attack any issues with your appetite head-on by increasing your protein and fat and the amount of fiber in your meals and snacks. Set an end goal of 50 grams of fiber every day, but don't add more than 5–10 grams a day as you work your way there. And remember to increase your water as you increase your fiber to keep things moving along.

Cravings are the very first thing the Sugar Impact Diet targets. There's no way forward with cravings. If you don't pull the nail out of the tire, you can never patch it up and go, right? The good news is that cravings let up quickly as you lower fructose, because doing so down-regulates the enzymes that help you absorb fructose. If you're better at absorbing fructose, you'll be hungrier and store fat easier—this is not something you want to be good at! Plus, eating less sweet means you'll crave less sweet.

Sugar-Withdrawal Strategies

Here are common signs of sugar withdrawal and ways to sidestep them.

Fatigue

1. Ensure that you're getting 7–9 hours of sleep every night
2. Take a 60-minute power nap in the early afternoon
3. Plan to do less during the first week of Cycle 2
4. Take a high-quality B complex vitamin with breakfast and lunch

Headaches

1. Keep emergency food with you
2. Eat by the Sugar Impact Plate and Sugar Impact Clock
3. Take magnesium (500 milligrams, 1–2 times a day). If a headache hits, open the capsule and put it under your tongue.
4. Take Epsom salt baths

Irritability

1. Carry emergency food with you
2. Eat by the Sugar Impact Plate and Sugar Impact Clock
3. Ensure that you're getting 7–9 hours of sleep every night
4. Drink green tea for a mild caffeine boost; it also has theanine, which helps mood and focus
5. Use supplements for stress support (go to http://sugarimpact.com/resources)

Cravings

If the Sugar-Attack Survival Strategies (page 182) aren't enough:

1. Try adding glutamine powder (1–3 grams) to your Sugar Impact Shake.
2. Drink Lemon-Aid throughout the day
3. Try 5-hydroxytryptophan, or 5-HTP (100 milligrams per day), to boost serotonin levels

Hunger

1. Eat by the Sugar Impact Plate and Sugar Impact Clock
2. Drink Lemon-Aid throughout the day
3. Increase your fiber slowly until you're having 50 grams per day
4. Ensure that you're getting 7–9 hours of sleep every night

BE A BOY SCOUT

If you've moved a little too quickly in swapping out high-SI foods and find yourself getting a little irritable or having headaches again, it usually means your blood sugar is low. So return to the basics: eat by the Sugar Impact Plate and control your snacks.

Even though I would prefer you not snack at all, you'll probably have a stretch of time during which you're relying on your optional snack in addition to breakfast, lunch, and dinner. Don't let that snack own you. You never know when you're going to get stuck, and if it's in a meeting where the only food lying around is biscotti, you're in trouble. I always want you to have emergency food with you—don't go anywhere without it! See page 63 for some smart options.

Sugar-Attack Survival Strategies

Burst train
Do yoga
Meditate
Pet the dog or cat
Walk the dog
Take a hot bath
Drink green tea
Watch a funny video
Listen to some uplifting music
Chat with a friend
Brush your teeth
Drink some Lemon-Aid
Join the Sugar Impact Diet Online Support Community
    (visit http://jjvirgincommunity.com and Resources online
    at http://sugarimpact.com/resources)
Read a juicy book

FATIGUE AND STRESS

Yep, it's that obvious. Make sure you get enough deep, restful sleep at night. I know it seems impossible, but it's not, no matter how busy you are. Take a 30–60 minute power nap in the early afternoon if you need one. And don't overschedule yourself, especially in Cycles 1 and 2.

You may also want to try a little green tea or coffee for a mild caffeine boost in the morning or afternoon. (See page 117 for more on caffeine.) Green tea has theanine in it, which is calming, good for your adrenal glands, and helps support a focused mood. If you prefer coffee for your jolt, make sure you're having clean, organic, mycotoxin-free coffee. Caffeine can be a double-edged sword, though, so be careful that you're not working against yourself. If you drink it, find your happy place—let it help you burn fat for fuel, sharpen your focus, and bump your energy—and stop there.

Stress lowers your dopamine and serotonin, amps up your hunger, and sends your sugar cravings through the roof. A good quality B complex vitamin can really help with low energy and stress. Check out the Supportive Supplements online at http://sugarimpact .com/resources for more ideas.

WATER

Sometimes cravings are just dehydration, and you're misreading thirst signals for hunger. When you get your fluids up, your hunger will back off. That makes water worth trying first almost every time you feel a craving coming on. Another major reason to love water is that you need it to burn fat.

To get the most bang for your water-drinking buck, drink according to this schedule. Yes, a schedule for water! No guess-work—it's all figured out for you. Just follow it and reap the rewards of fast and lasting fat loss.

Drinking Water by the Sugar Impact Clock

Within 30 minutes of waking up: 16 ounces
30 to 60 minutes before each meal: 16 ounces
During a meal: limit to 4 to 8 ounces
Start drinking water again 60 minutes after each meal
Before bed: 8 ounces (shuts down midnight hunger pangs)

> Daily total: 64 ounces minimum; more if you are in a hot climate, exercise heavily, or are heavier. You should be drinking approximately half your weight in ounces

And remember, what you measure, you can improve, so be sure to track how much water you're drinking every day until it becomes such a solid habit you couldn't imagine life without it.

If you're bored and want to sass it up a bit, make it sparkling mineral water, unsweetened coconut water, or Hint water. And don't forget about Lemon-Aid (see page 65). It's hydrating and there for you if a craving hits.

HELP! I HAVE ISSUES

If hypoglycemia is an issue, or if you're insulin-resistant or diabetic, there's a little more to talk about.

When you're dealing with hypoglycemia, you really can't go more than a few hours before crashing. Believe it or not, this program should help you with that, and one of the key ways is with the addition of more fiber to your diet. You also get a special dispensation to have 2 snacks and 3 meals a day, but I still want you to work on stretching out the time between each meal. And *always* carry emergency food with you, as a preemptive strike.

The same is true for you if you're a diabetic and on medication, but you'll need to be vigilant about monitoring your blood sugar levels, and you should be working closely with your doctor. The hope is that this program will help you reduce your medications, and I don't want you taking the wrong amount of medication. But working with your doctor is key to doing this safely and healthfully! If you're insulin-resistant or diabetic, I recommend staying in Cycle 1 for a second week.

If you have hypertension (high blood pressure), high cholesterol, or chronic pain, and are on medication, you may be pleasantly surprised to find that you can lower your medications while on the Sugar Impact Diet. Be sure you're working closely with your health care professional during this time.

For those with high blood pressure, make sure you're monitoring your blood pressure daily; you don't want it to get too low. If high cholesterol is your issue, I'd advise you to get another evaluation and blood draw after you have followed the Sugar Impact Diet for 4–6 weeks to re-check your levels.

If you're on pain medications, I'm going to recommend a slightly different path. If you haven't done the Virgin Diet yet, try it after you finish this program. You may see a substantial reduction in your pain and inflammation just by getting off gluten and high-SI foods, which this program will do for you. But on the Virgin Diet, you'll also remove dairy as well as four other potentially reactive and inflammatory foods. Pulling them out is a huge boost for gut healing and eliminating leaky gut, the genesis of many chronic conditions.

The entire SI program is designed to help you with inflammation and chronic disease. It's been nothing short of amazing to see so many people get off their medications, but I never want you to do that on your own. Make your doctor your partner in this—a member of your support team—and keep in close touch. If you'd like a referral to a doctor who recognizes the importance of food and healthy lifestyle behaviors in overall health, check out the Resources online at http://sugarimpact.com/resources.

GETTING THE FAMILY ON BOARD

I know you may have concerns about the tidal wave of kicking and screaming that will come from your family if you announce you're going on a diet. There are two ways to go at this. If you've got a family who's game, awesome. Build in rewards and involve them. If they're not going to come on board willingly, you may have to be a little sneaky. Hear me out.

If you're worried your family would organize and launch a revolt, don't make it World War III. Why not just wait until they notice? Because what they'll notice is that they're getting much better food (that's not a commentary on your cooking, I promise!). Kids don't have cars or wallets, right? So, if it's not there, they can't eat it. And the food in this program is delicious and is sure to satisfy the pickiest of kids (and partners). Won't you feel good knowing the whole family is getting healthier with you?

MY IMPACT!

Margaret Otis
Starting weight: 205 lbs.
Current weight: 180 lbs.
Total lost: 25 lbs.

I had been following the Virgin Diet since the end of January 2013. I removed sugar at that time and never added it back in. I noticed after being on a plateau for at least 2 months that maybe I was eating too much fruit and low-carb vegetables, even though they were allowed. I decided to cut back on these to see if that would make a difference. Then I discovered the Sugar Impact Diet, and it seemed made for me.

Thankfully, I started the program and never looked back. I don't feel deprived, and for the first time the holidays were not an issue. I stayed on plan and enjoyed the family time and made sure I provided foods on my plan. The few times I ate something that I didn't know had a trigger ingredient, I was in pain and my symptoms returned, so it was an easy decision to keep those foods out of my pantry.

I finally was able to break free of my plateau. I have a ways to go yet, but I had lost 95 pounds in 9 months on the Virgin Diet before I hit that plateau. I lost all my cravings, especially for sweets and chocolate, and was off medications within three days. I was never tempted to "go off" the plan because I felt so wonderful. I'm no longer pre-diabetic, am off my blood pressure as well as other medications, and have cleared many issues that I never connected to high SI. My lab values have improved, and my doctor was very proud of what I had accomplished in these short months.

I wish I had learned this years ago when I was living an unhealthy life with years of pain along with many medical issues. I had never expected to last more than three days when I started this journey because I was giving up all the foods I loved best. This is how I eat now, and I love the new foods I never would have eaten in the past. I still have certain foods that evoke fond memories, but not enough to undo all the work I've done.

My family and friends have been so impressed, and have even started changing some of their eating behaviors. When we get together, they are always looking for new recipes I'm using. Some of them have started following the Sugar Impact Diet, too. I have more energy, and my family and friends notice that I'm more outgoing than before. I have been an inspiration to them. I hope to show the next generation by my example that family is the main focus of our time together, not food.

RESOURCES AND TOOLS

You won't be left wanting for strategies and support to get you through the Sugar Impact Diet. Lean on me! I've put together a 1-week meal plan (see pages 188–192) and a shopping list (online at http://sugarimpact.com/resources) so you know exactly what to stock up on. You can use them as a bible and follow them exactly, if that's easiest for you. But even better, this program will teach you how to make great choices. Once you learn the principles, you don't have to follow my meal plans exactly—use them as a jumping-off point and be creative. That freedom does come with some responsibility, though—you have to make sure you're staying within the Sugar Impact Scales for your cycle.

To Make Shopping Easier...

The shopping lists and Sugar Impact Scales are online at http://sugarimpact.com/resources. I encourage you to take these tools to the grocery store with you. You're learning a new language, and turning the way you look at—and eat—sugar on its head. Rely on these tools until you're fluent.

CYCLE 1 MEAL PLANS

Putting Your Meals Together

- Refer to the Sugar Impact Plate and outline for amounts*
- Then, feel free to move things around
- Substitute one protein for another
- Substitute one slow, low carb for another
- Substitute one healthy fat for another
- Substitute one non-starchy veggie for another
- In other words, be creative!

Modify meals as needed for intolerances.

DAY 1

BREAKFAST:
Sugar Impact Shake (see recipe, page 239)

LUNCH:
Pan–Seared Salmon Lettuce Wrap made with Rice Tortilla (see recipe, page 247)

Easy Roasted Asparagus with Red Palm Fruit Oil (see recipe, page 264)

DINNER:
Spice-Rubbed Beef Tenderloin with Raw Tomato Salsa (see recipe, page 259)

½ baked sweet potato

Classic Creamed Spinach (see recipe, page 262)

SNACK:
Yogurt and Nut Parfait—add ½ cup of berries (see recipe, page 279)

DAY 2

BREAKFAST:
Sugar Impact Shake (see recipe, page 239)

LUNCH:
Bean and Bacon Minestrone Soup (see recipe, page 244)—add ½ cup cooked quinoa pasta to your serving

Arugula and Watercress Salad with a Poached Egg and Lemon-Dijon Vinaigrette (see recipe, page 243)

DINNER:
Mediterranean-Style Chicken Kabobs (see recipe, page 255) served on a bed of brown rice

Grilled Eggplant with Olive Relish (see recipe, page 264)

SNACK:
Pear and 2 ounces goat cheese

DAY 3

BREAKFAST:
  Sugar Impact Shake (see recipe, page 239)

LUNCH:
  Turkey Burger with Goat Cheese, Sautéed Onions, and
    Cucumber Salad (see recipe, page 251)
  Served on gluten-free English muffin

DINNER:
  Pesto-Topped Sea Scallops with Asparagus (see recipe, page 256)
    served on a bed of brown rice
  Warm Napa Slaw with Shallot Dressing (see recipe, page 267)

SNACK:
  Vanilla Spice Protein Popsicle (see recipe, page 283)

DAY 4

BREAKFAST:
  Sugar Impact Shake (see recipe, page 239)

LUNCH:
  Chicken Noodle Soup (see recipe, page 245)—Substitute
    cooked quinoa noodles for the shirataki noodles
  Mixed green salad with Simple Vinaigrette (see recipe, page 273)

DINNER:
  Italian Burgers with Tapenade (see recipe, page 254)
  Serve with ½ baked sweet potato

SNACK:
  Turkey, Bacon, Lettuce, and Tomato Roll-Up, sub rice wrap for
    lettuce, add lettuce in as more filler (see recipe, page 279)

DAY 5

BREAKFAST:
Sugar Impact Shake (see recipe, page 239)

LUNCH:
Shrimp and Shirataki Noodle Salad (see recipe, page 249)—
replace the Shirataki noodles with cooked al dente rice or
quinoa angel hair or spaghetti noodles

Serve on 2 cups of your choice of greens tossed with 1
tablespoon sesame oil and 1 tablespoon lime juice

DINNER:
Texas Bison Chili (see recipe, page 260), serve with mixed
green salad with Simple Vinaigrette

SNACK:
Honeydew with 4 ounces Greek-style coconut or dairy yogurt
and 1 ounce chopped almonds

DAY 6

BREAKFAST:
Sugar Impact Shake (see recipe, page 239)

LUNCH:
Vegetarian Lentil Soup (see recipe, page 253)
Serve with Pan-Fried Artichoke Hearts with Lemon and Garlic
(see recipe, page 266)

DINNER:
Pork Stir Fry with Snow Peas, Asparagus, and Peppers (see
recipe, page 256)
Serve on a bed of ½–1 cup brown rice

SNACK:
Roasted Garlic and Lemon Hummus with Bean Chips (see
recipe, page 278)

DAY 7

BREAKFAST:

Sugar Impact Shake (see recipe, page 239)

LUNCH:

Roast Beef and Vegetable Lettuce Wrap with Chipotle
Vinaigrette (see recipe, page 248)—make with rice tortilla
and keep lettuce in as filler

DINNER:

Spaghetti Squash alla Checca (see recipe, page 258)—substitute
quinoa pasta for the squash

Roasted Spice-Rubbed Chicken Thighs (see recipe, page 258)

Mixed green salad with Simple Vinaigrette

SNACK:

Apple slices with 2 tablespoons of almond butter

For Vegan Meal plan for Cycle 1 go to http://sugarimpact.com
/resources

YOU'RE JUST GETTING STARTED!

You can do this! You're on your way to cracking the code on your
sugar cravings. Part of the reason Cycle 2 will work so well is
because of the work you've done in Cycle 1. Tapering has inge-
niously and gradually prepared your system for the next 2 weeks.
Your body isn't on high alert, ready to shellac you with weapons of
craving and withdrawal to get its sugar. So it should hardly see the
transition coming.

You'll retrain your taste buds to restore your sensitivity to and
appreciation for sugar. You'll fire up your metabolism, control your
appetite, heal your digestive tract, and lose weight fast. You'll probably also notice a healthy, younger glow to your skin, too! Reversing
the effects of accelerated aging—and the seeds of chronic disease—is
one of the biggest benefits you'll see. Fat burner, here you come!

9

CYCLE 2: TRANSITION

Congratulations! You've made it through Cycle 1. Don't you feel awesome? You're breaking free of your cravings, regaining control of your appetite, and hopefully you're already feeling your energy come back and your brain fog lift. I hope you're excited for what's to come, because in Cycle 2 you're going to shift from sugar burner to fat burner and drop weight—fast.

STOP!

If you haven't gone through Cycle 1, do not try to cut in line here. You won't be gaining anything—certainly not the week you hoped to skip. You'll just set yourself up to wipe out, and you'll eventually give over to the idea that you have to start at the beginning. Go back and do it—it's just a week!

Cycle 2—Transition

Swap medium-SI foods for low-SI foods (see the Scales in part 2, starting on page 82, or online at http://sugarimpact.com/resources.)

Take the Sugar Impact Quiz at the beginning and end of this cycle

Eliminate fruit (except olives, avocados, tomatoes, lemons, and limes)

Total sugar consumption should be 25 grams or less per day; fructose should be less than 10 grams

Total carbs: 100–150 grams

Supplement as needed

Determine when you're ready to move into Cycle 3

HOW CYCLE 2 WORKS

Plan on committing at least 2 weeks to Cycle 2, your transition phase. You may notice changes quickly and feel like you can do it faster than 2 weeks, but I want you to prepare yourself to spend the time you need in Cycle 2, because there are some big payoffs. You'll stop craving sweet altogether—it won't even taste good to you anymore, so it will be really hard to miss it. Your symptoms will start to disappear: no more fatigue, achy joints, dull skin, gastric distress, and inflammation. Best of all, you'll finally break through that brick wall of weight-loss resistance. You've unlocked your body's fat-burning machinery, the gears are starting to turn, and they're about to accelerate.

You've unlocked your body's fat-burning machinery.

Cycle 2 will dramatically lower the amount of sugar, and especially fructose, that you eat for 2 weeks, which has the effect of "rebooting" your system. Think of it as a 2-week detox eliminating your drug of choice, sugar. Sugar activates a cravings and reward pathway, and the more sugar you eat, the more your body adjusts to it. By cutting out sugar for a period of time, you can reduce the hyperactive metabolic system that has developed and start over, transforming you from sugar burner to fat burner.

The key in Cycle 2 is to really tune in to how your body is responding and to pay attention to your own needs. If you find that you need more than 2 weeks to get through this cycle, that's completely fine. Everyone is different, and you'd rob yourself of a life-changing gift if you try to measure your progress against someone else's. So this is not about being arbitrarily locked into numbers on a chart—it's about you losing weight and feeling good fast.

In these 2 (or more) weeks, you're going to reclaim and reset your sugar sensitivity and retrain your taste buds to appreciate natural flavors. At the risk of having you call me crazy, you may even start to find some foods *too* sweet. Yes, your taste buds can truly be retrained—they can be brought back to life. Think of grass you run over with a car. If you keep retreading that same ground, the grass doesn't stand much of a chance. But when you stop running your tires over it and give it the care it needs, it pops back up, right as rain. Same with your taste buds—when you pave them over with unbearable sweetness meal after meal, day after day, they have nothing to live for. Okay, that's a bit dramatic, but you've pounded them with a single high intensity taste, and their calibration is shot. They can no longer respond to any subtle flavors, including sweetness. When you retrain your taste buds, you have a totally different response to what you used to think of as sweet. Isn't that exciting?!

LOWERING YOUR SUGAR IMPACT

The beauty of the Sugar Impact Diet is that it keeps things simple. During Cycle 2, you'll drop your total sugar consumption to 25 grams or less. Fructose, though, will drop to under 10 grams. Your total carbs will fall somewhere in the 100–150 gram range (up to 200 grams for larger men and athletes). You're still living by the

Sugar Impact Plate, and all of these calculations are guided by the portions on the Plate.

You know from Cycle 1 that this is not one of those sadistic, starvation, slow-your-metabolism-down diets that sends you spinning into a downward spiral. The same thing goes for Cycle 2: this is really about becoming aware of what your body needs and feeding it the right foods to crank up your metabolism until it's burning fat and soothing your insides the way it's meant to. The Sugar Impact Plate will take care of you, so you should never be hungry!

CYCLE 2 TOOLS

By now you're a pro with a lot of the Sugar Impact (SI) tools from Chapter 2. Keep checking in with the Sugar Impact Inventory to make sure you're not letting any of the enemies sneak back into your house. Your Sugar Impact Quiz will serve as a baseline for how well and quickly you're healing—take it again now, and again in 2 weeks. You'll be impressed with how far you've come! But if you score 20 or higher, consider using one or more of my Speed-Healing Techniques (see page 223) to help you reclaim your sugar sensitivity faster.

Then there's the scale. The one on your bathroom floor. You may have been avoiding the scale, but it's a really valuable tool, and a motivating one, too! Weigh in at least once a week, but if you want to weigh in daily, there's no penalty for that. But only do so during these weeks—once you're through the program, ditch the daily numbers check. I don't want you to become an obsessive weigher. This diet doesn't work any better if you eat standing on your scale.

The rule of thumb for maintenance is to get on the scale once a week, in the morning before you've eaten. If you get a funky result one day, just try it again another day. Don't freak out. Weekly waist and hip measurements will help you keep yourself in check over the long haul, too, but for now, if you want to do them daily to gauge your progress, feel free. Things tend to change very fast during this time, and it's fun to see those numbers drop.

And don't forget to journal! (Download a sample journal page online at http://sugarimpact.com/resources.) Journaling what you eat and how much water you drink will help you track your progress as you become low SI—especially during these 2 weeks as you start to hone in on the pattern of what foods are creating symptoms for you. There's really no better way to get at the heart of sugar's impact on your energy, mood, and achy joints, because sometimes that impact is delayed. When it is, we all tend to just grind on and deal with it, never thinking back to what we ate in the morning, or the day before.

But *if* some sugar happens to tiptoe back into your diet, you can easily ferret it out by connecting the dots between your food and notes like, "I feel awful today," or, "I'm so bloated, what the heck?" That's when it will jump out at you—there's a pattern! You can do a little light journal reading and see where the sugar got away from you.

WHAT TO EXPECT FROM CYCLE 2

Cycle 2 will function like an SI reset for you. After these two transition weeks, you'll be at a new baseline, and in the next cycle you'll discover which SI foods work for you and which don't. You'll be so much more sensitive to sugar that when you eat it, you'll feel lousy. That's exactly how you want to feel. When you're miserable after eating sugar, your body's trying to tell you something (can you guess what it is?). The only reason you didn't have that response before is because your addiction trumped your body's warning signals, and you kept beating those signals down until they gave up on you. But when you reset your system and get your sensitivity back, you'll feel fabulous all the time, until you do something that makes your body throw up a flag. Wouldn't you rather feel great and have a system that has your back than drag along with low-grade symptoms and weight creep, and not really notice?

The first few days will set your expectation for the rest of the cycle. Above all else, let go of the diet stigma that may have you believing you have to eat less food. You should not be hungry on the Sugar Impact Diet, or you'll become preoccupied with (the wrong kinds of) food, cravings will take root, and it will take some Herculean feats to keep you on course.

In fact, one of the most exciting things that's going to happen to you is the feeling of finally being not hungry—until your next mealtime, that is. If you're like most people, you've always had constant hunger hanging around because of the huge amount of fructose in your diet. So not being hungry will be new. Fructose creates high-wattage hunger that gnaws at you and demands immediate attention—and sweet makes you crave more sweet. As you're transitioning to a low-fructose way of life, you won't be hungry.

The increased protein and fiber from the Sugar Impact Plate have the biggest roles in curbing your appetite. And you're still eating by the Sugar Impact Clock (see page 61 for a refresher). But pay close attention to your body, and if you feel hungry here and there, nip it in the bud with some Supportive Supplements (online at http://sugarimpact.com/resources).

You should not be hungry on the Sugar Impact Diet.

I offer a lot of resources to make sure you succeed, so take the help you need.

Fructose-Free Shakes

You're transitioning to a low-fructose diet, so you'll have a shake in place of at least one meal every day. I have it listed as your breakfast, but it's not locked in—you can have it for lunch or dinner if that's easier for you. I've mixed the shake recipes up enough to keep them interesting, with lots of different flavors. But if they don't float your boat, you have the freedom to whip something else up to taste and be creative—just play by the rules.

One thing you'll notice right away is that the shake recipes in this cycle don't have any fruit. The only fruit allowed in shakes in Cycle 2 are lemons and limes, and fruit we sometimes think of as veggies, like avocadoes, tomatoes, and olives. The rule for the sweet ingredients in protein powder still applies, but for these 2 weeks, since you're transitioning to a very low sugar diet, the fruit has been modified to lower fructose.

Rest assured that the recipes were created with great care to make sure these shakes are still super yummy. You're not going to be falling on your sword to suffer through an undrinkable green concoction. I make mine with chocolate protein shake mix, avocado, coconut milk, chia seeds, and then I throw some raw cacao nibs on top. Does that sound like I'm giving up anything to you? No way, never. I like delicious, too. I have one every day, and I don't miss the fruit at all.

Even if shakes aren't your thing, I hope you'll at least give my Sugar Impact Shake a try before throwing in the towel. If you're still not keen on them, feel free to substitute any other meal for your shake—you're not locked into breakfast foods for breakfast! After all, most of them are high SI! Go ahead and have some wild salmon on a bed of lentils and sautéed spinach. Or you can be more traditional and have oatmeal, but be sure to add protein powder or a side of leftover protein from last night's dinner.

Experimentation is the order of the day with both meals, too. Play with your food! Test, have fun, swap in ingredients that get you jazzed about your next meal. Use the Sugar Impact Scales to guide you, and just make sure you're staying in bounds.

HOW LOW CAN YOU GO?

Let's have some fun with numbers. You've already come much further than you know (look back!). You've reached Cycle 2, which means a life free of sugar's grip is just around the corner.

The way there is through this calculation: 1 teaspoon = 4 grams. Keep it at your fingertips, because you'll live by it for the next 2 weeks. The total amount of sugar you have every day in your three meals and optional snack should not exceed 25 grams, or 6 teaspoons, *and* you'll limit your total carbs, which count as sugar, to a maximum of 100–150 grams. The 25 grams of sugar is included in that 100–150 gram total. Bigger men and athletes may go up to 200 grams, but keep that sugar low.

SUGAR IMPACT SCALES

Keep your Cycle 2 SI Scales handy (find them on pages 82, 89, 97, 110, 123, 135, 150 or download it online at http://sugarimpact .com/resources); you'll refer to it often. You're going to swap all the medium-SI foods you tapered to in Cycle 1 for low-SI foods in Cycle 2. This transition is true for each of the seven categories, and, as I mentioned earlier, in a few circumstances there are some low-SI foods like fruit that you'll leave out so that you can retrain your taste buds even faster.

In Cycle 1, you identified all the surprising sugar bombs slipping into your diet with the Sneaky Sugar Inventory. You figured out your portions by referring to the Virgin Sugar Impact Plate, which means you probably had to bring your slow, low carbs down a little. In these next 2 weeks, we're really going to get the amount of sugar from them under control.

CYCLE 2 MEAL PLANS

Here's the road map for Cycle 2 from start to finish. If you follow it exactly, it will drop you at your destination as a sugar-sensitive, fat-burning rock star. But don't feel fenced in—you always have the freedom to take creative license and change things up, if you play by the rules.

A note to athletes and big guys: take a close look at your portions. Wherever I specify 1–2 low-SI servings, as I do with slow, low carbs, you can go up to 3. Generally, you can increase your portions overall by 1.

Putting Your Meals Together

- Refer to the Sugar Impact Plate and outline for amounts
- Then, feel free to move things around
- Substitute one protein for another
- Substitute one slow, low carb for another
- Substitute one healthy fat for another
- Substitute one non-starchy veggie for another
- In other words, be creative!

Feel free to be creative here as long as you're sticking to the low-SI, Cycle 2 choices on the Scales. You can trade out proteins; switch a lunch option for a dinner; or eat a breakfast for lunch (who says you have to eat breakfast food for breakfast? Not me!).

If you want to replace a second meal with a shake, feel free. You can choose between the recommended shakes or have the Sugar Impact Shake with approved Cycle 2 fruit (see the recipe on page 239). And, of course, you can always add a mixed green salad and more non-starchy veggies to any meal.

For extra sweet tooth support, add a fermented food to your diet daily—choose kimchee, cultured veggies, coconut kefir, or sauerkraut. You only need ¼–½ a cup at lunch and dinner, and the easiest way to get it is with 4 ounces of coconut kefir. If you haven't had cultured foods, be patient: they take some getting used to. But when you're dying for sweets, they're worth a shot!

Vegetarians and vegans can find a customized meal plan at http://sugarimpact.com/resources. Modify the meals below as needed for intolerances.

DAY 1

BREAKFAST:
Coco-Cashew Shake (see recipe, page 239)

LUNCH:
Roast Beef and Vegetable Lettuce Wrap with Chipotle Vinaigrette (see recipe, page 248)
Simple Tomato Salad with Chick Peas and Feta Cheese (see recipe, page 250)

DINNER:
Mediterranean-Style Chicken Kabobs (see recipe, page 255)
Lentils alla Rustica and Pan-Fried Artichoke Hearts with Lemon and Garlic (see recipes, pages 268 and 266)

OPTIONAL SNACK:
Turkey, Bacon, Lettuce, and Tomato Roll-Up (see recipe, page 279)

DAY 2

BREAKFAST:
   Mushroom and Spinach Omelet with Feta Cheese (see recipe, page 241)
   Add sliced tomatoes

LUNCH:
   Sugar Impact Shake with approved Cycle 2 fruit (see recipe, page 239)

DINNER:
   Pesto-Topped Sea Scallops with Asparagus (see recipe, page 256)
   Mushroom and Onion Wild Rice Pilaf (see recipe, page 269)

OPTIONAL SNACK:
   Yogurt and Nut Parfait (see recipe, page 279)

DAY 3

BREAKFAST:
   Coco-Cashew Shake (see recipe, page 239)

LUNCH:
   Shrimp and Shirataki Noodle Salad (see recipe, page 249)
   Serve on a bed of 2–4 cups of mixed greens tossed with 1 tablespoon sesame oil and 1 tablespoon freshly squeezed lime juice

DINNER:
   Italian Burgers with Tapenade (see recipe, page 254)
   Pan-Roasted Brussels Sprouts with Almonds (see recipe, page 265)

OPTIONAL SNACK:
   Homemade Cashew Butter on Celery (see recipe, page 277)

DAY 4

BREAKFAST:
Creamy Cinnamon-Spiced Quinoa with Slow-Roasted Almonds (see recipe, page 240)
Add 2–4 chicken breakfast sausages or 2–4 ounces of last night's leftover protein

LUNCH:
Lean and Green Shake (see recipe, page 241)

DINNER:
Grilled Chicken Breasts with Puttanesca Sauce (see recipe, page 261)
Quinoa with Shallots, Tomato, and Asparagus (see recipe, page 270)

OPTIONAL SNACK:
Lemony Frozen Greek-Style Yogurt (see recipe, page 282)

DAY 5

BREAKFAST:
Sugar Impact Shake with approved Cycle 2 fruit (see recipe, page 239)

LUNCH:
Chicken Noodle Soup (see recipe, page 245)
Arugula and Watercress Salad with a Poached Egg and Lemon-Dijon Vinaigrette (see recipe, page 243)

DINNER:
Spice-Rubbed Beef Tenderloin with Raw Tomato Salsa (see recipe, page 259)
Classic Creamed Spinach (see recipe, page 262)

OPTIONAL SNACK:
Vanilla Spice Protein Popsicle (see recipe, page 283)

DAY 6

BREAKFAST:
  Lean and Green Shake (see recipe, page 241)

LUNCH:
  Bean and Bacon Minestrone Soup (see recipe, page 244)
  2–4 cups mixed green salad with Simple Vinaigrette (see recipe, page 273)

DINNER:
  Roasted Spice–Rubbed Chicken Thighs (see recipe, page 258)
  Zucchini, Snow Pea, Sugar Snap, and Celery Skillet (see recipe, page 268)

OPTIONAL SNACK:
  Roasted Garlic and Lemon Hummus served with crudités (see recipe, page 278)

DAY 7

BREAKFAST:
  Sugar Impact Shake with approved Cycle 2 fruit (see recipe, page 239)

LUNCH:
  Turkey Burger with Goat Cheese, Sautéed Onions, and Cucumber Salad (see recipe, page 251)
  Simple Tomato Salad with Chick Peas and Feta Cheese (see recipe, page 250)

DINNER:
  Spaghetti Squash alla Checca (see recipe, page 258)
  Serve with a simple grilled chicken breast on the side (for directions, see Grilled Chicken Breasts with Puttanesca Sauce, page 261)

OPTIONAL SNACK:
  Cumin and Chili Roasted Cashews (see recipe, page 276)

DAY 8

BREAKFAST:
Mushroom and Spinach Omelet with Feta Cheese (see recipe, page 241)
Add sliced tomatoes

LUNCH:
Coco-Cashew Shake (see recipe, page 239)

DINNER:
Grilled Chicken Breasts with Puttanesca Sauce (see recipe, page 261), Grilled Eggplant with Olive Relish (see recipe, page 264), mixed green salad with Lemon-Dijon Vinaigrette with Macadamia Nut Oil (see recipe, page 273)

OPTIONAL SNACK:
Turkey, Bacon, Lettuce, and Tomato Roll-Up (see recipe, page 279)

DAY 9

BREAKFAST:
Creamy Cinnamon-Spiced Quinoa with Slow-Roasted Almonds (see recipe, page 240)
Add 2–4 chicken breakfast sausages or 2–4 ounces of last night's leftover protein

LUNCH:
Lean and Green Shake (see recipe, page 241)

DINNER:
Mediterranean-Style Chicken Kabobs (see recipe, page 255)
Lentils alla Rustica (see recipe, page 268) and Pan-Fried Artichoke Hearts with Lemon and Garlic (see recipe, page 266)

OPTIONAL SNACK:
Homemade Cashew Butter on Celery (see recipe, page 277)

DAY 10

BREAKFAST:
 Coco-Cashew Shake (see recipe, page 239)

LUNCH:
 Vegetarian Lentil Soup (see recipe, page 253)
 Mixed green salad with Lemon-Dijon Vinaigrette with
  Macadamia Nut Oil (see recipe, page 273)

DINNER:
 Roasted Spice-Rubbed Chicken Thighs (see recipe,
  page 258)
 Zucchini, Snow Pea, Sugar Snap, and Celery Skillet (see
  recipe, page 268)

OPTIONAL SNACK:
 Lemony Frozen Greek-style Yogurt (see recipe, page 282)

DAY 11

BREAKFAST:
 Sugar Impact Shake with approved Cycle 2 fruit (see recipe,
  page 239)

LUNCH:
 Arugula and Watercress Salad with a Poached Egg and Lemon-
  Dijon Vinaigrette (see recipe, page 243)
 Bean and Bacon Minestrone Soup (see recipe, page 244)

DINNER:
 Pork Stir Fry with Snow Peas, Asparagus, and Peppers (see
  recipe, page 256)
 Serve with a side of quinoa

OPTIONAL SNACK:
 Yogurt and Nut Parfait (see recipe, page 279)

DAY 12

BREAKFAST:
  Lean and Green Shake (see recipe, page 241)

LUNCH:
  Pan-Seared Salmon Lettuce Wraps (see recipe, page 247)
  Quinoa with Shallots, Tomato, and Asparagus (see recipe,
    page 270)

DINNER:
  Italian Burgers with Tapenade (see recipe, page 254)
  Easy Roasted Asparagus (see recipe, page 264)

OPTIONAL SNACK:
  Vanilla Spice Protein Popsicle (see recipe, page 283)

DAY 13

BREAKFAST:
  Coco-Cashew Shake (see recipe, page 239)

LUNCH:
  Double-Chopped Chicken and Vegetable Salad with Creamy
    Pesto Dressing (see recipe, page 247)

DINNER:
  Texas Bison Chili (see recipe, page 260)
  Warm Napa Cabbage Slaw with Shallot Dressing (see recipe,
    page 267)

OPTIONAL SNACK:
  Roasted Garlic and Lemon Hummus served with crudités (see
    recipe, page 278)

DAY 14

BREAKFAST:
Sugar Impact Shake with approved Cycle 2 fruit (see recipe, page 239)

LUNCH:
Vegetarian Lentil Soup (see recipe, page 253)

2–4 cups mixed green salad with Simple Vinaigrette (see recipe, page 273) with 1 tablespoon chopped walnuts

DINNER:
Spice-Rubbed Beef Tenderloin with Raw Tomato Salsa (see recipe, page 259)

Classic Creamed Spinach (see recipe, page 262)

OPTIONAL SNACK:
Cumin and Chili Roasted Cashews (see recipe, page 276)

CYCLE 2: THE INTENSIFY WEEK

If you've completed Cycle 1 and at least one week of Cycle 2, *and* your scores for the Sugar Impact Quiz are 2 or less in any category or 12 or less overall, you're a Virgin Diet graduate or if you have already improved by 50% or more and feel great, then I have an optional bonus week for you.

This intensify week is more of a challenge, but it's a great tool for breaking through a plateau and getting to the next level, if you choose. Even though it's tempting to skip ahead, you shouldn't attempt this until you meet the criteria above—doing this before you're ready will lead to cravings, stress and, ultimately, disaster. Don't set yourself back! Only do this if you're really ready.

How the Intensify Week works:

- Eat from all of the low-SI foods approved for Cycle 2
- Drink 1–2 shakes daily in place of meals

- Limit your slow, low carbs to 1 per meal (strive for none if you can do it) and increase your non-starchy veggies to 8–10 servings a day
- Drink water between meals, and use Lemon-Aid as needed (with chia or freshly ground flaxseed)
- Your non-shake meal should consist of 5 or more veggie servings, 1 protein serving, and 2 fat servings
- Your snack should consist of 1 or more veggie servings, 1 fat serving, and a small amount of protein (2–3 ounces)
- Eat 50 grams of fiber a day

Intensify Tips

Keep a pot of Chicken "Noodle" Soup, Intensify Version (see recipe, page 246), around for easy, filling meals and snacks, and keep Vanilla Spice Protein Popsicles (see recipe, page 283) in the freezer as a great snack and sweet-tooth soother.

INTENSIFY MEAL PLANS

Here are a few sample days to help guide you. Design your Intensify days based around what works best for your schedule.

SAMPLE DAY 1

UPON RISING:
Hot water with lemon, green tea, or coffee

BREAKFAST:
Lean and Green Shake (see recipe, page 241)

BETWEEN BREAKFAST AND LUNCH:
Water, Lemon-Aid (see page 65), Green tea

LUNCH:
Sugar Impact Shake with approved Cycle 2 fruit

BETWEEN LUNCH AND DINNER:
Water, Lemon-Aid (see page 65)

DINNER:
1 serving of Chicken "Noodle" Soup, Intensify Version (see recipe, page 246)

4 cups of mixed green salad with your choice of 2 tablespoon Lemon-Dijon Vinaigrette, Red Wine Vinaigrette, or extra virgin olive oil and fresh-squeezed lemon juice

1 8-ounce glass of water before bed

OPTIONAL SNACK:
Celery sticks with 2 tablespoons cashew cheese (see recipe, page 242)

SAMPLE DAY 2

UPON RISING:
Hot water with lemon, green tea, or coffee

BREAKFAST:
Sugar Impact Shake (see recipe, page 239) with approved Cycle 2 fruit

BETWEEN BREAKFAST AND LUNCH:
Water, Lemon-Aid (see page 65), or green tea

LUNCH:
Shrimp and Shirataki Noodle Salad—make ahead and chill (see recipe, page 249)

Serve on 4 cups of your favorite greens tossed with 1 tablespoon sesame oil and 1 tablespoon lime juice

Or salad at a restaurant: 4 cups mixed greens, any non-starchy low-SI veggies you can add, sliced chicken breast or grilled salmon, a few slices of avocado, 1 tablespoon extra virgin olive oil, and lemon juice or red wine vinegar

BETWEEN LUNCH AND DINNER:
Water, Lemon-Aid (see page 65)

DINNER:
1 serving Chicken "Noodle" Soup, Intensify Version (see recipe, page 246)

4 cups of mixed green salad with your choice of 2 tablespoon Lemon-Dijon Vinaigrette, Red Wine Vinaigrette, or extra virgin olive oil and fresh-squeezed lemon juice

1 8-ounce glass of water before bed

OPTIONAL SNACK:
Cup of Chicken "Noodle" Soup, Intensify Version (see recipe, page 246)

SAMPLE DAY 3

UPON RISING:
Hot water with lemon, green tea, or coffee

BREAKFAST:
Sugar Impact Shake (see recipe, page 239) with approved Cycle 2 fruit

BETWEEN BREAKFAST AND LUNCH:
Water, Lemon-Aid (see page 65), Green tea

LUNCH:
Turkey Burger with Goat Cheese, Sautéed Onions, and Cucumber Salad (see recipe, page 251)

Warm Napa Cabbage Slaw with Shallot Dressing, 2 servings (see recipe, page 267)

BETWEEN LUNCH AND DINNER:
Water, Lemon-Aid (see page 65)

DINNER:
1 serving Chicken "Noodle" Soup, Intensify Version (see recipe, page 246)

4 cups of mixed green salad with your choice of 2 tablespoon
Lemon-Dijon Vinaigrette, Red Wine Vinaigrette, or extra
virgin olive oil and fresh-squeezed lemon juice

1 8-ounce glass of water before bed

OPTIONAL SNACK:
Vanilla Spice Protein Popsicle (see recipe, page 283)

RE-ENTRY AFTER INTENSIFY WEEK

Once you've come through the Intensify week, proceed to Cycle
3 and do the assessments as instructed to make sure you're ready.
In Cycle 3, you'll test whether your long-term, low-SI life can
include a sweet treat now and then. If it can, great; if it can't, you
can always return to Cycle 2 and stay here for life.

IF YOU GET KNOCKED OFF COURSE IN CYCLE 2

Look, life happens. If something beyond your control knocks you
off course, engage one of my Sugar-Attack Survival Strategies in
Chapter 8 and get yourself back on track. Even if some sugar snuck
past you or you collapsed under the weight of a craving, look at it
with a cold eye. Ask yourself what happened. You know how bad
it made you feel physically, emotionally, and mentally, so it's worth
figuring out. Once you do, focus on how you can make sure it
never happens again. Put a strategy in place to protect yourself from
it the next time, and you'll be stronger than ever. Look at those
moments as opportunities to become bulletproof, and you win.

GIVE IT YOUR ALL—YOU'LL GET EVEN MORE BACK

You get out of the Sugar Impact Diet exactly what you put into it.
In that way, it's like a lot of other things in life. The moments that
transform us are the ones we're most deeply connected to, the ones

we invest in, the ones where we care about the outcome. In these 2 weeks, I want you to go for it!

The payoff is coming. After these 2 weeks, you'll move into Cycle 3 for your final week. In Cycle 3, you'll put everything to the test. You'll retake your Sugar Impact Quiz to compare where you are with where you've been. You'll reintroduce some sugar to see how much you can handle before you set off cravings. It's the big reveal, and it will set the stage for your relationship with sugar for the rest of your life. It's so empowering to have that information.

You'll connect the dots between what you're eating and how you feel, so you'll understand where on the Sugar Impact Scales feeling fabulous lives for you: can you be low and medium with an occasional high? I can't wait to find out!

10

CYCLE 3: TRANSFORMED!

You did it! You're through the tapering and transitioning weeks—don't you feel great?! Not to mention all the weight you've already lost! Now that you've transformed your relationship to sugar, there's just one step left. Cycle 3 is all about discovering whether you're fully sugar-sensitive.

After the Sugar Impact Diet, you'll understand how sugar works in your body and the impact it has on how you feel every single day. When you've lost weight and have amazing energy, I bet you'll look at that afternoon biscotti in a completely different way. Those things are just not worth it. So you can stay in Cycle 2 forever if you want or need to; stick with all low-Sugar Impact (SI) foods (go ahead and add 1–2 servings of fruit as well), and an occasional medium-SI choice (1–2 servings a day max) is okay, too.

But for now, in Cycle 3, we'll figure out whether you're in a place to have an occasional piece of cake without sliding backward, or if you have to spend a bit more time in Cycle 2, possibly even a month, before you get there.

YOU *CAN* HANDLE THE TRUTH!

It's time to know how far you've come and how much sugar you can handle before you set off your system's alarm and before cravings see a chink in your armor, so you won't dive face-first into a plate full of powdered donuts. Cycle 3 will walk you through the responsible reintroduction of medium-SI foods, and maybe a few high-SI foods as well.

In Cycle 3, the lightbulb will really come on. You'll connect the dots between the amount of sugar in what you eat and how you feel. What combination of low-, medium-, and high-SI foods is best for you? For your energy, your mood, your skin, your weight? This is your chance to write your personal sugar roadmap, unique to you. After this last piece of the puzzle, you'll know exactly what your sugar-sensitive life should look like, and you'll really be able to make the best choices for the long term. It's so empowering!

You'll connect the dots between the amount of sugar in what you eat and how you feel.

Are You Ready?

Move into Cycle 3 when your Sugar Impact Quiz scores are 2 or less per symptom, 12 or less total, or your overall score is reduced by 50% from your starting score.

Before you start:

1. Weigh and measure yourself
2. Take the Sugar Impact Quiz

Cycle 3 Blueprint

- Swap 3–4 low-SI servings for medium-SI servings; 1–2 of these servings should be from fruit for 7 days
- Follow the recommended servings on the Sugar Impact Plate
- Have one high-SI serving at the end of the week
- Journal daily
- Weigh, measure, and retest at the end of the week. Decide whether you can stay in Cycle 3 or need to return to Cycle 2

  Plan to do Cycles 1 and 2 once a year as a reset, or if you "fall off the wagon."

ARE YOU READY?

This isn't like that class in college. It's not pass or fail. But there are two possible paths, and one is that you're ready for Cycle 3—you've passed, get to move on, and can incorporate some medium- and high-SI foods in your life. The other is that you'll simply stay in Cycle 2 a little longer until you're ready for Cycle 3.

It can be tough to risk sliding backward when you're looking and feeling great. Still, if you're ready, and you probably are, I want you to go for it. Knowledge is power. Besides, you've worked really hard...wouldn't it be nice to know you can have a little treat now and then?

SO HOW DO YOU KNOW?

What really determines whether you move to Cycle 3 is how you feel. You'll identify this by retaking the Sugar Impact Quiz as you reintroduce medium-SI foods. Here's a hint: your score should have improved. Let me tell you where I'd like you to be. Ideally, you'll score 2 or lower for each of the seven symptoms—low or unstable energy, sugar and carb cravings, appetite, poor mood and focus, gas and bloating, difficulty losing weight, and belly fat. My hope is that you'll be 12 or below overall. Or, if you've got a higher score than that, then you at least have had a 50% improvement from your original score.

If you've seen a big change, fantastic! You're ready to move to Cycle 3, and you can skip to the nuts and bolts of how Cycle 3 works: go to Start Me Up, page 223. If you aren't quite there yet, let me help.

TURN THAT FROWN UPSIDE DOWN

First of all, don't be discouraged. You've done a lot of worthwhile work getting to a low-SI diet, and since most of you have lost weight, no doubt you feel great about that alone. If you haven't hit the benchmarks to move into Cycle 3, it will just take a bit more time. For now, let's look into what else could be going on.

Let's go over some of the biggest metabolic challenges that can keep you from truly getting out from under the grip of sugar. If you find out you're dealing with any of them, my advice would be to visit a functional medicine doctor to dig deeper on how best to address them. You can also hook up with a health and nutrition coach. I've got recommendations for both in the Resources online at http://sugarimpact.com/resources.

If you're still feeling some fatigue or moodiness, cravings haven't completely left you, or, worse, you're flat-out frustrated that the weight hasn't come off as much or as fast as you hoped, you may find out why very soon. There are six common issues I've found that can really shut down weight loss. Thankfully, all of them can be fixed.

1. Insulin Resistance or Diabetes

If you have:

> High blood pressure
> Elevated triglycerides or an elevated TG/HDL ratio
> High fasting glucose, insulin, or hemoglobin A1c, and/or
> A high waist circumference

...you may be struggling with insulin resistance or diabetes. If so, your fasting insulin is higher than it should be, which signals your body to create inflammation and store fat rather than burn it off. This makes weight loss difficult, and sometimes downright impossible. If you suspect you have insulin resistance or diabetes, refer to the recommended Lab Tests online at http://sugarimpact .com/resources and ask your doctor to run them. Consider supportive supplements, too, which can also be found online at http:// sugarimpact.com/resources. Some that can help are fish oil, Vitamin D, lipoic acid, chromium, magnesium, vanadium, zinc, berberine, and fiber. Resistance training and sleep also help restore insulin sensitivity.

2. Low Thyroid

Low thyroid function, or hypothyroidism, is a biggie, and often goes un- or underdiagnosed. The thyroid gland has a huge responsibility—it manufactures the hormones that regulate the speed of your metabolism. When it's dragging, it can rob you of energy, lead to depression, make your skin dry and your hair fall out, cause your LDL cholesterol to rise, make you constipated and cold, and cause weight gain. There are a lot of reasons you might have hypothyroidism, including stress, genetics, toxicity and diet, but most are not your fault. It tends to run in families, and is more common in women. If you rely on soy as a "healthy" protein source, you could be contributing to a thyroid problem, as soy can impair thyroid function. Ask your doctor for a complete thyroid panel and be sure to include free T3 and thyroid antibodies. Combine your symptoms with ideal thyroid lab markers, because you can still have low function and be in the "normal" test range.

3. Adrenal Exhaustion

You also might have adrenal exhaustion. Adrenal problems can be masked as thyroid problems, but the two often go hand in hand. If you're constantly going nonstop, besieged by stress and pounding coffee to get through the day, you're crushing your adrenal glands (you were beating them up even worse when you were hoovering sugar all day). Your adrenals regulate the stress hormones cortisol and adrenaline. When you're stressed, your adrenals release more stress hormones, which causes your blood sugar to increase, so insulin increases. That's how you gain belly fat. In fact, increased cortisol alone can cause you to eat more. Stress also depletes serotonin, which will also make you crave sugar. If you're chronically stressed, your adrenals will eventually get fatigued. Then you're tired all of the time, which of course makes you go for more... sugar.

When you're exhausted, it's even harder to lose weight. You should be getting at least 7–9 hours of quality sleep a night—yes, that means you! According to a 2010 study in the *Journal of Clinical Endocrinology and Metabolism*, just one night without enough sleep can trigger insulin resistance, which is linked to type 2 diabetes. It can also make you hungrier, especially for sugar. The fastest way to heal your adrenals is to make time for sleep. Burst training–style exercise also helps your body handle stress faster. Don't overschedule yourself, and make sure you have some downtime. Vitamin C, the B vitamins, fish oil, and healing herbs, including rhodiola, can also help you de-stress (for more tips, go online at http://sugarimpact.com/resources).

4. Toxicity

We're all walking vessels of toxicity, to one degree or another. There's no avoiding some toxins in the air or in our homes. But clean eating and exercising go a long way toward flushing most toxins out of your system, and if you're still hanging on to yours, they can get in the way of you being able to lose weight and set you up for chronic disease.

> *Clean eating and exercising go a long way toward flushing most toxins out of your system.*

Toxicity creates brain fog and fatigue, makes you hold on to fat, and slows down your metabolism. A National Health and Nutrition Examination Survey study found that obesity by itself wasn't the cause of diabetes. It was the toxicity—in this case, phthalates—stored in the fat of the women studied. If you're toxic and it's the cause of your weight-loss resistance, you may have to go through detoxification with a functional medical doctor before you'll start to see improvements.

5. Gastrointestinal Conditions

You may also be dealing with a gastrointestinal issue like leaky gut. Leaky gut can lead to food intolerances, Candida, and small intestinal bacteria overgrowth (SIBO). It's unbelievably common, and just as commonly goes undiagnosed. Leaky gut is the condition of having a permeable small intestine, and it can be caused by issues like stress, gluten, fructose, toxicity, certain medications, and altered gut flora. When your gut is leaky, food particles slip into places they don't belong. They then trigger an immune response, which can make you inflamed, gain weight, and crave the very food that is hurting you. Addressing and fixing these food intolerances is the foundation of my book, *The Virgin Diet*. If you haven't done the Virgin Diet yet, I highly recommend moving onto that next.

SIBO is a condition marked by large numbers of bad bacteria in your small intestine. Our bodies are actually made up of more bacteria than cells, and it's critical to have the right balance of bacteria in your gut—about 80% good bacteria to 20% or less of the bad guys. Poor diet, especially sugar and processed foods, stress (again!), and antibiotic use can contribute to SIBO. It gives you presents like gas, bloating, diarrhea, and weight gain. Depending on the severity of your SIBO, you might need a doctor to prescribe a special antibiotic. I also like berberine, a good probiotic, and a daily dose of a fermented food like kimchee, cultured veggies, or coconut kefir. They'll all help restore the balance of bacteria in your gastrointestinal tract.

Candida overgrowth creates a variety of symptoms, including brain fog, sugar cravings, and bloating. Candida yeast in your gut needs sugar to survive, but if you've got a severe case, you may not be able to starve it out without some supplements or other support. My favorite nutrients are antifungal herbs and probiotics (go online at http://sugarimpact.com/resources for Supportive Supplements).

6. Hormonal Issues

If you're 40 or older, you might be struggling with sex hormone imbalances. This happens to both men and women and can make it nearly impossible to lose weight. For men, it means low testosterone and possibly elevated estrogen, and for women, low testosterone and an imbalance of estrogen and progesterone. An imbalance in your sex hormones can lead to depression, low energy, joint pain, low sex drive, and an inability to put on muscle or lose weight. If you're struggling with any of these symptoms, I recommend you see a functional medicine doctor (go to http://sugarimpact.com/resources).

Speed-Healing Techniques

If you score at 20 or above on your Sugar Impact Quiz, consider using one or more of these techniques to help you reclaim your sugar sensitivity faster.

- Burst train to blast fat and improve stress tolerance (see page 220)
- Resistance train to improve insulin sensitivity
- Sleep 7–9 hours a night to reduce appetite and improve insulin sensitivity
- Meditate to lower stress hormones
- Eat by the Sugar Impact Plate: protein, healthy fat, and slow, low carbs help balance blood sugar
- Drink green tea to improve insulin sensitivity
- Take Supportive Supplements for specific concerns (online at http://sugarimpact.com/resources)

START ME UP: CYCLE 3

Welcome to Cycle 3! I'm going to walk you through the nuts and bolts of how the cycle works and what to expect.

First things first. You're here because you've redone your Sugar Impact Quiz and scored each symptom a 2 or lower, or you've improved overall by 50% or more. Next, do a weigh-in and measure. Measure your hips and your waist. From here on out, you'll measure both every week. It's extremely important to journal through this cycle, or you'll miss out on the heart of what the Sugar Impact Diet can do for you—help you connect the dots between the amount of sugar you're eating and how you feel. You don't want to miss that—it's such a gift to your weight and health!

You'll still be eating by the Sugar Impact Plate in Cycle 3, and really paying attention to portions, so keep that diagram close and commit it to memory. The same rules apply for meal timing, too— be sure to eat by the Sugar Impact Clock.

THE SWAPS

Cycle 3 is a test week to see whether you're fully sugar-sensitive. The Scales pendulum is swinging back from the direction it went in Cycle 2. You're going to take 3–4 low-SI foods and swap them for 3–4 medium-SI foods every day. That's it. Simple, right?

The exception is fruit, since you weren't having any fruit in Cycle 2. In this cycle, you'll get back to 1–2 fruits a day, and real fruit, not just avocados, olives, lemons, and limes! Just add which- ever low- or medium-SI ones you choose. Toss berries in your shake, have some grapefruit in your salad, or have a couple small tangerines with your almonds as a snack.

Let's take a closer look at how these swaps work. For dinner, an example of an acceptable trade would be to have quinoa pasta in place of quinoa, if that was your low-SI choice in the grains cat- egory. It doesn't mean portions go out the window, though. A cup of pasta should count as 2 slow, low carb servings.

For the roots category, try adding a starchy carb rather than swapping it outright for a vegetable, because I still want you to have those veggies. Add beets to your salad. Or you might choose sweet potatoes in place of legumes. Be sure to keep up with your 5 or more servings of non-starchy vegetables, but live a little and bring in a couple of foods from the medium-SI list.

The news for low and no-fat foods in Cycle 3, especially dairy, is short and sweet (a pun!). Stay out of the high SI. That keeps it easy, right? (PS—that doesn't mean you can't have no-sugar-added coconut milk ice cream! or unsweetened coconut or almond milk yogurts—all of which are in most grocery stores these days . . . okay, I'll stop.)

As for beverages, bring back the libations! Yes, you can now start having a little bit of dry red or white wine, if you'd like. Or tequila, or a little gluten-free beer. Keep it to 1 drink a day for women, 2 drinks for men. And what's my rule? Don't save all your allotted drinks for the week for just one day! I always have to say that, right? Enjoy.

In the sauces category, you can bring back no-sugar-added marinara sauce, which is on the medium-SI list. You'll notice that sugar-added marinara sauce is on the high-SI list, so stay away from that still. Different dressings straddle those columns, too, because some have more sugar than others.

Finally, the sweeteners. This is where I want you to be really careful. Sweeteners are a slippery slope—a sugar gateway. I'm betting sweeteners will all taste too sweet to you now, but even so, I'd prefer you not dip into the high-SI sweeteners at all and that you limit the mediums to no more than one a day. Maybe your walk on the wild side is 72% dark chocolate (if this is a weakness, keep yourself together—break off a small piece and walk away!). For those of you who want to use honey for homeopathic reasons, local, organic raw is back in play. And if there's a little added coconut sugar or honey in something, you don't have to avoid it; just make sure you count it.

Or better yet, go with a natural flavoring to sweeten up your food. There are more than a few. Sweeten with spices like cinnamon, vanilla, or nutmeg, or add cumin, cardamom, allspice, mace, star anise, or clove. Try extracts like vanilla, almond, hazelnut, orange, or coconut. You can also add in zests of orange, lemon, or lime.

And just a snack quickie—if you were noshing on guacamole and veggies, you can move to guacamole and bean chips. There's just something liberating about that. If you like a dry crunch, you can swap from dehydrated, low-roasted nuts to rice chips as a Cycle 3 indulgence, in small amounts.

Detailed Cycle 3 Blueprint

In Cycle 3:

- Be sure to journal daily (download a sample journal page online at http://sugarimpact.com/resources)
- Swap 3–4 low-SI servings for medium-SI servings
- 1–2 of these servings should be from fruit

EXAMPLE 1:

- Add 1 cup of berries to your shake
- Swap your quinoa for quinoa pasta
- Have a glass of dry red wine with dinner

EXAMPLE 2:

- Have guacamole with bean chips for a snack
- Toss an orange in your shake (vanilla + orange—think 50/50 bar!)
- Trade your legumes for a sweet potato

Add one high-SI serving at the end of the week and deploy the three-bite rule (take three polite bites—bites you'd be comfortable having if you were being watched on national live TV—and put the fork down!)

At the end of the week, reevaluate:

- Weigh and measure
- Retake the Sugar Impact Quiz

If you feel the same or have continued to improve, then follow the Sugar Impact Cycle 3 guidelines.

If your Sugar Impact Quiz score increased by 3 or more points overall or 2 points in any category; you stopped losing weight; or you gained back 1–2 pounds or an inch around your waist: choose from low-SI foods most of the time. Limit yourself to 1 medium-SI choice daily, and limit high SI to 1 per week until your Quiz scores improve or you start losing weight again.

This will keep you at:

- 10 grams of fructose
- 25 grams of sugar overall
- 150–200 grams of carbs overall

Depending on your biochemistry—if you don't tolerate sugar well because of your genetics or a very damaged metabolism—this may be where you have to stay. But most of you will move to the next level, below.

You're Sugar-Sensitive

If you are in good health, have reached or are close to your ideal body composition, and are physically active, stay at:

- 25 grams fructose total per day
- 50 grams of sugar total per day
- 150-200 grams of carb total per day
- 3–4 medium-SI choices (or less) per day
- 1–2 fruit servings per day
- 1–3 high-SI servings (or less) per week

Plan to do Cycles 1 and 2 once a year as a reset or if you "fall off the wagon."

MEAL PLAN: CYCLE 3

In Cycle 3, make the Sugar Impact Shake with one fruit serving, and modify meals for intolerances.

DAY 1

BREAKFAST:
Sugar Impact Shake (see recipe, page 239)

LUNCH:
Pan-Seared Salmon Wrap made with Rice Tortilla (see recipe, page 247)
Easy Roasted Asparagus with Red Palm Fruit Oil (see recipe, page 264)

DINNER:
Spice-Rubbed Beef Tenderloin with Raw Tomato Salsa (see recipe, page 259)
½ baked sweet potato
Classic Creamed Spinach (see recipe, page 262)

SNACK/DESSERT:
Strawberry Avocado Mousse (see recipe, page 283)

DAY 2

BREAKFAST:
Sugar Impact Shake (see recipe, page 239)

LUNCH:
Bean and Bacon Minestrone Soup (see recipe, page 244)
Arugula and Watercress Salad with a Poached Egg and Lemon-Dijon Vinaigrette (see recipe, page 243)

DINNER:
Mediterranean-Style Chicken Kabobs (see recipe, page 255) served on a bed of brown rice
Grilled Eggplant with Olive Relish (see recipe, page 264)
Snack/Dessert: Cherry-Berry Fruit Salad with Shaved Dark Chocolate (see recipe, page 281)

DAY 3

BREAKFAST:
Sugar Impact Shake (see recipe, page 239)

LUNCH:

Turkey Burger with Goat Cheese, Sautéed Onions, and Cucumber Salad (see recipe, page 251)

Serve on Gluten-free English Muffin

DINNER:

Pesto-Topped Sea Scallops with Asparagus (see recipe, page 256) served on a bed of brown rice

Warm Napa Cabbage Slaw with Shallot Dressing (see recipe, page 267)

SNACK:

Homemade Cashew Butter on Celery (see recipe, page 277)

DAY 4

BREAKFAST:

Sugar Impact Shake (see recipe, page 239)

LUNCH:

Chicken Noodle Soup (see recipe, page 245)

Substitute brown rice or quinoa noodles for the shirataki noodles (2 cups brown rice for 4 servings)

Mixed green salad with Simple Vinaigrette (see recipe, page 273)

DINNER:

Italian Burgers with Tapenade (see recipe, page 254)

Serve with ½ baked sweet potato

SNACK:

Apple slices with 2 tablespoon almond butter

DAY 5

BREAKFAST:

Sugar Impact Shake (see recipe, page 239)

LUNCH:
  Shrimp and Shirataki Noodle Salad (see recipe, page 249)
  Serve on 2–4 cups of your choice of greens tossed with
    1 tablespoon sesame oil and 1 tablespoon lime juice

DINNER:
  Pork Stir Fry with Snow Peas, Asparagus, and Peppers (see
    recipe, page 256) served with 1 cup of brown rice

SNACK:
  Sliced honeydew (approximately 1 cup) topped with Lemony
    Frozen Greek-Style Yogurt (see recipe, page 282)

DAY 6

BREAKFAST:
  Sugar Impact Shake (see recipe, page 239)

LUNCH:
  Roast Beef and Vegetable Lettuce Wrap with Chipotle
    Vinaigrette (see recipe, page 248)—make with rice tortilla
    and keep lettuce in as filler

DINNER:
  Texas Bison Chili (see recipe, page 260), serve with mixed
    green salad with Simple Vinaigrette

SNACK:
  Roasted Garlic and Lemon Hummus with Bean Chips
    (see recipe, page 278)

DAY 7

BREAKFAST:
  Sugar Impact Shake (see recipe, page 239)

LUNCH:

Vegetarian Lentil Soup (see recipe, page 253)

Serve with Pan-Fried Artichoke Hearts with Lemon and Garlic (see recipe, page 266)

DINNER:

Spaghetti Squash alla Checca—substitute quinoa pasta (see recipe, page 258)

Roasted Spice-Rubbed Chicken Thighs (see recipe, page 258)

Mixed green salad with Simple Vinaigrette (see recipe, page 273)

SNACK/DESSERT:

Test one serving of a high-SI food of your choice

TRACK HOW YOU FEEL

For this week, as you dabble in medium-SI foods, choose wisely—you only get 3–4 servings each day. You could also decide to have a double serving of a medium-SI food, which would count as 2 servings.

Tune in to how you feel as you swap those 3–4 low-SI foods for 3–4 medium-SI foods. Pay attention and journal your results. What happens? Does your weight stay the same, or do you start to gain weight? How's your energy level? Do you get bloated? Is your waist measurement going up? How's your focus? What about your mood? Are you getting hungry or struggling with cravings again?

Check the way you're feeling against your scores on the Sugar Impact Quiz at the beginning of the week. I know it can be frightening to feel yourself slipping, but you'll course-correct in no time, and then you'll know how to avoid ever going back.

And the only way that happens is if you pay attention to how you feel when you eat. It's the key to unlocking you from the prison of overweight and nagging symptoms. When you discover a trigger food—say, when you eat a sweet potato and suddenly start scrounging for what's left in the casserole dish—it's just easier to stay off them entirely, right? The risk is too big. I know this; I've been there. I don't ever want to visit again.

At the end of the week, take another look at your Sugar Impact Quiz, your weight, and your waist—see what happens.

WHERE TO GO WITH WHAT YOU KNOW

There are two possible outcomes: You either stayed the same (or continued to improve), or you took a few steps backward. It's the difference between discovering you'll be fine having a high-SI treat once in a while, or that you have to stay low SI—at least for a while longer—to keep the weight off and feel your best. Let your outcome direct you to the right path, below.

IF YOU'RE STAYING THE SAME (OR CONTINUING TO IMPROVE)

Congratulations—you've graduated! You've become sugar-sensitive, and you're exactly where you should be. See if this describes you: you're in overall good health, you've got your weight close to or where you want it to be, you're active, and you don't have a lot of stress.

Here are the specific guidelines for managing your daily sugar consumption going forward (don't worry, if things didn't go as well for you, I'll help you chart your course in just a bit).

- 25 grams fructose overall
- 50 grams of sugar overall
- 150–200 grams carbohydrates overall

The total daily sugar tallied above translates to 3–4 medium-SI foods maximum a day. Stay mostly with low-SI foods, and monitor your medium-SI choices based on your weight and what your body tells you in response to those foods, with symptoms. You can also sneak in a high–SI food once or twice a week.

The American Heart Association (AHA) recommends that only 10% of total daily calories (based on a 2,000 calorie a day diet) come from added sugar. In 2002, the World Health Organization suggested the same, but it has since proposed that you reduce your total daily calories from added sugars to below 5%, or about 6 teaspoons daily, for more benefit. The AHA refines its guidelines further, suggesting only 5 teaspoons maximum of added sugar a day for women and 9 for men. Of course, most people are getting way more than that, but don't feel like you need to hit the AHA recommended amount, either. If you must use one, be sure to use a product with low- or medium–SI sugar.

As for high–SI foods, when you have to have one, go with my three-bite rule. You can have three bites of something normally off limits when it's really, really worth it. A diet cookie or a gluten-free muffin do not pass the "really, really" test. But something delicious, amazing, to-die-for worth it gets the three-bite blessing. (Only if it won't set off your food intolerances, though. No matter how sensational a treat, if it's made with a food you're intolerant to, like gluten or dairy, that trumps the three-bite go-ahead.)

But as a newly crowned Sugar Impact Diet graduate, you can implement the three-bite rule one to three times a week. Whether your food crack is a muffin or red velvet cake, you can have three *polite* bites—not three how much can I shove in my mouth bites, okay? Then get rid of it.

DE-FRIEND YOUR TRIGGERS

If you have those three bites of that awesome high–SI treat and it triggers a reaction for you, or a craving, it's out. For good. You're breaking up with that food. You don't want to have any food in your life that sends you back into the downward spiral of cravings and crashes and weight gain, right? Moderation is a slippery slope, because so often people really believe they can have just one cookie. This is the beauty of connecting the dots, and a giant dot is when you figure out that a food triggers your cravings. That means it counts as a high-SI food for you—and it's gone, baby, gone.

HELP! I GOT WORSE!

If your symptoms get worse by swapping 3–4 low-SI foods for 3–4 medium-SI foods this week, don't stress. You're just not fully sugar-sensitive, at least not yet. Go back to Cycle 2 and re-challenge again in 4 weeks to see if you can move into Cycle 3. By the way, you can live in Cycle 2 forever. I live in a modified Cycle 2—it's just where I feel best. This means that I might have a piece of fruit or a medium-SI food several times a week, but the majority of my food comes from the low-SI categories. So know that's an option for you, too. And guess what? The longer you live in it, the less you want any of those medium- and high-SI foods anyway!

Cycle 2 is also your place to live a little longer if you're dealing with any more serious health problems, such as hypertension, insulin resistance, heart disease, metabolic syndrome, autoimmune diseases, or cancer.

Remember, you can live in Cycle 2 forever. There's no reason to leave a place that helps you feel good and lose weight. It's easier than you think, and you won't have any cravings! The dots that connect there seem to point to not messing with a good thing, and I don't want you to end up in a situation where all of a sudden you're eating your trigger foods, you feel crappy, and you go down a deep dark rabbit hole and never come out again.

Plan to do Cycles 1 and 2 once a year as an annual reset—it's an awesome plateau buster, and we all need that on occasion. You should also go back and do Cycles 1 and 2 again if you really "fall off the wagon."

MY IMPACT!

Kelly Doerr
Starting weight: 158.6 lbs.
Current weight: 148.4 lbs.
Total lost: 10.2 lbs.

I have struggled and struggled my whole life with my weight. Putting it on, taking it off, and putting it right back on as soon as I alter one little step. I would exercise 2 hours a day, cut my calories back to 700, and would literally get nowhere except more frustrated. I even had a doctor tell me to start smoking! But something told me to not give up. I think it was fate that I stumbled across JJ Virgin.

I am 45 years old and dealing with the usual hot flashes, joint pain, skin problems, high blood pressure, gas, bloating, constipation, fatigue, and weakness. At least, I used to think these were usual—I don't deal with them anymore!

Before I started the Sugar Impact Diet I had been following the Virgin Diet. I had been on it for 7 months. I had lost a good deal of weight—43 pounds, to be exact. Easily, too, I might add. I was feeling pretty good, I thought, but I still struggled with certain things.

Then I found the Sugar Impact Diet. In all honesty, I wasn't that excited. What I was doing was working for me. I hadn't been losing any more weight, but I wasn't gaining. However, after spending 4½ weeks following the Sugar Impact Diet, I was astonished. I was down 10 pounds and almost 3" on my waist and 4" on my hips.

Now I'm healthy! I feel great! And it was easy! The Sugar Impact Diet gets you to where you need to be without you even knowing it! JJ's plan steps you down, bit by bit, and before you know it, you're doing it, and loving it! It's like the Sugar Impact

Diet targets major problem areas like your waist and belly, because that's where I see the most difference! I've lost more inches on my waist on the Sugar Impact Diet in one month than in the previous 6–7 months!

My energy is at an all-time high. I'm a part of this world again, not just someone who watches it as it goes by. I find myself dancing as I'm washing dishes. I'm getting more done in a day than I ever have. When I do laundry, I pull out something that looks small and think, whose is this? Then I realize, it's mine! My confidence is high, my skin glows, my hair shines, my attitude is brighter, my blood pressure is down, my joints don't hurt. But most important I think what I love the most is that I can now trust my body. I don't think about doing things now. I just do them.

Taking the sugar out of my diet has allowed me to realize the effects (and limitations) it had on my life. If sugar slips in my diet now, I immediately get a headache. The next day, my knees are killing me. I'm grumpy and miserable. It's not worth it.

I've been inspired to try to help others as well. I want to shout it from the top of a mountain that this plan works! It's easier than you think. If I did this with ease, then anybody can do it. So make a lifelong change and do the Sugar Impact Diet. You won't regret it.

WELCOME TO YOUR NEW LIFE

You've had an enlightening, empowering journey. You've come a long way, baby! Now what?

When you look at food from here on out, think about its SI. Where does it fall on the Scales? Will it have a low, medium, or high impact on your blood sugar, your energy, your weight? Remember, if broccoli isn't available, it's not necessary to default immediately to the mashed potatoes!

Cycle 3 has clearly outlined the amount of sugar you can handle so you know how to make sure you feel fantastic for the rest of the great life ahead of you. I'm willing to bet you couldn't have even imagined being here before you started. And it gets even better. With your new appreciation of food's subtle, natural sweetness and the rich contribution of savory and spicy flavors, your food will explode with flavor. Your cravings and extra pounds will never find their way back. But the new you is here to stay.

> *Your cravings and extra pounds will never find their way back.*

You've used the recipes for each of the cycles, but don't toss them out now—enjoy them regularly to keep burning fat, looking great, and living a low-SI life, symptom-free. Keep eating by the Sugar Impact Plate and the Sugar Impact Clock and relying on the Sugar Impact Shake as your go-to breakfast. Create your own yummy path forward. Mix it up and share what you discover—you're carrying the torch now!

11

LOW-SUGAR IMPACT RECIPES

Fire up the kitchen, strap on your apron...you can even go for the big hat, if you like to make a statement. You're in charge! It's so empowering to take your health back, and you're about to know just how great that really feels.

These sumptuous meals taste more like treats, and that's a good thing. They're going to be your friend in the foxhole over the next few weeks (and more likely, for life). They'll help you extend the time you can go between meals and get you through your transition from high-Sugar Impact (SI) foods to low-SI foods. They're the key to breaking your sugar addiction, kissing cravings goodbye, and reclaiming your sensitivity to sugar. Prepare to wonder what you're going to do with all your new energy. I know—you can cook!

Note: these are Cycle 2 recipes unless otherwise designated, but wherever possible I've included modifications to make them fair game for Cycles 1 and 3, too.

BREAKFAST

I would crow this if I could: breakfast is the most important meal of the day. No skipping on this one! I want you losing weight, not short-circuiting your metabolism. These delicious, protein-rich breakfasts will support your shift from sugar burner to fat burner and fuel you all the way to lunch. My rule is to eat within an hour of waking up, and it's hard to argue that could be any easier than with a shake. If you prefer to have something warm in the morning, I've got you covered there, too!

The Sugar Impact Shake

I recommend you start your day with a shake, whether you're on the run or reading the paper. It's rich and flavorful, revs your metabolism, and keeps you full and happy right till lunch. Hard to beat that.

Makes 1 serving

- 1–2 scoops protein blend (per package instructions)
- 1 serving fiber blend (see Resources online at http://sugarimpact.com/resources)
- 1–2-tablespoons chia, hemp or freshly ground flaxseeds, ½ small avocado or 1 tablespoon nut butter
- 8–10 ounces unsweetened coconut, cashew, or almond milk (such as So Delicious)
- 4–5 ice cubes

Combine the protein blend, extra fiber, chia seeds, coconut milk, and ice cubes in a blender. Mix on high until smooth. Thin with additional cold water if desired.

Cycles 1 and 3 variation—add 1 serving low- or medium-SI fruit.

Nutrition facts per serving: 424 calories, 21.3 g fiber, 31.9 g carbs, 2.6 g sugar, 27 g fat, 7 g saturated fat, 26 g protein, 55 mg sodium

Coco-Cashew Shake

This nutrient powerhouse is packed with protein and fiber to perk you up and get fat-burning off to an early start. Quick and easy, it's a great breakfast on the run.

Makes 1 serving

> 1–2 scoops chocolate protein blend (per package instructions)
> 1 serving fiber blend
> 1 tablespoon freshly ground flaxseed
> 1 tablespoon cashew butter
> 8–10 ounces unsweetened coconut milk (such as So Delicious)
> 5–6 ice cubes

Combine the shake mix, fiber blend, ground flax, cashew butter, coconut milk, and ice cubes. Mix on high until smooth. Thin with additional cold water if desired.

Nutrition facts per serving: 437 calories, 13.5 g fiber, 31.7 g carbs, 3.6 g sugar, 28 g fat, 8 g saturated fat, 29 g protein, 180 mg sodium

Creamy Cinnamon-Spiced Quinoa with Slow-Roasted Almonds

This dish is so decadent, you'll have to remind yourself you're not having dessert for breakfast. It's a truly mouthwatering way to start your morning. If you're dairy-sensitive, substitute ¾ cup plain, no-sugar, cultured coconut milk for the yogurt.

Makes 2 servings

> ½ cup quinoa, rinsed
> 1 cup water
> ½ teaspoon vanilla extract
> ½ teaspoon ground cinnamon
> ⅛ teaspoon ground nutmeg
> ⅛ teaspoon sea salt
> ¾ cup organic full-fat Greek-style yogurt
> 1 teaspoon monk fruit extract
> 20 Slow-Roasted Nuts (use almonds; see page 276), coarsely chopped

Combine the quinoa, water, extract, cinnamon, nutmeg, and salt in a medium saucepan. Bring to a boil over medium-high heat, then reduce heat to medium-low. Cover and simmer until tender, about 15 minutes. Remove from heat and let stand 5 minutes. Fluff with a fork, then stir in the yogurt and monk fruit extract. Divide between 2 bowls and top each with the almonds.

Nutrition facts per serving: 330 calories, 4 g fiber, 32 g carbs, 3 g sugar, 16 g fat, 7 g saturated fat, 14 g protein, 220 mg sodium

Lean and Green Shake

Looking to go green? Here's your chance. Introduce the ingredients to one another at high speed for an omega-3 and potassium-rich jump-start.

Makes 1 serving

   2 scoops vanilla-flavored protein blend (per package instructions)
   1 serving fiber blend
   ¼ small avocado
   2 cups baby spinach
   1 tablespoon raw almond butter
   ⅛ teaspoon ground cinnamon
   8–10 ounces unsweetened cashew milk (such as So Delicious)
   5–6 ice cubes

Combine the protein blend, fiber blend, avocado, spinach, almond butter, cinnamon, cashew milk, and ice cubes. Mix on high until smooth. Thin with additional cold water if desired.

Nutrition facts per serving: 384 calories, 16 g fiber, 30 g carbs, 2 g sugar, 22 g fat, 2.5 g saturated fat, 27 g protein, 385 mg sodium

Mushroom and Spinach Omelet with Feta Cheese

The egg just got a lot more exciting! This healthy, hearty omelet delivers the immune-boosting benefits of phytonutrients and antioxidants in every bite and is perfect for breakfast or brunch. Hunger, you have no place here.

If you're dairy-sensitive, substitute 1 ounce of cashew or other nut cheese for the feta. (The recipe follows if you'd like to make your own, or you can buy it in your local specialty or health food store.)

Makes 1 serving

> 1 cup baby spinach
> 1 tablespoon olive oil, divided
> 2 ounces white mushrooms, thinly sliced
> 1 garlic clove, minced
> 2 large eggs, lightly beaten with 2 teaspoons water
> ¼ teaspoon sea salt
> ⅛ teaspoon ground black pepper
> 1 ounce feta cheese, crumbled, or 1 ounce of cashew cheese (see
> below)

Heat an 8-inch nonstick skillet over medium-high heat until hot. Add the spinach and cook, turning often, until wilted; transfer to a bowl. Return the skillet to the heat and add 2 teaspoons of the oil. Stir in the mushrooms and garlic; cook, stirring occasionally, until lightly browned, 4–5 minutes. Remove from the skillet.

Combine the eggs, salt, and pepper in a bowl. Return the skillet to the stove over medium heat. Add the remaining 1 teaspoon oil, then pour in the egg mixture and cook until the eggs begin to set in the center, about 3 minutes, using a silicone spatula to lift up the set edges and allow the uncooked mixture to run underneath. Flip the eggs over; top one-half with the feta cheese, mushrooms, and spinach. Carefully loosen the omelet with the spatula and fold the empty half over the filling. Transfer to a plate and let stand 1 minute before serving.

Nutrition facts per serving: 360 calories, 2 g fiber, 9 g carbs, 2 g sugar, 29 g fat, 9 g saturated fat, 18 g protein, 1070 mg sodium

Cashew Cheese

Stores well in the refrigerator for up to 10 days.

Makes 1 cup (8 servings)

> 1½ cups raw cashews
> 1 tablespoon lemon juice
> 1 tablespoon extra virgin olive oil
> ½ teaspoon sea salt
> ⅛ teaspoon cayenne pepper

Combine cashews in a bowl with enough cold water to cover by 3 inches. Let cashews soak at least 5 hours or overnight.

Drain cashews and place in the bowl of a food processor with the lemon juice, oil, salt, and cayenne pepper. Process the ingredients, stopping to scrape down the sides of the bowl occasionally, until the mixture is smooth and begins to hold together. Transfer to a bowl and serve.

Nutrition facts per serving: 160 calories, 1 g fiber, 9 g carbs, 1 g sugar, 14 g fat, 2.5 g saturated fat, 4 g protein, 140 mg sodium

LUNCHES

Your patience—and good breakfast—have paid off. Food is information, and these lunches are going to make you one smart cookie (okay, maybe not a cookie). They're fresh, satisfying, soothing, and popping with flavor. They'll help you power up and on, so you don't slam into a brick wall mid-afternoon and find yourself staring down a sugar craving.

Arugula and Watercress Salad with a Poached Egg and Lemon-Dijon Vinaigrette

This simple and elegant salad is transformed with a protein-rich egg and the sophisticated complement of vinaigrette. If you're sensitive to eggs, substitute four 4-ounce, cooked, boneless and skinless chicken breast halves for the poached eggs.

Makes 4 servings

 4 cups baby arugula
 4 cups watercress
 4 radishes, halved and thinly sliced
 ½ small red onion, thinly sliced
 3 tablespoons Lemon-Dijon Vinaigrette (see page 273)
 4 large organic cage-free eggs

Combine the arugula, watercress, radishes, onion, and vinaigrette in a large bowl; toss well. Divide the salad among four plates.

Meanwhile, bring 2 inches of water to a boil in a medium skillet over high heat. Reduce the heat to medium-low and let simmer. Carefully break the eggs into the skillet just above the water so the yolks don't break. Cook until the egg whites are firm and the yolks barely start to set, about 3½–4 minutes. One at a time, lift the eggs out of the water with a slotted spoon and set each on top of a salad.

Nutrition facts per serving: 150 calories, 1 g fiber, 4 g carbs, 1 g sugar, 12 g fat, 2.5 g saturated fat, 7 g protein, 180 mg sodium

Bean and Bacon Minestrone Soup

Minestrone isn't just for vegetables anymore. Liven up this cornerstone of Italian cooking with creamy cannellini beans and rich, flavorful bacon. The bacon adds depth and character, but the beauty of this ancient dish is that you can really make it your own. For a vegan option, leave out the bacon and sauté the vegetables in 1½ tablespoons olive oil, then substitute 3 cups organic, low-sodium vegetable broth for the chicken broth.

Makes 4 servings (about 2 cups per serving)

    5 slices uncured nitrate-free bacon
    1 medium red onion, chopped
    3 celery ribs, chopped
    6 garlic cloves, chopped
    1 teaspoon chopped thyme
    ½ teaspoon dried oregano
    1 medium zucchini, about 12 ounces, cut into ½-inch dice
    1 (14.5-ounce) can organic no-salt-added diced tomatoes
    3 cups organic low-sodium chicken broth
    3 cups chopped kale
    1 (15-ounce) can organic no-salt-added cannellini beans, drained and rinsed
    ¾ teaspoon sea salt
    ¼ teaspoon ground black pepper

Heat a Dutch oven over medium heat. Add the bacon and cook until crisp, turning once, 6–7 minutes. Transfer to a plate covered with paper towel and drain; crumble.

Pour off all but 2 tablespoons bacon fat from the Dutch oven. Return to the stove over medium-high heat. Add the onion, celery, garlic, thyme, and oregano; cook, stirring occasionally, until slightly softened, 4–5 minutes. Add the zucchini and cook until slightly softened, about 5 minutes. Stir in the diced tomatoes and cook 2 minutes. Add the broth, bring to a boil, then stir in the kale. Reduce heat to medium and simmer, uncovered, 25 minutes. Add the beans, salt, and pepper and cook until heated through, 2–3 minutes. Divide among four bowls and top with the reserved bacon.

Cycles 1 and 3 variation—add 2 cups cooked quinoa noodles and 1 additional cup chicken broth.

Nutrition facts per serving: 300 calories, 7 g fiber, 33 g carbs, 9 g sugar, 13 g fat, 4.5 g saturated fat, 15 g protein, 990 mg sodium

Chicken Noodle Soup

An American classic, dating back to Colonial times. It makes you warm all over just thinking about it, doesn't it? But you don't need to be under the weather to enjoy this pure homemade goodness—shirataki noodles give it heft without the high SI of pasta noodles, and organic free-range chicken checks the clean, lean protein box. I even slipped in some spinach for good measure.

Makes 4 servings

6 cups organic low-sodium chicken broth

2 (12-ounce) organic free-range bone-in chicken breast halves

1 tablespoon olive oil

2 medium onions, chopped

3 celery ribs, chopped

3 garlic cloves, minced

8 parsley sprigs

3 dill sprigs

1 bay leaf

1 (8-ounce) package shirataki noodles, rinsed and drained

2 cups baby spinach

1 teaspoon sea salt

¼ teaspoon ground black pepper

Combine the broth and chicken breast halves in a Dutch oven over medium-high heat. Bring to a boil, cover, reduce the heat to medium low, and simmer until chicken is cooked through, 20 minutes. Transfer chicken to a bowl and let cool 10 minutes. When cool enough to handle, discard the skin and bones, then shred the chicken; reserve.

Heat the oil in a large nonstick skillet over medium heat. Add the onion, celery, and garlic; cook, stirring occasionally, until slightly softened, 5–6 minutes. Transfer mixture to the Dutch oven with the broth, then stir in the parsley, dill, and bay leaf. Bring to a boil over medium-high heat; cover, reduce the heat to medium-low, and simmer 10 minutes. Remove the parsley, dill, and bay leaf and stir in the noodles; return to a simmer and cook 3 minutes. Add the chicken and cook until heated through, about 2 minutes. Stir in the spinach and cook 2 minutes. Remove from the heat and season with the salt and pepper.

Cycles 1 and 3 variation—substitute 2 cups cooked quinoa noodles for the shirataki noodles.

Nutrition facts per serving: 364 calories, 2.8 g fiber, 10 g carbs, 4 g sugar, 6 g fat, 1.4 g saturated fat, 40 g protein, 640 mg sodium

Chicken "Noodle" Soup—Intensify Version

Keep everything the same as in Chicken Noodle Soup (recipe above), but add the following:

   1 head shredded green cabbage (about 1" strips; feel free to add more if
      you are a cabbage fan)
   4 cups chicken broth
   5 additional celery ribs, chopped (or rest of the celery stalks)

Add the extra chicken broth to step 1, and add the cabbage and extra celery to step 2 when you add the onion, celery, and garlic.

Make enough for at least half the week, and then make a second batch midweek.

Nutrition facts per serving: 414 calories, 6.6 g fiber, 19.5 g carbs, 10 g sugar, 6 g fat, 1.4 g saturated fat, 24 g protein, 740 mg sodium

Double-Chopped Chicken and Vegetable Salad with Creamy Pesto Dressing

There's a huge payoff in this uber-satisfying salad; you'll love the way the pesto and mayo work together, slathered over all those veggies.

Makes 4 servings (about 1½ cups per serving)

- ¼ cup Sugar Impact Pesto (see page 274)
- 2 tablespoons Sugar Impact Mayonnaise (see page 274)
- ¼ teaspoon sea salt
- 1 pound cooked organic free-range boneless skinless chicken breasts, cut into ½-inch cubes
- 1 large red bell pepper, chopped
- 1 large cucumber, seeded and chopped
- 3 celery ribs, chopped
- 2 plum tomatoes, seeded and chopped
- 4 radishes, chopped
- 4 romaine lettuce leaves, chopped
- ½ medium red onion, finely chopped

Combine the pesto sauce, mayo, and salt in a small bowl. Combine the chicken, bell pepper, cucumber, celery, tomatoes, radishes, lettuce, and onion in a bowl. Add the pesto mixture and toss well to coat.

Nutrition facts per serving: 260 calories, 4 g fiber, 13 g carbs, 4 g sugar, 13 g fat, 2.5 g saturated fat, 22 g protein, 867 mg sodium

Pan-Seared Salmon Lettuce Wraps

The beauty of this salmon dish is in its simplicity. It's light and easy to prepare, and it's loaded with essential omega-3 oils. Some of them come from the avocado, which also adds great texture and loads of heart-healthy potassium. Wrap the lettuce leaf around the salmon to pick it up, sandwich-style.

Makes 2 servings

    1 teaspoon red palm fruit oil, sustainably farmed
    2 (6-ounce) wild-caught king or sockeye salmon filet
    ¼ teaspoon sea salt
    ⅛ teaspoon ground black pepper
    ½ ripe avocado, sliced
    1 tablespoon chopped basil
    2 large romaine lettuce leaves
    3 tablespoons Lemon-Dijon Vinaigrette (see page 273)

Heat the oil in a medium nonstick skillet over medium-high heat. Season the salmon with salt and pepper and add to the skillet and cook until fish flakes easily with a fork, about 5 minutes per side.

Meanwhile, combine the avocado and basil in a small bowl. Place a lettuce leaf on each of two plates. Top each leaf with 1 salmon filet and the avocado mixture. Drizzle the vinaigrette over the top of each and serve warm or at room temperature.

Cycles 1 and 3 variation—substitute rice wrap for lettuce wrap.

Nutrition facts per serving: 480 calories, 4 g fiber, 6 g carbs, 1 g sugar, 39 g fat, 6 g saturated fat, 27 g protein, 550 mg sodium

Roast Beef and Vegetable Lettuce Wraps with Chipotle Vinaigrette

Bring the deli to you! If you're a fan of a classic roast beef sandwich, make this trade for a lower-SI lunch without sacrificing any of the taste. The Mexican-inspired chipotle vinaigrette gives it just the right kick. Make it ahead of time and have it ready when friends come over for lunch.

Makes 2 servings

- 1 tablespoon lime juice
- 1 tablespoon chopped cilantro
- ¼ teaspoon sea salt
- ⅛ teaspoon ground chipotle pepper
- 2 tablespoons walnut oil
- 2 romaine lettuce leaves
- 8 ounces nitrate-free sliced roast beef
- ¼ medium cucumber, thinly sliced
- ¼ medium red bell pepper, thinly sliced
- 2 tablespoons thinly sliced white onion

Combine the lime juice, cilantro, salt, and chipotle pepper in a small bowl. Slowly whisk in the oil. Place a lettuce leaf on each of two plates. Top each with half the roast beef, cucumber, bell pepper, and onion. Drizzle with lime mixture and serve.

Cycles 1 and 3 variation—substitute rice wrap for lettuce wrap.

Nutrition facts per serving: 330 calories, 2 g fiber, 4 g carbs, 2 g sugar, 20 g fat, 6 g saturated fat, 33 g protein, 330 mg sodium

Shrimp and Shirataki Noodle Salad

You say shrimp, I say prawn. Either way works; once those tasty crustaceans make their way into this salad, pad thai may become a distant memory. Give this salad a whirl to scratch that occasional craving for take-out.

Makes 4 servings (about 1½ cups per serving)

- 1 pound peeled and deveined wild-caught spot prawns or shrimp
- 2 (8-ounce) packages shirataki noodles, drained and rinsed
- 1 tablespoon red palm fruit oil, sustainably farmed
- 1 tablespoon minced ginger
- 8 ounces sugar snap peas
- 2 cups shredded red cabbage
- 1 mini or Persian cucumber, halved lengthwise and sliced
- 3 green onions, thinly sliced on a diagonal
- 3 tablespoons chopped cilantro
- 2 tablespoons wheat-free tamari (or coconut aminos if soy-sensitive)
- 2 tablespoons lime juice

Bring a large pot of lightly salted water to a boil over high heat. Add the prawns and cook until opaque, about 1½–2 minutes. Transfer prawns to a bowl with a slotted spoon; rinse with cold water and drain well.

Return the water to a boil and add the noodles. Cook noodles according to package directions; drain, rinse and pat dry with paper towels. Add to the bowl with the prawns.

Heat the oil in a large nonstick skillet over medium-high heat. Add the ginger and cook, stirring, until fragrant, 30 seconds. Add the sugar snap peas and cook, stirring occasionally, until bright green, about 2 minutes. Add the cabbage and cook until just starting to wilt, 2 minutes. Transfer to the bowl with the prawns and stir in the cucumber, green onions, cilantro, tamari, and juice. Serve warm or at room temperature.

Cycles 1 and 3 variation—substitute 2 cups cooked quinoa noodles for the shirataki noodles.

Nutrition facts per serving: 170 calories, 3 g fiber, 13 g carbs, 4 g sugar, 5 g fat, 1.5 g saturated fat, 19 g protein, 616 mg sodium

Simple Tomato Salad with Chick Peas and Feta Cheese

The Mediterranean vibe of this salad just screams with flavor, but it's the underappreciated chick pea that steals the show. Cultivated for over 7,000 years, chick peas are a nutrient rock star, loaded with protein, iron, and fiber. It's ideal to make this dish when tomatoes are at their peak in the summer.

Makes 4 servings

1 pint grape tomatoes, halved

1 pint yellow pear tomatoes, halved

6 ounces feta cheese, crumbled (or 4 ounces cashew cheese if
    dairy-sensitive)

2 green onions, chopped

2 tablespoons chopped parsley

1 tablespoon chopped mint

1 (15-ounce) can organic no-salt-added chick peas, drained and rinsed

1 tablespoon sherry wine vinegar

2 tablespoons extra virgin olive oil

½ teaspoon sea salt

¼ teaspoon ground black pepper

2 beefsteak tomatoes, cut into 8 slices each

Combine the grape tomatoes, pear tomatoes, feta cheese, green onions, parsley, mint, chick peas, vinegar, oil, salt, and pepper in a large bowl. Arrange 4 tomato slices on each of four plates, then top with the salad.

Nutrition facts per serving: 290 calories, 5 g fiber, 24 g carbs, 8 g sugar, 17 g fat, 7 g saturated fat, 12 g protein, 790 mg sodium

Turkey Burgers with Goat Cheese, Sautéed Onions, and Cucumber Salad

In the mood for a burger? Is there more than one answer to that question? Still, sometimes it's just fun to mix it up, and white turkey meat is not only tasty, it has less saturated fat than beef. Combined with the creamy texture of goat cheese and succulent sautéed onions, these lean protein burgers will knock you out. If you're dairy-sensitive, leave out the goat cheese or substitute 1–2 ounces of crumbled nut cheese.

Makes 4 servings

CUCUMBER SALAD:

3 mini or Persian cucumbers, thinly sliced
1 teaspoon white wine vinegar
2 teaspoons extra virgin olive oil
⅛ teaspoon sea salt

ONIONS:

1 tablespoon olive oil
2 medium onions, thinly sliced
⅛ teaspoon sea salt

BURGERS:

1½ pounds lean ground turkey
¾ teaspoon dried basil
½ teaspoon garlic powder
½ teaspoon sea salt
¼ teaspoon ground black pepper
4 large romaine lettuce leaves
2 ounces goat cheese, crumbled

For the cucumber salad, combine the cucumbers, vinegar, oil, and salt in a small bowl.

For the onions, heat the oil in a large nonstick skillet over medium-high heat. Add the onions and cook, stirring occasionally, until golden, 8–10 minutes. Season with salt.

For the burgers, combine the turkey, basil, garlic powder, salt, and pepper in a bowl. Form into four ¾-inch-thick patties. Heat a nonstick grill pan over medium-high heat and add the burgers. Cook, turning once, until an instant-read thermometer registers 165°F, about 5–6 minutes per side.

Place a lettuce leaf on each of four plates and top with a burger. Top each with ¼ of the onions and ¼ of the goat cheese.

Cycles 1 and 3 variation—serve on a gluten-free English muffin.

Nutrition facts per serving: 350 calories, 4 g fiber, 12 g carbs, 5 g sugar, 21 g fat, 6 g saturated fat, 31 g protein, 610 mg sodium

Vegetarian Lentil Soup

For Cycles 1 and 3

I'm hearing some big cheers from the vegetarians, but you guys are going to have to share! This is some seriously good soup, and it's loaded with protein, fiber, and iron (thank you, lentils). The seasoning strikes the perfect balance with the lentils' nutty favor.

Makes 4 servings

> 3 tablespoons olive oil
> 2 medium onions, finely chopped
> 6 garlic cloves, minced
> 3 ribs celery, finely chopped
> 1 teaspoon chopped thyme
> 1 bay leaf
> 1½ cups organic sprouted green lentils, such as TruRoots
> 5 cups organic low-sodium vegetable broth
> 3 tablespoons tomato paste
> ½ teaspoon sea salt
> ¼ teaspoon ground black pepper

Heat the oil in a Dutch oven over medium heat. Add the onion, garlic, celery, thyme, and bay leaf; cook, stirring occasionally, until tender, about 10–12 minutes. Add the lentils, broth, and tomato paste. Increase the heat to medium-high and bring to a boil, then cover and reduce heat to medium-low; simmer until the lentils are tender, 28–30 minutes. Season with salt and pepper.

Cycle 2 variation—leave out the tomato paste and substitute 1 cup organic unsalted diced tomatoes.

Nutrition facts per serving: 380 calories, 16 g fiber, 56 g carbs, 13 g sugar, 12 g fat, 1.5 g saturated fat, 16 g protein, 570 mg sodium

DINNERS

Say goodbye to the nutritiously suspect fire drills you used to call dinner. Even with the chaos of a busy family life swirling around you, these mouthwatering dishes will help you find your zen. They're fast (I'll never tell), nutrient-rich, and do a lot of the heavy lifting toward covering the protein and non-starchy veggie portions of the Sugar Impact Plate. Now we're both smiling!

Italian Burgers with Tapenade

Ahhh, Italia! Can you think of anything better than a good ol' fashioned burger souped up with the spices of the old country? The seasoning in the meat gives these big, juicy burgers even more savory flavor. This recipe will have you saying "delizioso" in no time.

Makes 4 servings

- 1½ pounds grass-fed lean ground beef
- 2 tablespoons chopped parsley
- 1 teaspoon dried basil
- ½ teaspoon dried oregano
- ½ teaspoon garlic powder
- ½ teaspoon sea salt
- ¼ teaspoon ground black pepper
- 4 large romaine lettuce leaves
- 4 tomato slices, each about ¼-inch thick
- 4 tablespoons tapenade spread

For the burgers, combine the beef, parsley, basil, oregano, garlic powder, salt, and pepper in a bowl. Form into four ¾-inch-thick patties. Heat a grill pan over medium-high heat and add the burgers. Cook, turning once, 4–5 minutes per side for medium rare or until desired doneness.

Place a lettuce leaf on each of four plates and top with a burger. Top each with a tomato slice and 1 tablespoon tapenade.

Cycles 1 and 3 variation—serve on a gluten-free English muffin.

Nutrition facts per serving: 300 calories, 1 g fiber, 4 g carbs, 1 g sugar, 15 g fat, 6 g saturated fat, 35 g protein, 590 mg sodium

Mediterranean-Style Chicken Kabobs

Feeling a little exotic? With advanced prep, you can get these sumptuous grilled chicken kabobs in front of a hungry family in no time. Make more than you need—leftovers for lunch are easy to reheat.

Makes 4 servings

1½ pounds organic free-range boneless skinless chicken thighs, trimmed
    and cut into 40 pieces
1 medium red bell pepper, cut into 16 pieces
1 medium green bell pepper, cut into 16 pieces
2 tablespoons extra virgin olive oil
1 garlic clove, minced
1 teaspoon dried oregano
½ teaspoon dried basil
¾ teaspoon sea salt
¼ teaspoon ground black pepper
Lemon wedges for serving

Combine the chicken, bell peppers, oil, garlic, oregano, and basil in a bowl. Refrigerate 30 minutes. Then preheat the broiler and lightly oil a broiler pan.

Remove from the refrigerator and alternately skewer 5 chicken pieces and 4 bell pepper pieces on to each of 8 skewers. Season with salt and pepper and place skewers on the prepared pan. Broil chicken 5 inches from the heat source until cooked through, about 8–10 minutes, turning every 2 minutes. Serve skewers with lemon wedges.

Cycles 1 and 3 variation—serve on a bed of brown rice.

Nutrition facts per serving: 310 calories, 2 g fiber, 5 g carbs, 2 g sugar, 18 g fat, 4 g saturated fat, 31 g protein, 550 mg sodium

Pesto-Topped Sea Scallops with Asparagus

So decadent! This elegant and beautiful dinner is as fit for a busy weeknight as it is for impressing dinner guests. It's abundant in protein, B-12, and omega-3s. But it's the soft texture and mild sweetness of the succulent scallops that will elicit "Mmms" all around.

Makes 4 servings

  1 pound asparagus, trimmed
  1 tablespoon extra virgin olive oil
  4 teaspoons olive oil
  1½ pounds wild-caught sea scallops
  ½ teaspoon sea salt
  ¼ teaspoon ground black pepper
  4 tablespoons Sugar Impact Pesto (see page 274)

Bring a large pot of salted water to a boil. Add the asparagus, return to a boil, and cook until tender, 1–2 minutes. Drain and drizzle with extra virgin olive oil.

Meanwhile, heat 2 teaspoons of the olive oil in a large nonstick skillet over medium-high heat. Season scallops with salt and pepper and add half to the skillet. Cook until scallops are nicely browned and opaque in the center, 2–3 minutes per side. Transfer scallops to a plate and keep warm. Wipe out skillet with a paper towel and repeat with remaining 2 teaspoons oil and scallops.

Divide asparagus and scallops among four plates. Top each scallop with some of the pesto sauce.

Cycles 1 and 3 variation—serve on a bed of brown rice.

Nutrition facts per serving: 321 calories, 3 g fiber, 11.7 g carbs, 2 g sugar, 17.6 g fat, 2.9 g saturated fat, 30.3 g protein, 927 mg sodium

Pork Stir Fry with Snow Peas, Asparagus, and Peppers

If you're ever tempted to call for takeout in a weak moment, think about the fact that you can probably have this sassy dish on your table in less time. And it's not just faster than delivery—the nutrient content is higher, too. Pork is a great source of clean, lean protein, and it's high in B vitamins. Preparation is easy, and you'll be able to enjoy the wonderful aromas in your kitchen along the way. If you're sensitive to soy, swap the tamari for coconut aminos.

Makes 4 servings

- 1 pound pork tenderloin, trimmed, cut into ¾-inch pieces
- 2 tablespoons wheat-free tamari, divided
- 2 tablespoons toasted sesame oil, divided
- 1 tablespoon minced ginger
- 3 garlic cloves, minced
- 2 cups broccoli florets
- 8 ounces asparagus, trimmed, cut into 1-inch pieces
- 1 medium red bell pepper, chopped
- 4 ounces snow peas
- 4 green onions, chopped

Toss the pork with 1 tablespoon of the tamari in a medium bowl and let stand 5 minutes. Heat 1 tablespoon of the oil in a large nonstick skillet over medium-high until very hot. Add the pork and cook, stirring occasionally, until lightly browned and almost cooked through, 3–3½ minutes. Transfer pork to a plate and reserve.

Return skillet to the heat and add the remaining 1 tablespoon oil. Stir in the ginger and garlic and cook, stirring, until fragrant, about 15 seconds. Add the broccoli and ¼ cup water and cook 1 minute. Add the asparagus and bell pepper and cook 2 minutes. Stir in the snow peas and cook until bright green, about 2 minutes. Add the reserved pork and any juices on the plate and cook, stirring occasionally, 1 minute. Add the remaining 1 tablespoon tamari and green onions and cook, stirring, 30 seconds longer.

Cycles 1 and 3 variation—serve on a bed of brown rice.

Nutrition facts per serving: 250 calories, 4 g fiber, 11 g carbs, 4 g sugar, 10 g fat, 2 g saturated fat, 29 g protein, 430 mg sodium

Roasted Spice-Rubbed Chicken Thighs

This may be just the meal you need to help you push through tired to inspired. You can always count on chicken—it's mouthwatering with nothing more than a little roasting. Double or triple the versatile spice rub and keep the extra in a bottle or plastic bag with your spices.

Makes 4 servings

- 1 teaspoon ground coriander
- 1 teaspoon paprika
- ¾ teaspoon garlic powder
- ¼ teaspoon ground cinnamon
- ¾ teaspoon sea salt
- ¼ teaspoon ground black pepper
- 8 organic free-range bone-in skinless chicken thighs, about 2–2¼ pounds, trimmed
- 1 tablespoon red palm fruit oil, sustainably farmed

Preheat the oven to 400°F. Lightly oil a large shallow roasting pan. Combine the coriander, paprika, garlic powder, cinnamon, salt, and pepper in a small bowl. Toss the chicken and oil in a separate bowl. Pour the coriander mixture over the chicken and mix well to coat. Place chicken on the prepared roasting pan.

Roast chicken in the center of the oven until an instant-read thermometer inserted into the thickest part of the thigh registers 165°F. It should take approximately 23–25 minutes. Let rest 5 minutes before serving.

Nutrition facts per serving: 313 calories, 1 g fiber, 1 g carbs, 0 g sugar, 15 g fat, 5 g saturated fat, 41 g protein, 580 mg sodium

Spaghetti Squash alla Checca

A tasty twist on a Tuscan classic. Spaghetti squash makes an ideal low-SI swap for pasta, and after one twirl of your fork in the pure, fresh flavor burst of checca, you'll never go back to sugary marinaras. This dish is great year-round, but it's an especially wonderful option for a warm summer night. Grazie, Italia! If you're dairy-sensitive, substitute 4 ounces of cashew or other nut cheese for the mozzarella.

Makes 4 servings

  1-3 pound spaghetti squash, halved lengthwise and seeded
  4 tablespoons extra virgin olive oil
  ½ small garlic clove, minced
  5 plum tomatoes, seeded and chopped
  5 ounces fresh mozzarella cheese, cut into ½-inch cubes
  ⅓ cup thinly sliced fresh basil
  ¾ teaspoon sea salt
  ¼ teaspoon ground black pepper

Preheat the oven to 350°F. Lightly oil a large shallow roasting pan. Place the squash, cut sides down, on the prepared pan. Prick all over with the tip of a knife. Bake until very tender, 28–30 minutes. Remove from the oven and let cool 5 minutes. Turn the squash over and, with the tines of a fork, scrape out the flesh—it will come out in long, thin spaghetti-like strands. You should have about 3 cups. Transfer to a bowl and add the oil, garlic, tomatoes, cheese, basil, salt, and pepper; toss well.

Cycles 1 and 3 variation—replace spaghetti squash with rice or quinoa pasta. One serving is 1 cup cooked pasta.

Nutrition facts per serving: 310 calories, 5 g fiber, 20 g carbs, 9 g sugar, 23 g fat, 7 g saturated fat, 8 g protein, 500 mg sodium

Spice-Rubbed Beef Tenderloin with Raw Tomato Salsa

Spice up your night! The flavors dance in this salsa-drenched beef tenderloin. Ketchup doesn't even come close to matching fresh salsa's nutrition or taste, not to mention the gulf between their SIs. Bonus—you'll spend more time enjoying it than preparing it. Feel free to spread the love around and also use this salsa as a salad dressing, on grilled chicken, or as a dip for your crudités.

Makes 4 servings

SALSA:

> 4 plum tomatoes, seeded and chopped
> ½ ripe avocado, chopped
> ½ small red onion, finely chopped
> 1 serrano pepper, seeded and finely chopped
> 2 tablespoons chopped cilantro
> 1 tablespoon lime juice
> 2 teaspoons olive oil
> ¼ teaspoon sea salt

BEEF:

> 1 teaspoon chili powder
> 1 teaspoon ground cumin
> ½ teaspoon smoked paprika
> ½ teaspoon garlic powder
> ½ teaspoon salt
> 4 (6-ounce) grass-fed beef tenderloin steaks, about 1-inch thick

For the salsa, combine the tomatoes, avocado, onion, serrano pepper, cilantro, lime juice, oil, and salt in a small bowl.

For the beef, combine the chili powder, cumin, paprika, garlic powder, and salt in a bowl. Rub the mixture over both sides of each steak.

Heat a nonstick grill pan over medium-high heat until very hot. Add the steaks and cook, 6–8 minutes per side, turning once, until medium-rare, or until desired doneness. Place a steak on each of four serving plates. Top with the salsa.

Nutrition facts per serving: 360 calories, 3 g fiber, 7 g carbs, 3 g sugar, 27 g fat, 9 g saturated fat, 26.8 g protein, 500 mg sodium

Texas Bison Chili

Straight from the heart of Texas, so you know it's BIG—big flavor, big benefits. Good stuff will be sticking to your ribs, too—lean, omega-3–rich, grass-fed bison, antioxidant-rich veggies, and anti-inflammatory spices.

While you're at it, why not make an extra batch and squirrel it away in the freezer for a cold winter night?

Makes 4 servings (about 1¼ cups per serving)

  1 tablespoon red palm fruit oil, sustainably farmed
  1 pound grass-fed ground bison
  2 medium onions, chopped
  3 garlic cloves, minced
  1 medium green bell pepper, chopped
  2 tablespoons chili powder
  1 teaspoon dried oregano
  1 teaspoon ground cumin
  ¼ teaspoon ground chipotle pepper
  2 (14.5-ounce) cans organic no-salt-added fire-roasted diced tomatoes
  1 (15-ounce) can organic no-salt-added red kidney beans, drained and
      rinsed
  ¾ teaspoon sea salt
  ¼ teaspoon ground black pepper

Heat the oil in a Dutch oven over medium-high heat. Add the bison and cook, breaking into smaller clumps with a spoon, until no longer pink, about 4–5 minutes. Stir in the onions, garlic, bell pepper, chili powder, oregano, cumin, and ground chipotle; cook, stirring occasionally, until the vegetables are slightly softened, 3–4 minutes. Add the diced tomatoes; bring to a boil, reduce heat to medium-low, cover, and simmer, stirring occasionally, 30 minutes.

Stir in the beans, return to a simmer and cook 5 minutes. Remove from the heat and stir in the salt and pepper.

Nutrition facts per serving: 440 calories, 18 g fiber, 47 g carbs, 13 g sugar, 12 g fat, 5 g saturated fat, 36.8 g protein, 566 mg sodium

Grilled Chicken Breasts with Puttanesca Sauce

When you serve chicken in puttanesca sauce, it's going to be a sassy night. Slightly pound the chicken breasts with the heel of your hand to get them to a uniform thickness, which will allow them to cook evenly.

Serves 4

> 4 (6-ounce) organic free-range boneless chicken breast halves
> 1 tablespoon olive oil
> ½ teaspoon dried oregano
> ¼ teaspoon dried basil
> ½ teaspoon sea salt
> ¼ teaspoon ground black pepper
> 2 cups Puttanesca Sauce (see page 275)

Heat a grill pan over medium. Brush chicken breasts with the remaining oil, then season with oregano, basil, salt, and pepper; place on the grill pan. Cook chicken, turning once, until well-marked and an instant-read thermometer inserted into the thickest portion of the breast registers 165°F, about 5–6 minutes per side. Serve topped with puttanesca sauce.

Cycles 1 and 3 variation—serve on a bed of quinoa or rice pasta.

Nutrition facts per serving: 400 calories, 2 g fiber, 10 g carbs, 3 g sugar, 8 g fat, 1 g saturated fat, 23 g protein, 1820 mg sodium

VEGETABLE SIDES

Love your vegetables, and they'll love you back—and the good news is, they tend to give more than they receive. When you eat this close to nature, your food is at its most nutrient-dense and flavorful. These sides pair some of nature's greatest fast foods with low-maintenance dressing, oils, pesto, and relish that will send your taste buds to the moon. Your main dish may not even make it to the plate.

Classic Creamed Spinach

Everything tastes better creamed, right? Well, that's especially true of Popeye's favorite. By making your own, you'll dodge the heavy calories and saturated fat of most restaurant versions. If you're dairy-intolerant, see below for a dairy-free version.

Makes 4 servings (½ cup per serving)

4 (5-ounce) bags baby spinach
¾ cup plus 3 tablespoons organic grass-fed whole milk, divided
½ small onion, thinly sliced
⅛ teaspoon ground nutmeg
½ teaspoon sea salt
⅛ teaspoon ground black pepper
1 tablespoon arrowroot

Heat a large nonstick skillet over medium-high heat. Add the spinach in batches and cook, turning often, until wilted. Transfer to a strainer and let cool. With your hands, squeeze as much liquid out of the spinach as possible. Transfer to a cutting board and coarsely chop.

Combine ¾ cup of the milk, onion, nutmeg, salt, and pepper in a medium saucepan over medium-high heat. Bring just to a simmer, remove from the heat, and let stand 10 minutes. Strain the milk into a bowl and discard the solids. Return the milk to the saucepan and bring just to a simmer over medium heat. Dissolve the arrowroot in the remaining 3 tablespoons milk and whisk it into the warm milk. Cook, stirring, until the mixture thickens, about 1–2 minutes. Stir in the spinach and cook until hot, 1–2 minutes.

Nutrition facts per serving: 120 calories, 7 g fiber, 23 g carbs, 4 g sugar, 2 g fat, 1 g saturated fat, 6 g protein, 540 mg sodium

For a dairy-free version, use ¾ cup plus 3 tablespoons unsweetened coconut milk and make the following modifications.

Combine ¾ cup of the coconut milk, onion, nutmeg, salt, and pepper in a medium saucepan over medium heat. Heat the coconut milk until it is hot and bubbles just begin to form at the edges of the pan; remove from the heat and let stand 10 minutes. Strain the mixture into a bowl and discard the solids. Return the coconut milk to the saucepan. Dissolve the arrowroot in the remaining 3 tablespoons milk, whisking it in. Bring to a simmer over medium heat, stirring occasionally. Once the coconut milk begins to bubble, cook, stirring, until the mixture thickens, about 1 minute. Stir in the spinach and cook until hot, 1–2 minutes.

Nutrition facts per serving: 170 calories, 7 g fiber, 19 g carbs, 0 g sugar, 11 g fat, 10 g saturated fat, 5 g protein, 510 mg sodium

Easy Roasted Asparagus with Red Palm Fruit Oil

Asparagus is a nutrient rock star and one of those veggies that needs little doctoring. The red palm fruit oil only serves to support it, but handle the oil with care. It's packed with color-altering carotenes, so try to avoid dying your cuticles or doing any other inadvertent redecorating.

Makes 4 servings

  1 pound asparagus, trimmed
  1 tablespoon red palm fruit oil, sustainably farmed
  ¼ teaspoon sea salt
  ⅛ teaspoon ground black pepper

Preheat the oven to 425°F. Lightly oil a shallow roasting pan. Combine the asparagus, oil, salt, and pepper in a medium bowl. Arrange in a single layer on the prepared pan. Roast asparagus, shaking pan occasionally, until lightly browned in spots and tender, about 9–10 minutes.

Nutrition facts per serving: 50 calories, 2 g fiber, 4 g carbs, 2 g sugar, 3.5 g fat, 1.5 g saturated fat, 7 g protein, 150 mg sodium

Grilled Eggplant with Olive Relish

As if you needed an excuse to fire up the grill. This simple side dish perfectly pairs the meaty canvas of eggplant with the rich oils of olives. Make a double batch of the relish to serve with grilled fish and meat, too!

Makes 4 servings

RELISH

10 pimento stuffed olives, chopped

10 pitted Kalamata olives, chopped

1 plum tomato, seeded and finely chopped

½ small red bell pepper, finely chopped, about ⅓ cup

2 teaspoons finely chopped shallots

1 tablespoon chopped parsley

2 teaspoons extra virgin olive oil

½ teaspoon grated lemon zest

⅛ teaspoon ground black pepper

EGGPLANT

1 large eggplant, about 1½ pounds, trimmed and cut into ½-inch thick
   slices

2 tablespoons olive oil

¼ teaspoon sea salt

Preheat the grill to medium heat. For the relish, combine the olives, tomato, bell pepper, shallots, parsley, oil, zest and pepper in a bowl; set aside.

Brush the eggplant slices lightly with the oil, then season with salt. Place the eggplant on the grill rack directly over the heat. Grill until nicely marked and tender, about 4–5 minutes per side. Transfer eggplant to a platter and spoon the relish over the top. Serve hot or at room temperature.

Nutrition facts per serving: 160 calories, 5 g fiber, 13 g carbs, 6 g sugar, 12 g fat, 1.5 g saturated fat, 2 g protein, 430 mg sodium

Pan-Roasted Brussels Sprouts with Almonds

Brussels sprouts fall in the love 'em or hate 'em camp. They're so dense with nutrients and flavor, my hope (fingers crossed!) is that if you're not a fan, this dish will change all that. But, if not, substitute bite-size pieces of cauliflower, and you won't miss out.

Makes 4 servings

> 2 tablespoons olive oil
> 6 garlic cloves, sliced
> 1 medium onion, sliced
> ½ teaspoon dried basil
> 1 pound Brussels sprouts, trimmed and quartered
> ½ cup water
> 3 tablespoons Slow-Roasted Nuts (use almonds; see page 276), coarsely
> chopped
> ¼ teaspoon sea salt
> ⅛ teaspoon ground black pepper

Heat the oil in a large nonstick skillet over medium. Add the garlic, onion, and basil; cook, stirring occasionally, until translucent, 3–4 minutes. Increase the heat to medium-high and stir in the Brussels sprouts; cook, stirring occasionally, 3 minutes. Add ½ cup water and continue to cook until the liquid evaporates and the Brussels sprouts are lightly browned and tender, 5–6 minutes. Stir in the almonds and cook 1 minute. Remove from heat and season with salt and pepper.

Nutrition facts per serving: 190 calories, 6 g fiber, 18 g carbs, 6 g sugar, 11 g fat, 1 g saturated fat, 5 g protein, 220 mg sodium

Pan-Fried Artichoke Hearts with Lemon and Garlic

I have to say it—your heart will run wild for this scrumptious dish. It's a straightforward side, but don't let its simplicity fool you. Artichoke hearts have subtle, succulent flavor and are dense with nutrients like vitamins, minerals, phytonutrients, and antioxidants. Be sure to buy frozen artichokes with no added ingredients.

Makes 4 servings (about ½ cup per serving)

> 2 tablespoons olive oil
> 3 garlic cloves, thinly sliced
> 12 ounces frozen artichoke hearts, thawed
> 1 teaspoon grated lemon zest
> 1 tablespoon chopped parsley
> ¼ teaspoon sea salt

Heat the oil in a large nonstick skillet over medium-high heat. Add the garlic and cook until starting to brown, 1–1½ minutes. Remove garlic with a slotted spoon and reserve. Return skillet to the heat and let the oil get very hot. Add the artichokes; cook, stirring occasionally, until nicely browned, about 5–6 minutes. Remove from the heat and stir in the reserved garlic, lemon zest, parsley, and salt.

Nutrition facts per serving: 100 calories, 5 g fiber, 8 g carbs, 0 g sugar, 8 g fat, 1 g saturated fat, 2 g protein, 200 mg sodium

Warm Napa Cabbage Slaw with Shallot Dressing

Bathed in a warm shallot dressing, this salad works year-round. But for a summer version, make it with raw cabbage and allow it to sit for 20 minutes so the cabbage softens. You'll get a full spectrum of flavors in every bite.

Makes 4 servings (about 1 cup per serving)

    1 small shallot, finely chopped
    2 tablespoons white wine vinegar
    1 teaspoon Dijon mustard
    ½ teaspoon sea salt
    ⅛ teaspoon ground black pepper
    2 tablespoons olive oil
    1 medium red bell pepper, cut into thin 1½-inch-long strips
    6 cups shredded Napa cabbage

Combine the shallot, vinegar, mustard, salt, and pepper in a small bowl. Slowly whisk in 1 tablespoon of the oil until well combined. Heat the remaining 1 tablespoon oil in a large nonstick skillet over medium-high heat. Add the bell pepper and cook 30 seconds. Stir in the cabbage and cook, stirring, until slightly wilted, about 1 minute. Stir in the shallot mixture, then remove from the heat and serve warm.

Nutrition facts per serving: 100 calories, 2 g fiber, 9 g carbs, 4 g sugar, 7 g fat, 1 g saturated fat, 2 g protein, 340 mg sodium

Zucchini, Snow Pea, Sugar Snap, and Celery Skillet

If you don't share, your friends will be green with envy. This lovely green medley of vegetables looks and tastes like a celebration of spring.

Makes 4 servings

2 tablespoons red palm fruit oil, sustainably farmed
4 garlic cloves, minced
1 medium zucchini, about 8 ounces, cut into ½-inch cubes
2 celery ribs, cut into ½-inch-thick slices
8 ounces sugar snap peas, trimmed
4 ounces snow peas, trimmed
¼ teaspoon sea salt
⅛ teaspoon ground black pepper

Heat the oil in a large nonstick skillet over medium-high heat. Add the garlic and cook, stirring, until just starting to brown slightly, 45 seconds. Stir in the zucchini and celery and cook until starting to soften, about 2 minutes. Add the sugar snaps and cook until bright green, 1 minute. Stir in the snow peas and cook 1 minute longer. Remove from heat and season with the salt and pepper.

Nutrition facts per serving: 120 calories, 3 g fiber, 9 g carbs, 4 g sugar, 7 g fat, 3 g saturated fat, 4 g protein, 150 mg sodium

STARCHY SIDES

There's no need to feel uninspired when it comes to filling the slow, low carb section of the Sugar Impact Plate. These starchy sides will round out your plate and are sure to be crowd pleasers, too.

Lentils alla Rustica

These lentils are a protein-rich, hearty and satisfying side dish. Serve them over lettuce or as the perfect pairing with virtually any meat or fish dish as a great slow, low carb. Vegans can substitute veggie broth for the chicken broth.

Makes 4 servings

- 1 tablespoon olive oil
- 1 medium onion, chopped
- 1 celery rib, chopped
- 3 garlic cloves, minced
- ½ teaspoon dried basil
- 2 cups organic low-sodium chicken broth
- ½ teaspoon sea salt
- ¼ teaspoon ground black pepper
- 1 cup sprouted green lentils, such as TruRoots

Heat the oil in a medium saucepan over medium-high heat. Add the onion, celery, garlic, and basil; cook, stirring occasionally, until slightly softened, 4–5 minutes. Pour in the broth, salt, and pepper and bring to a boil. Stir in the lentils, reduce heat to medium, and cook 5 minutes. Remove from the heat, cover, and let stand 8 minutes to allow lentils to become tender. Lentils will be slightly wet; drain if desired.

Nutrition facts per serving: 220 calories, 9 g fiber, 34 g carbs, 5 g sugar, 4.5 g fat, 0.5 g saturated fat, 12 g protein, 350 mg sodium

Mushroom and Onion Wild Rice Pilaf

Time to live on the wild side. The umami, or savory, properties of the mushrooms give this simple dish deep flavor, and the wild rice is packed with protein and fiber. It's a taste bud party that's easy on your blood sugar and keeps you satisfied for hours.

Makes 4 servings

- ¾ cup wild rice
- 2 tablespoons red palm fruit oil, sustainably farmed
- 1 medium onion, chopped
- 8 ounces white mushrooms, sliced
- 3 garlic cloves, minced
- 1 teaspoon chopped thyme
- 2 tablespoons chopped parsley
- ½ teaspoon sea salt
- ¼ teaspoon ground black pepper

Cook rice according to package directions. Heat the oil in a large nonstick skillet over medium-high heat. Add the onion, mushrooms, garlic, and thyme; cook, stirring occasionally, until onion and mushrooms are lightly browned, about 8–9 minutes. Stir in the wild rice and cook 1 minute. Remove from the heat and add the parsley, salt, and pepper.

Cycles 1 and 3 variation—substitute brown rice for wild rice.

Nutrition facts per serving: 230 calories, 4 g fiber, 36 g carbs, 3.6 g sugar, 5 g fat, 3 g saturated fat, 7 g protein, 300 mg sodium

Quinoa with Shallots, Tomato, and Asparagus

Don't worry, you only have to eat it, not spell it. Quinoa is a gluten-free source of protein and fiber that makes the perfect canvas for the shallots, tomato, and asparagus in this dish. You can't judge asparagus flavor by how thick or thin the spears are, but to judge freshness, choose asparagus with tightly closed tips.

Makes 4 servings (about 1 cup per serving)

    ¾ cup quinoa, rinsed
    2 tablespoons olive oil
    1 large shallot, finely chopped
    3 garlic cloves, minced
    8 ounces asparagus, trimmed and cut into 1-inch pieces
    2 plum tomatoes, seeded and chopped
    ¼ cup chopped basil
    ½ teaspoon sea salt
    ¼ teaspoon ground black pepper

Cook the quinoa according to package directions. Heat the oil in a large nonstick skillet over medium-high heat. Add the shallot and garlic; cook, stirring occasionally, until starting to soften, 1–2 minutes. Add the asparagus and cook until bright green, about 2 minutes. Stir in the tomatoes and cook until starting to wilt, 1–2 minutes. Add the quinoa and cook, stirring, 1 minute. Remove from the heat and stir in the basil, salt, and pepper.

Nutrition facts per serving: 210 calories, 4 g fiber, 27 g carbs, 2 g sugar, 9 g fat, 1 g saturated fat, 7 g protein, 290 mg sodium

Shirataki Sesame Scallion Noodles

Did you forget the side dish? This tasty complement to just about any meal can be on your table faster than anyone will notice. While this is listed in starchy sides, shirataki noodles are nearly a free food since they are so low in calories, and a great alternative to higher-SI noodles.

Makes 4 servings

> 2 (8-ounce) packages shirataki noodles, drained and rinsed
> 3 tablespoons wheat-free lower-sodium tamari (or coconut aminos if soy-sensitive)
> 1 tablespoon unseasoned rice vinegar
> ½ teaspoon monk fruit extract
> 2 tablespoons toasted sesame oil
> 3 garlic cloves, minced
> 1 tablespoon minced fresh ginger
> ⅛ teaspoon crushed red pepper flakes
> 3 scallions, thinly sliced on a diagonal

Bring a large pot of water to a boil over high heat. Add the noodles, return to a boil, and cook 3 minutes. Drain the noodles, rinse under cold water; drain again. Pat noodles dry with paper towels. In a small bowl, combine the tamari, vinegar, and monk fruit extract.

Heat the oil in a large nonstick skillet over medium-high heat. Add the garlic, ginger, and red pepper flakes; cook, stirring, until just starting to brown slightly, about 1 minute. Add the noodles and cook, tossing, until heated through, 1 minute. Pour in the tamari mixture and cook 30 seconds longer. Remove from the heat and stir in the scallions.

Cycles 1 and 3 variation—substitute 2 cups cooked quinoa or rice noodles for the shirataki noodles.

Nutrition facts per serving: 80 calories, 0 g fiber, 6 g carbs, 1 g sugar, 5 g fat, 1 g saturated fat, 2 g protein, 530 mg sodium

Warm Black Bean and Avocado Salad

BACON! This nutrient-dense salad is a tasty low-SI touch on your plate, especially as a swap for baked beans or other starchy, high-SI sides. Plus, bacon! For a vegan alternative, simply take out the bacon, increase the oil to 1 tablespoon, and add a pinch of smoked paprika.

Makes 4 servings (½ cup per serving)

  4 slices uncured nitrate-free bacon
  1 red onion, chopped
  2 garlic cloves, minced
  1 jalapeño pepper, seeded and finely chopped
  ½ teaspoon ground cumin
  1 (15-ounce) can organic no-salt-added black beans, drained and rinsed
  ½ ripe avocado, cut into ¼-inch dice
  2 tablespoons lime juice
  2 tablespoons chopped cilantro
  1 teaspoon extra virgin olive oil
  ½ teaspoon sea salt

Heat a medium nonstick skillet over medium. Add the bacon and cook, turning once, until crisp, 6–7 minutes. Transfer bacon to a plate covered with paper towels and drain.

Pour off all but 1 tablespoon bacon fat from skillet and return to the stove over medium heat. Add the onion, garlic, jalapeño, and cumin; cook, stirring occasionally, until slightly softened, 2–3 minutes. Stir in the beans and cook until heated through, 1–2 minutes. Remove from heat and add the avocado, lime juice, cilantro, oil, and salt.

Nutrition facts per serving: 190 calories, 6 g fiber, 16 g carbs, 2 g sugar, 11 g fat, 3 g saturated fat, 8 g protein, 440 mg sodium

DRESSINGS AND SAUCES

Dressings and sauces are two of the sneakiest, slipperiest slopes for sugar in your diet. They can put you in a spin all by themselves. Do you really think they're worth the meltdown in aisle 7? Lose the side of stress with your salad and make one of these guilt-free, nourishing toppings instead.

Simple Vinaigrette with Extra Virgin Olive Oil

Make this your go-to. It's like the little black dress of the dressing world, so keep it on hand for salads or as a marinade.

Makes about ¾ cup

> 2 tablespoons red wine vinegar
> 1 teaspoon Dijon mustard
> ½ teaspoon sea salt
> ¼ teaspoon ground black pepper
> ½ cup extra virgin olive oil

Combine the vinegar, mustard, salt, and pepper in a small bowl. Slowly whisk in the oil until well combined. Store in an airtight container in the refrigerator.

Nutrition facts per 2 tablespoon serving: 160 calories, 0 g fiber, 0 g carbs, 0 g sugar, 19 g fat, 2.5 g saturated fat, 0 g protein, 210 mg sodium

Lemon-Dijon Vinaigrette with Macadamia Nut Oil

Is it a dressing or a marinade? Why not both? Combine the zest of lemons with the sweet and buttery essence of the macadamia nut for a delicious and healthy alternative to your usual dressing, or to what you might normally drizzle over fish or a chicken breast.

Makes ¾ cup

> 3 tablespoons lemon juice
> 1 teaspoon grated lemon zest
> 1 tablespoon Dijon mustard
> ½ teaspoon sea salt
> ¼ teaspoon ground black pepper
> ½ cup macadamia nut oil

Combine the juice, zest, mustard, salt, and pepper in a small bowl. Slowly whisk in the oil until well combined. Store in an airtight container in the refrigerator.

Nutrition facts per 2 tablespoon serving: 170 calories, 0 g fiber, 1 g carbs, 0 g sugar, 19 g fat, 2 g saturated fat, 0 g protein, 250 mg sodium

Sugar Impact Mayonnaise

Shelve the mayo without sacrificing flavor with this healthy, creamy variation of its artery-clogging (distant) cousin. You can also use it as a starter for sauces or dressings, so it's a must in your fridge. Refrigerate up to 3 weeks.

Makes 1 cup

¼ cup unsweetened cashew or coconut milk (such as So Delicious)
½ cup raw cashews
4 teaspoons fresh lemon juice
1 tablespoon Dijon mustard
½ teaspoon sea salt
½ cup olive or macadamia nut oil

Combine the cashew milk, cashews, lemon juice, mustard, and salt in a blender. Puree. With the blender running, add the oil in a slow, steady stream until the mixture is thick and creamy.

Nutrition facts per 1 tablespoon serving: 80 calories, 0 g fiber, 1 g carbs, 0 g sugar, 8 g fat, 1 g saturated fat, 1 g protein, 95 mg sodium

Sugar Impact Pesto

You don't have to live without pesto! The basil and garlic offer actual health benefits, but I'm guessing you'll be more focused on flavor than health benefits when you enjoy this. Refrigerate up to 2 weeks, or freeze up to 2 months. If you're dairy-sensitive, leave out the cheese and increase the salt by ¼ teaspoon.

Makes about 1 cup

4 cups loosely packed basil leaves
1 garlic clove
¼ cup Slow-Roasted Nuts (use almonds; see page 276)
⅓ cup grated Pecorino Romano cheese
1 teaspoon grated lemon zest
¼ teaspoon sea salt
½ cup olive oil

Combine the basil, garlic, almonds, cheese, zest, and salt in the bowl of a food processor. Process until the basil mixture is finely chopped. With the machine running, add the oil in a steady stream until a thick puree forms. Store in the refrigerator in an airtight container.

Nutrition facts per 2 tablespoon serving: 170 calories, 1 g fiber, 2 g carbs, 0 g sugar, 17 g fat, 3 g saturated fat, 3 g protein, 170 mg sodium

Puttanesca Sauce

Straight to you from the shores of Napoli. It's well known that this Italian staple is easy to prepare and this version will make it fun, too—it's very fragrant, with just the right amount of spice. A perfect complement to chicken, fish, pork, shirataki noodles, or, of course, spaghetti squash!

Makes 3 cups (six ½ cup servings)

    2 tablespoons olive oil
    1 medium onion, chopped
    3 garlic cloves, minced
    ½ teaspoon dried oregano
    ⅛ teaspoon crushed red pepper flakes
    10 pitted Kalamata olives, halved
    2 pints cherry tomatoes, halved
    ¼ cup thinly sliced fresh basil
    ¼ teaspoon sea salt

Heat the oil in a large nonstick skillet over medium-high heat. Add the onion, garlic, oregano, and pepper flakes; cook, stirring occasionally, until translucent, about 2 minutes. Add the olives and cook 1 minute. Stir in the tomatoes and cook until barely starting to wilt, about 2½–3 minutes. Remove from the heat and stir in the basil and salt.

Nutrition facts per serving: 100 calories, 2 g fiber, 10 g carbs, 3 g sugar, 6 g fat, 1 g saturated fat, 2 g protein, 210 mg sodium

SNACKS

Are snacks where you crack? Don't twitch. I'm about to give you snacks that redefine the role of snacking as you know it. They're guardrails on the road between your meals to keep you moving toward your goals. They support blood sugar balance and cool cravings, while pumping you up with steady, sustained energy. In short—snacking as you always hoped it could be!

Slow-Roasted Nuts

Time to go nuts! This great snack takes a bit of time, but it will be worth the wait. Nuts are an excellent source of protein, fiber, and heart-healthy fats. Best of all, they're a great-tasting, nutritious option when you're on the move. Choose your favorite, or mix it up. Note: If your oven doesn't go to 140°F, you can use a dehydrator instead.

  1½ cups raw nuts (cashews, walnuts, almonds, pecans, macadamia)
  Water
  ½ teaspoon sea salt

Combine the nuts and enough water to cover by 3 inches, then stir in the salt. Let the nuts soak overnight.

Preheat the oven to 140°F. Drain nuts and spread onto a baking sheet or place in a dehydrator. Bake nuts for 8 hours. Remove from the oven or dehydrator and let cool completely (nuts will crisp up as they cool). Store nuts in a resealable plastic bag in the refrigerator for best results.

Nutrition facts per ¼ cup serving: 140 calories, 2 g fiber, 4 g carbs, 1 g sugar, 13 g fat, 1.5 g saturated fat, 4 g protein, 150 mg sodium

Cumin and Chili Roasted Cashews

There's a lot more to this snack than meets the eye in the interplay of flavors between the sweet cashews and spices. So tasty! Plus, the slight sweetness of the cashews can really help blunt a sugar craving and quiet hunger pangs. Keep them close!

Makes 8 servings (3 tablespoons per serving)

1½ cups Slow-Roasted Nuts (use cashews; see page 276)
½ teaspoon olive oil
½ teaspoon ground cumin
½ teaspoon chili powder
½ teaspoon sea salt
⅛ teaspoon ground chipotle pepper

Preheat the oven to 200°F. In a medium bowl, combine the cashews and oil. Add the cumin, chili powder, salt, and pepper; toss well. Place the nuts in a single layer on a shallow baking pan. Bake 15 minutes, remove from the oven, and cool 10 minutes before serving. Store in an airtight container.

Nutrition facts per ¼ cup serving: 120 calories, 1 g fiber, 6 g carbs, 2 g sugar, 9 g fat, 1.5 g saturated fat, 4 g protein, 290 mg sodium

Homemade Cashew Butter on Celery

Cashew butter, especially homemade, is a better choice than peanut butter because of cashews' superior fatty acid profile and the fact that they're less likely to cause an allergic reaction. Try this versatile, high-protein spread in the trench of some crunchy celery.

This recipes makes ⅔ cup cashew butter, but you'll only have 4 tablespoons as a snack. Keep the extra refrigerated in an airtight container for up to 2 weeks.

Makes 4 servings

1 cup Slow-Roasted Nuts (use cashews; see page 276)
5 teaspoons coconut butter
⅛ teaspoon salt
4 ribs celery

Combine the cashews, coconut butter, and salt in the bowl of a food processor. Process mixture to a paste, stopping occasionally to scrape down the bowl. Fill each of the celery ribs with 1 tablespoon cashew butter. Store the remaining in an airtight container in the refrigerator.

Cycles 1 and 3 variation—serve with sliced apple or rice chips.

Nutrition facts per serving: 170 calories, 2 g fiber, 9 g carbs, 3 g sugar, 13 g fat, 5 g saturated fat, 4 g protein, 280 mg sodium

Roasted Garlic and Lemon Hummus

If I had to pick one snack to win the blue ribbon, hummus would be the one. Hummus is the sum of all the goodness that's in it—the protein in chick peas, the omega-3s in olive oil, the calcium in tahini. Add garlic and lemon, and need I say more? For a twist, serve it with vegetables you might not usually think to eat with dip: fennel, radishes, and jicama.

Makes 8 servings (3 tablespoons per serving)

    6 unpeeled garlic cloves
    1 (15-ounce) can organic no-salt-added chick peas, drained
    4 teaspoons tahini paste
    Grated zest of 1 lemon
    2 tablespoons lemon juice
    3 dashes Tabasco sauce
    2 tablespoons extra virgin olive oil
    ¼ teaspoon sea salt

Preheat the oven to 425°F. Wrap the garlic in a small sheet of aluminum foil. Place garlic packet directly on an oven rack and roast until fragrant and tender, 30 minutes. Remove from the oven and cool 10 minutes.

Unwrap the garlic cloves and squeeze each clove to remove the garlic. Transfer the garlic to the bowl of a food processor. Add the chick peas, tahini, lemon zest, lemon juice, and Tabasco sauce; puree. Stir in the oil and salt, then transfer to a bowl to serve. Can be made up to 4 days in advance, then refrigerated in an airtight container.

Cycles 1 and 3 variation—serve with bean or rice chips.

Nutrition facts per serving: 90 calories, 2 g fiber, 9 g carbs, 0 g sugar, 5 g fat, 0.5 g saturated fat, 3 g protein, 85 mg sodium

Turkey, Bacon, Lettuce, and Tomato Roll-Up

How happy are you? This is simply a deconstructed diner BLT, with all the same great flavors...and it's a snack! Throw in a slice of avocado, because everything's better with avocado.

Makes 2 servings if you're having it as a snack to share; otherwise, 1 serving counts as a meal

  2 slices uncured nitrate-free bacon
  2 medium romaine lettuce leaves
  4 teaspoons Sugar Impact Mayonnaise (see page 274)
  4 ounces nitrate-free sliced turkey breast
  1 plum tomato, cut into 8 slices
  ¼ ripe avocado, sliced

Heat a small nonstick skillet over medium. Add the bacon and cook, turning once, until crisp, about 6-7 minutes. Transfer to a plate covered with paper towel and drain.

Place a lettuce leaf on each of 2 plates. Spread each down the center lengthwise with the mayonnaise. Top with the bacon, turkey, tomato slices, and avocado.

Cycles 1 and 3 variation—substitute lettuce leaf with half of a rice wrap.

Nutrition facts per serving (meal size): 400 calories, 6 g fiber, 15 g carbs, 5 g sugar, 25 g fat, 5 g saturated fat, 31 g protein, 670 mg sodium

Yogurt and Nut Parfait

In French, parfait means perfect. That sounds about right. You'll find it hard to believe something this tasty could be part of your plan to lose weight fast. Don't ask, just enjoy! If you're dairy-sensitive, substitute 1 cup plain, no-sugar cultured coconut milk for the yogurt.

Makes 1 serving

    1 cup organic full-fat plain Greek-style yogurt
    ¼ teaspoon vanilla extract
    1 teaspoon grated lemon zest
    ⅛ teaspoon ground cinnamon
    1–1½ teaspoons monk fruit extract
    1 tablespoon cacao nibs
    5 Slow-Roasted Nuts (use almonds or cashews; see page 276), coarsely
       chopped

Combine the yogurt, vanilla extract, zest, cinnamon, and monk fruit extract in a small bowl. Spoon half the yogurt mixture into a parfait glass. Sprinkle with half the cacao nibs and half the nuts. Repeat layering. Serve, or cover and refrigerate up to 24 hours.

Cycles 1 and 3 variation—add ½ cup of berries as you layer.

Nutrition facts per serving: 385 calories, 3 g fiber, 11 g carbs, 7 g sugar, 29.9 g fat, 22 g saturated fat, 17 g protein, 80 mg sodium

DESSERTS

Gimme some sugar! If you've got a sweet tooth, dessert can be kryptonite. So I don't think it's too much to ask that you get dessert that doesn't give you cravings, cause blood sugar crashes, create headaches, increase brain fog, or drain you with fatigue. Oh, and it should also taste great and satisfy your sweet tooth, right? You got it. Enjoy!

Blueberry Ice Cream

For Cycles 1 and 3

They'll all scream for ice cream when you put this creamy indulgence on the table. Reward your crew with the all-natural goodness of blueberries and coconut for the perfect end to dinner, or as an afternoon treat.

Makes 9 servings (about ⅓ cup per serving)

If dairy-sensitive, leave out the heavy cream and use 2 cups full-fat coconut milk.

> 1½ cups unsweetened organic non-GMO full-fat coconut milk
> ½ cup heavy cream
> 12-ounce bag frozen organic blueberries
> 3 tablespoons monk fruit extract
> ¼ teaspoon vanilla extract

Combine the coconut milk, cream, and blueberries in a medium saucepan over medium heat. Bring to a simmer and cook, stirring occasionally, until the blueberries are tender, 10 minutes. Remove from the heat and let stand 10 minutes. Transfer to a blender and puree. Pour into a bowl and stir in the monk fruit extract and vanilla extract. Cover and chill 2 hours.

Pour the mixture into an ice cream maker and freeze according to the manufacturer's directions. Transfer to a freezer-safe container and allow to harden in your freezer at least 1 hour. If frozen longer, let stand at room temperature 10–15 minutes to soften slightly before serving.

Nutrition facts per serving: 139 calories, 1.1 g fiber, 6 g carbs, 3.3 g sugar, 13.2 g fat, 10.2 g saturated fat, 1.3 g protein, 10 mg sodium

Cherry-Berry Fruit Salad with Shaved Dark Chocolate

For Cycles 1 and 3

Even kids will enjoy this fruit salad for dessert. It's as beautiful to look at as it is delicious to eat. The rich cherry syrup will satisfy the most incorrigible sweet tooth, but there's shaved chocolate, just to be sure. And it's rich in antioxidants! It's almost too good to be true.

Makes 4 servings

  1 cup fresh blueberries
  1 cup fresh raspberries
  1 cup fresh blackberries
  1 cup frozen dark sweet cherries, thawed
  1 tablespoons water
  ¼ teaspoon almond extract
  1 teaspoon monk fruit extract
  1 ounce 85% dark chocolate, shaved

Combine the blueberries, raspberries, and blackberries in a bowl. Combine the cherries, water, almond extract, and monk fruit extract in a small saucepan over medium heat. Bring to a gentle boil, stirring occasionally, and cook until the cherries have softened and the liquid has thickened slightly, about 5 minutes. Remove from the heat and let cool 1 minute, then pour over the berries; mix well. Divide the berry mixture among 4 bowls and sprinkle each with some of the chocolate.

Nutrition facts per serving: 130 calories, 4 g fiber, 28 g carbs, 18 g sugar, 3.5 g fat, 1.5 g saturated fat, 2 g protein, 0 mg sodium

Lemony Frozen Greek-Style Yogurt

The neighborhood yogurt shop is in trouble. Homemade doesn't get any easier, and this one is everything you'd want from frozen yogurt and more. It's tangy with sweet undertones, which makes it satisfying but not cloying. Waiting for the freezer to do its job is the hardest part. If you're dairy-sensitive, substitute an equal amount of plain, no-sugar cultured coconut milk for the yogurt.

Makes 8 servings (about 4 cups)

  32 ounce container full-fat organic plain Greek-style yogurt
  2 tablespoons lemon juice
  1 tablespoon grated lemon zest
  ¼ cup monk fruit extract
  ¼ teaspoon vanilla extract
  ¼ teaspoon sea salt

Combine the yogurt, juice, zest, monk fruit extract, vanilla extract, and salt in a medium bowl. Whisk until well blended. Transfer to the bowl of an ice cream maker and freeze according to manufacturer's directions. Transfer to a freezer-safe container and allow to harden in your freezer at least 1 hour. If frozen longer, let yogurt stand 10–15 minutes to soften before serving.

Nutrition facts per serving: 160 calories, 0 g fiber, 4 g carbs, 4 g sugar, 12 g fat, 9 g saturated fat, 8 g protein, 105 mg sodium

Strawberry Avocado Mousse

For Cycles 1 and 3

We just can't get enough avocado. And we certainly can't pass up a dessert that will satisfy our sweet tooth, support stable blood sugar, and keep us on track with fast fat-loss goals. I think you may be starting dinner with dessert! If you're dairy-sensitive, substitute 1 cup plain, no-sugar cultured coconut milk for the yogurt.

Makes 4 servings

1 ripe avocado, peeled, pitted, and mashed
1 cup organic plain full-fat Greek-style yogurt
1½ teaspoons monk fruit extract
1 cup strawberries, hulled and cut into ¼-inch dice

Combine the avocado, yogurt, and monk fruit extract in a medium bowl. Beat with an electric mixer on the highest setting until light and fluffy. Gently fold in the strawberries. Divide among four bowls and refrigerate at least 1 hour before serving.

Nutrition facts per serving: 170 calories, 4 g fiber, 10 g carbs, 5 g sugar, 13 g fat, 6 g saturated fat, 5 g protein, 20 mg sodium

Vanilla Spice Protein Popsicle

Random fact—the Popsicle was invented in 1905 by an 11-year-old. So right there you have some evidence that this might be a good dessert swap for kids. But you can have one, too! Enjoy this sophisticated version of the summertime favorite, which has a delicious combination of spices. Perfect on a hot summer day—or anytime you need to tame your sweet tooth.

Makes 6 servings

2 scoops vanilla-flavored protein powder

10 ounces unsweetened coconut milk (such as So Delicious)

1 teaspoon ground cinnamon

¼ teaspoon ground nutmeg

1 teaspoon vanilla extract

Whisk together the shake powder, coconut milk, cinnamon, nutmeg, and vanilla extract in a bowl until well blended. Pour into 6 Popsicle molds and freeze overnight. Dip mold into warm water to remove. Store in a resealable plastic container in the freezer.

Nutrition facts per serving: 36 calories, 1 g fiber, 2.9 g carbs, 0.5 g sugar, 1.5 g fat, 1 g saturated fat, 4 g protein, 0 mg sodium

12

THE FINAL FRONTIERS: EATING OUT AND WORKING OUT

Eating out is not as scary as it seems! By now you've gotten the hang of being low Sugar Impact (SI), or if you're just starting out, you'll catch on quickly—and you're stronger than you think. Besides, when you misstep and let in a little too much sugar, your body is going to let you know it, so you'll fall right back in line. Isn't that awesome? You're a Sugar Impact player now—a self-regulating machine.

Still, menus can make your eyes spin, so a little guidance couldn't hurt. I want you to be able to zero in on the best low-SI options and be done with it so you can focus on having fun—no matter what cycle you're in. Consider this section a little security blanket, chock full of tips, to make sure you're dining, not whining.

I FACE IT, TOO

If there's one thing years of trial and error have taught me, it's that restaurants don't have to be a food-hazard obstacle course or a head-banging exchange with waitstaff. But they're also not a free-pass zone where good sense and all your hard work goes out the window. Sorry, you don't get to dive into deep-fried appetizers or sugary desserts just because someone brought them to the table. Despite the famous line in *When Harry Met Sally*, you do not have to have what she's having.

You can follow the Sugar Impact Diet anywhere, even at fast-food restaurants. But since you can't bring your own food or easily pop out of your seat and go to another restaurant, I want you to be fully prepared. You shouldn't break into a cold sweat about what to order, and you won't. You'll be able to relax and enjoy what's great about eating out—someone else is doing the cooking, and the dishes!

With this dining out guide, I've removed the guesswork by giving you specific directions about what to choose and avoid. You're not going to lose 15 minutes of your life reading a menu like you're a detective going over a crime scene, trying to figure out whether "healthy" options are actually sugar bombs. (Why do restaurant menus always get that wrong?)

Having this guide is the next best thing to having me sit across the table and point out your best options for low-SI foods. Once you get the hang of it, navigating any menu will be a breeze.

TRAVEL IS INCLUDED

If you're stranded in an airport with a 3-hour layover, you may be eating out whether you want to or not. If you have time, choose a restaurant and meal according to these guidelines. If not, visit the kiosk with the veggies (86 the ranch dressing) over the cinnamon bun (don't even smell it, just walk on by . . .). When you're on the go, you're not stuck. You don't have to sacrifice healthy for convenient. Believing you do is only going to cost you more later, in more ways than one. A little planning can save you time, money, and your waistline. Take these with you!

Portable Meals

- Turkey and avocado slices on a coconut wrap
- A Tupperware of chopped kale and romaine salad topped with chicken, avocado, tomato, olive oil, and vinegar
- A shaker cup of protein powder (just add water)

Portable Snacks

- Dehydrated nuts and seeds
- Trail mix: dehydrated nuts and seeds, unsweetened coconut slivers, and raw cacao nibs
- Celery slices with almond butter
- Jicama with hummus
- Crudités with guacamole
- No-sugar-added jerky
- Virgin Diet Bar (see Resources online at http://sugarimpact .com/resources)
- Goat cheese slices
- Hard-boiled egg
- Turkey roll-up with avocado and tomato
- Cultured coconut milk with cucumbers and chopped walnuts

FAST-FOOD OPTIONS

If you're on the run, grab a portable snack like a bag of almonds or jerky on your way out the door, and when a craving hits or you've stretched the time between meals, choose the nuts over the burger joint to get you by. If you end up at a fast-food restaurant, though, you do have options:

- Burger without the bun with side salad
- Grilled chicken breast without the bun with side salad
- Salad topped with grilled chicken (check dressing for added sugar)

LOW-SUGAR IMPACT STRATEGIES WHEN YOU'RE OUT AND ABOUT

- **Mix and match.** Look over the entire menu when you sit down. Let's say you want wild salmon, but it comes with garlic-cheddar risotto, while the filet comes with sautéed spinach and garlic. Just ask your server to switch sides—simple, done. If you're away from home, experience local culture when you make a swap and try the homegrown favorites.

- **Start your meal with a salad.** One study showed people who started with a salad ate less food during their meal. Keep it simple and top it with olive oil and vinegar or freshly squeezed lemon.

- **Bypass the gargantuan dinner salads.** Candied walnuts, bacon, taco strips, dried fruit, rice noodles, and wontons dumped on top of entrée salads are sugar bombs. Skip the sugary vinaigrettes and creamy dressings, too. Customize your salad with avocado or guacamole, salsa, chicken, and black beans (Chipotle does a fab job of this). Ask for a low-sugar vinaigrette or oil and vinegar or lemon on the side.

- **Beware of red flags.** Any entrée described as breaded, fried, crunchy, crispy, glazed, or creamy slams you into a fast fat-loss brick wall. Order your lean protein and non-starchy veggies grilled, baked, or broiled.

- **Speak up! You know what assuming does . . .** Remember you're in charge; ask your server questions before you order so you know your meal is Sugar Impact Diet–compliant. There's no reason to be afraid to ask to have something modified. If you don't ask and your chicken dish shows up drowning in a syrupy soy glaze (why didn't the menu say that!?), you're the only one who gets hurt—and the only one responsible if you eat it.

- **Don't invite the enemy to the table.** Say no thanks to the breadbasket before your server even puts it down. If your dining companions insist, lay into them about the dangers of gluten and stare judgmentally as they eat the bread. Kidding. *Kidding!* If you need something to munch on before your salad, ask for a small bowl of olives or crudités. Or try having one of the veggie sides as an appetizer. It's a great way to up your veggies, and roasted asparagus makes an awesome starter.

- **Double up.** Having two appetizers as your main course gives you better portion control than a single gigantic entrée does. Think about the difference between eating hummus with veggies and grilled chicken kabobs with salsa, instead of chicken cordon bleu and all its sides.

- **Share or cut it in half.** Split that super-sized, broccoli and garlic–stuffed chicken breast in half and share it with your dining partner, or get it to go before you even dive in. You'll save money and calories.

- **Three bites and fork down.** If you're getting pressure from the sugar pusher at the table to try the chocolate upside-down cake, and you have reason to give in (trying to score his six-figure account?), have three polite bites. When you're in Cycle 3 of the Sugar Impact Diet, three polite bites is legal. But we're talking bites you would eat on *The Rachael Ray Show*, not during an 11 p.m. fridge raid. Once you're done, ask your server to remove your plate. Trust me: your dining partner will have no problem finishing that cake.

- **Do some reconnaissance—check out menus online.** Most restaurants have menus posted on their websites. It's a great way to think through your options and head off panicky decisions when it's your turn to order. Call ahead with questions if you have any doubts.

I'M IN THE MOOD FOR...

Since you've eaten out once or twice, you know that it often starts with someone asking what everyone's in the mood for. Don't panic. Whatever you want, I've got you covered. One of the treats of eating out is to get ethnic food you don't make at home, so go for it. And don't sweat the menus—I've already made the best low-SI choices for you. Here they are, in black and white. You don't have to commit them to memory (there will not be a quiz), but check in with this list when you're on your way out so you can feel good about wherever you end up.

MEXICAN

BEST CHOICE:
   Guacamole with raw veggies, chicken fajitas (see criteria
      below)

WORST CHOICE:
   Chips and salsa with a margarita to start and then a giant burrito

SUGGESTIONS:
   - Carne or Chicken Asada, Shrimp Diablo, Snapper Veracruz
   - Ask for salsa to top dishes rather than sauces. If you're not dairy-sensitive and can handle cheese and/or sour cream, opt for full-fat varieties, and go easy!
   - Be wary of any sauces—many are loaded with sugar
   - Avocado and guacamole (ask for veggies to dip)
   - Green vegetables if they serve them (some Mexican restaurants even serve sautéed spinach)

   If you're craving authentic Mexican, order fajitas:
      - Stick with lean meats, salsa, guacamole, onions, and peppers
      - Put this all on top of a big salad

- o Skip the rice and tortillas
- o If you aren't dairy-sensitive, you can include small amounts of full-fat cheese and/or sour cream

WATCH OUT FOR:

- Anything breaded or deep-fried, including burritos, deep-fried beans, and quesadillas
- Sugary, creamy sauces, including mango salsa, mole, and creamy green chile sauce
- Refried beans, rice, and other side dishes
- Any kind of syrup
- Agave in any form
- Alcohol in any form (in Cycle 2)
- Other sugars and artificial sweeteners
- Chips (don't even let your server put them down!)
- Any kind of tortillas (gluten-free, non–corn-based are acceptable in Cycles 1 and 3)
- Any kind of dessert, including flan, custards, and fried ice cream

CHINESE

BEST CHOICE:
Steamed chicken with broccoli

WORST CHOICE:
Orange Chicken (I call this "chicken candy"!)

SUGGESTIONS:

- Beef, chicken, or veggie skewers (skip the sauce)
- Steamed chicken, beef, pork, or fish
- Broccoli, bok choy, eggplant, and other non-starchy veggies
- Ask to substitute double veggies instead of rice

WATCH OUT FOR:

- Asian salad dressings—almost all are full of sugar
- Anything breaded or deep-fried, including egg rolls, "crispy" chicken, and General Tso's chicken
- Rice (including brown rice in Cycle 2)
- MSG
- Corn starch thickener
- Hoisin, brown sauce, hot and sour sauce, and any other sugary or sticky sauces—assume they are full of sugar, MSG, or both
- Fortune cookies and any other dessert
- Other sugars and artificial sweeteners

FAST FOOD

BEST CHOICE:
Grilled chicken breast on a salad

WORST CHOICE:
Double bacon cheeseburger with fries

SUGGESTIONS:

- Many fast-food places now offer customized salads. Don't be afraid to specify exactly what you do and don't want on your salad. Ask for yours topped with grilled chicken or steak, avocado, salsa, veggies, tomatoes, onions, and cucumbers. Specify romaine, spinach, or other green-leaf lettuce. Many fast-food chains have been criticized for using iceberg lettuce
- Grilled chicken breast without the bun
- Burger without the bun—make sure it is 100% beef with no fillers. If you're not dairy-sensitive, you can add full-fat mozzarella or other cheese, but *not* American processed cheese
- Green veggies (if they have them!)

WATCH OUT FOR:

- Anything breaded or deep fried
- Sweet pickles
- Sugary or creamy sauces like BBQ sauce, honey mustard, spicy buffalo, sweet 'n sour, and creamy ranch—assume any sauce other than mustard is sugary and off-limits
- Most salad dressings like honey mustard and raspberry vinaigrette, which are full of sugar; opt for olive oil and vinegar or lemon instead
- Salad toppings—anything crunchy, creamy, or crispy is usually a red alert. Always ask and tell your server exactly what you want
- "Healthy" foods like sweet potato fries, fruit-added oatmeal, and granola or berry yogurt
- Any kind of bread, including "healthy" whole wheat wraps and buns
- Sugar—it lurks in nearly everything in fast food restaurants as a preservative and flavor enhancer
- Artificial sweeteners

THAI

BEST CHOICE:
Chicken coconut soup; chicken, scallops, or shrimp and veggies with red or green curry sauce. Careful, though—curry sauces vary

You can find commercial brands with low or no sugar added to make your own curry at home. In restaurants, they often contain more sugar than you should have, so unless you know the chef, save them for Cycle 1 or 3

WORST CHOICE:
Tofu pad thai

SUGGESTIONS:

- Chicken satays (no peanut sauce); get red or green curry sauce instead
- Brown rice (Cycles 1 and 3)
- Coconut soup with chicken
- Red or green curry (Cycles 1 and 3)

WATCH OUT FOR:

- Anything breaded or deep fried
- Sugary or creamy sauces
- Anything that comes with noodles (sometimes the menu does not alert you)
- Peanut sauces

FRENCH

BEST CHOICE:
Nicoise salad (skip the potatoes), Chicken Provençale

WORST CHOICE:
French Onion Soup, quiche (unless you can tolerate eggs and dairy, in which case opt for crustless veggie and full-fat cheese quiche; if ordering crustless isn't available, eat everything except the crust)

SUGGESTIONS:

- Grilled meat and/or veggies appetizer
- Bouillabaisse
- Swap the French bread for olives
- Lentil soup
- Salad, with oil and vinegar dressing on the side
- Avocado (great to top a salad)
- Mussels or other steamed or grilled shellfish
- Grilled steak, chicken, or fish as entrée

- Load up on as many green veggies as possible, including spinach and broccoli
- Quinoa, legumes, or wild rice
- Full-fat dairy (including ricotta, cream cheese, and goat cheese) is fine in small amounts (say, goat cheese to top a salad) if you can tolerate dairy
- For sauces, opt for hot sauce, Tabasco or vinegar (not balsamic)

WATCH OUT FOR:

- Anything breaded or deep fried
- Tomato soup
- Any kind of soufflé or other dish that includes bread
- Croissants (basically dessert)
- Sweet, creamy, or syrupy sauces, including Béchamel and brown sauce, which are often thickened with cornstarch
- Be aware many French sauces are cream-based if you are dairy-sensitive
- Honey mustard and other salad dressings—safest bet is olive oil and vinegar
- If you're dairy-sensitive, be aware many French dishes are cooked with butter
- Pastries and other desserts
- Other forms of sugar

STEAKHOUSE

BEST CHOICE:
Salad and filet with steamed broccoli

WORST CHOICE:
Wedge salad and a steak drowned in sugary sauce with creamed spinach and battered onion rings

SUGGESTIONS:

- Swap the bread for olives
- Salad with olive oil and vinegar dressing (not balsamic)
- Shrimp cocktail (without the sauce)
- Grilled meat and/or veggie appetizer
- Filet or other lean steak
- Broccoli, spinach, cauliflower, or other veggie—many steak-houses offer these à la carte, so use this as an opportunity to get more delicious veggies!
- Quinoa, legumes, or wild rice
- For sauces, opt for hot sauce, Tabasco, and vinegar

WATCH OUT FOR:

- Caesar and other salads with creamy dressings
- Steak sauce and other sugary dressings—if they give you the bottle, read labels for added sugar!
- Crunchy, crispy, and other "illegal" salad toppings, including fried onions, candied walnuts, and dried cranberries
- Anything breaded or deep fried
- Dinner rolls (don't even let your server put them down!)
- Breaded veggies and other "legal" foods (steakhouses love to fry anything for added appeal)
- Baked potatoes (these things are gargantuan at steakhouses and easily equal 3–4 servings)
- Baked sweet potatoes—always ask; these often are swimming in butter and added sugar (like they really need it!)
- Mashed potatoes, French fries, and other typical steakhouse sides
- Giant lettuce wedge—basically a pesticide bomb drenched with creamy dressing
- Any form of dessert

AMERICAN

BEST CHOICE:
Salad; grilled chicken breast topped with peppers, onions, and mushrooms; steamed green veggies; gluten-free healthy starches

WORST CHOICE:
Bacon cheeseburger with fries and soda

SUGGESTIONS:
- Salad with olive oil and vinegar dressing
- Steamed veggies—load up on as many varieties as possible. Good choices include green beans, asparagus, broccoli, tomatoes, and spinach
- Omelet with veggies (if you can tolerate eggs) with a side salad
- Grilled, broiled, or baked steak, chicken, pork, or seafood
- Large, customized entrée salad
- Legumes, wild rice, or quinoa
- Opt for olive oil and red wine vinegar for salads
- For sauces, opt for hot sauce, Tabasco, red wine vinegar, and salsa

WATCH OUT FOR:
- Anything crunchy or deep fried
- Any form of potato
- Corn on the cob
- Balsamic vinegar
- Salads with words like creamy and crunchy
- Anything breaded—always ask, because I've seen breaded green beans, asparagus, and otherwise healthy foods on menus
- Meats drowning in sugary, syrupy sauces
- Ketchup, BBQ sauce, and other sugary sauces to dip in
- Any kind of dessert

- Hidden sugars, including vegetable casseroles and steak sauces (just because it doesn't taste sweet doesn't mean it doesn't have sugar)

JAPANESE

BEST CHOICE:
Sashimi and cucumber salad

WORST CHOICE:
Edamame, rolls with special sauce (usually they are full of sugar), vegetable or meat tempura

SUGGESTIONS:
- Sashimi
- Bring your own coconut aminos instead of soy sauce
- Hibachi grill: scallops, shrimp, or chicken with double veggies
- Side salad with ginger dressing
- Shirataki noodles
- Choose traditional rice wine vinegar with no added sugar
- Unsweetened hot green tea
- Marinated cucumbers

WATCH OUT FOR:
- Almost all Asian salad dressings except ginger are full of sugar, so avoid
- Any kind of rice, including brown rice during Cycle 2
- Tempura and anything else crunchy, breaded, or deep-fried
- Soy (tofu, etc., but also from hidden sources) unless you can tolerate it
- Sugary, creamy sauces
- Teriyaki sauce

ITALIAN

BEST CHOICE:
Cioppino (fish stew); mussels in garlic and olive oil

WORST CHOICE:
Fettuccine Alfredo with garlic bread

SUGGESTIONS:
- Mussels
- Salad drizzled with tomatoes and olive oil
- Grilled or baked chicken, pork chop, or other dish
- Steamed veggies
- Checca sauce

WATCH OUT FOR:
- Anything breaded or deep-fried
- Marinara sauce (generally this is high in sugar)
- Tomato soup
- Fish sauce
- Pasta (even with meat, some restaurants slide it in)
- Rice or gluten-free pasta (during Cycle 2)
- Sugary or creamy sauces
- Sorbet, gelato, and other sugary desserts
- Garlic bread (don't even let them set it down!)

SEAFOOD

BEST CHOICE:
Grilled or poached wild salmon or halibut; mixed veggies; jumbo shrimp appetizer

WORST CHOICE:
Fried shrimp with French fries

SUGGESTIONS:

- Salad with olive oil and vinegar
- Mussels or other shellfish appetizer
- Grilled or poached wild seafood—salmon, shrimp, etc. Always look for lower-mercury fish and avoid shark, swordfish, and other larger fish
- Steamed veggies
- Wild rice, quinoa, or legumes

WATCH OUT FOR:

- Anything breaded or deep-fried—always ask if your fish is breaded or battered in any way
- Creamy or sugary salad dressings
- Fish sauce
- Any form of potato—mashed, sweet, etc.
- All forms of rice, including brown rice in Cycle 2
- Sugary sauces (e.g., cocktail sauce)
- Cocktail, tartar sauce, and other dipping sauces

MEDITERRANEAN

BEST CHOICE:
Roasted fish with peppers, onions, and artichokes

WORST CHOICE:
Couscous (it's gluten)

SUGGESTIONS:

- Ask for olives instead of bread
- Salad with cucumber, onions, and peppers topped with olive oil and vinegar
- Hummus with crudités
- Lentils and other legumes
- Lentil soup
- Grilled fish (choose lower-mercury options)

- Grilled chicken or red meat if you're not a fish fan
- Roasted peppers and artichokes

WATCH OUT FOR:

- Anything crunchy, breaded, or deep-fried—not really Mediterranean foods, but more common as Mediterranean becomes more Americanized
- Salad dressings—many have added sugar, so stick with olive oil and vinegar
- Couscous (gluten)
- Pita
- Pasta
- Fish sauce
- Sugary, syrupy sauces

GET A MOVE ON!

If you want to lose weight, don't focus on exercise. Did you just drop the book? Okay, pick it up and I'll explain. First of all, I'm not telling you *not* to exercise...far from it. But I don't emphasize exercise until you've gotten your diet totally under control. Otherwise, you're hit with information overload, and when you're overwhelmed you can't do anything at all.

Research shows that diet is most critical for initial weight loss, while exercise is key for long-term weight management and overall health. So don't worry, eventually I'm going to insist you exercise, because I don't want you to become "TOFI," or thin outside, fat inside. You'll be TOFI if you try to maintain your weight by diet alone. No exercise means you won't be building lean muscle, so you'll have a higher body fat percentage relative to your weight. Even if you think you look good, without exercise you put yourself at a higher risk for disease. TOFI fat is the fat that's packed around vital organs and in underused muscles, and it's different than the fat lying below your skin. It sends out chemical signals that can ultimately lead to insulin resistance and diabetes, among other conditions.

Exercise is one of my strategies for sugar withdrawal. It can provide the endorphin boost you were looking for in the cookie jar, and it's also great for speed healing because it helps quickly restore insulin sensitivity in the muscles. It's critical for long-term weight management because it helps burn up your fat-storing enzymes, and it boosts your metabolism so you burn more calories from fat throughout the day. And, of course, it'll help you look better naked. Had to say it.

Just as I talk you through the right types of sugars, I'll do the same with the right types of exercise. It isn't enough just to exercise, you want to make sure that what you're doing is sending the messages to your body to build muscle, burn off fat, and maintain strong bones—all without taking your adrenals down in the process. Yes, it can be done! And the good news is that doing exercise correctly is actually a major time-saver, since it takes just minutes a day.

Did I just get your attention?

MOVE MORE AND BURST TRAIN

First, we need to move more. You know you're always being told to park farther away, take the stairs, walk to work. Yes, you really need to do that. We should be moving at least an hour a day. If that sounds daunting, it shouldn't be—everything counts! That jaunt to grab your green tea from Starbucks, the hike up the escalators to get to the sale rack before anyone else, the long trek from one gate to another at the airport (no moving sidewalks for you!) . . . they all count as part of your daily movement. But what these don't count as is exercise. So I want you to move more, but movement only counts as exercise when you get hot and sweaty and it hurts a little bit. For me, this means burst-style training and resistance training (yes, they can be done together). Of course, these also count toward your daily movement total.

So start slowly—just move more, and measure it. What you measure, you can improve. The easiest way to do that is to throw on some kind of tracking device, which can be as low-tech as a simple $20 pedometer or as high-tech as a Fitbit. All you need to know is how many steps you actually take each day. Count them every day for a week, add them up, divide by 7, and you have your average steps per day. Add 10% to your total, and that will be your new goal each week. If you were averaging 4,000 steps a day, add 400 to it for a target of 4,400 for the week. The following week, the goal will be 4,840. This way you don't even notice the extra effort, but your body will! Do that until you're hitting at least 6,000 steps a day. The more the merrier, so don't hold back.

Once you're moving more, up the intensity. I like to say burst to blast fat! Four minutes of bursting, or high-intensity interval

Burst to blast fat!

training, is worth 20 minutes of regular aerobic training. You can get a beach body in just 15 minutes, three times a week. Researchers at the University of New South Wales (UNSW) asked women to exercise either three times a week for 20 minutes, alternating 8 seconds of sprinting on a bike with 12 seconds of exercising lightly, or at a regular pace for 40 minutes.

Fifteen weeks later, the women who did high-intensity interval training lost three times as much fat as the women doing 40 minutes at a regular pace. Steve Boutcher, head of the Health and Exercise Science program in the School of Medical Sciences at UNSW, said, "Intermittent sprinting produces high levels of chemical compounds called catecholamines, which allow more fat to be burned from under the skin and within the exercising muscles."

Burst training is also de-stressing and anti-aging, and it's the most efficient, effective exercise for balancing blood sugar levels. One study in the *Journal of Applied Physiology* showed that bursting could improve blood sugar levels and reduce complications for people who already have diabetes.

Here's a snapshot of the benefits you'll get with burst training:

- Improved stress tolerance
- Increased testosterone and HGH, the fountain of youth hormone
- Less oxidative stress than in endurance training
- Endorphin release
- Muscle-building support
- Post-workout fat-burning

CHEAP AND FAST

One of the best things about burst training is that you don't have to buy any fancy equipment or join any expensive clubs. You can do it anywhere. And in just 15–20 minutes. With all the benefits it delivers, it's hard to imagine choosing any other way to go. Does anyone really wish they could spend more time getting fewer results? Plus, that 15–20 minutes includes the warm up and cool down!

Here's how it goes: choose any type of exercise that uses as much of your body as possible. Begin by doing a fast-paced warm-up for several minutes. Then burst! Go all out for 30 to 60 seconds. Leave it all out there—when you're done, you should be ready to drop, as if you can't go another second. Feel the burn! Allow yourself to actively recover by doing the "light" version of your burst for twice as long, then do it again. Work your way up to 4 to 8 minutes of total bursting time in 30–60 second increments, 3 days a week.

If you're currently a runner, here's an easy example of how to shift your routine to bursting: warm-up with a walk and easy jog;

sprint all out for 30–60 seconds; walk it off for twice as long; and then repeat, until you've done 4–8 total minutes of bursting. Follow with a cool-down. Every time I have someone do this, they're blown away by how much better a workout they get in so much less time.

Some of my favorite ways to burst are:

- Step-ups
- X-iser
- Stair climbing
- Sprinting
- Cycling
- Turkish get-ups
- Burpees
- Squat thrusts
- Plyometrics
- Swimming
- Jump rope
- Jumping jacks

If you don't own an X-iser (my favorite burst-training machine; see Resources online at http://sugarimpact.com/resources), your nearest park, hill, or stairwell can provide all the "equipment" you need to get your burst on.

RESIST!

I also recommend resistance training. When you build more muscle, you do a few really amazing things for your body—you raise your metabolic rate all day long, you improve insulin sensitivity in your muscles immediately so you're better at burning off fat, and you protect your bones, both because exercise improves bone density and because stronger muscles safeguard the bones.

Your body also uses sugar as its primary fuel source during both resistance training and burst training, which means you burn off glycogen reserves, so your body has a place to shuttle glucose when you eat sugar and carbs.

You can resistance train with weight machines, free weights, kettle bells, your own body weight, and suspension cables. I definitely prefer cables, body weight, and free weights to machines, because we're not exactly bolted to the floor in real life, are we? The more unstable you are—sitting on a ball instead of sitting in a chair, standing instead of sitting, standing on one leg, and so on—the more you'll activate your core muscles, and the more muscles you'll use overall. I also prefer to do more multi-joint exercises like push-ups, squats, and pull-ups as opposed to single-joint exercises like bicep curls, triceps extensions, and leg extensions because you use so many more muscles. Plus, full-body exercises are much more applicable to everyday life, so they'll help you do more throughout the day with less effort.

The ideal repetition range for hypertrophy, or muscle growth, is 8–12 repetitions. A repetition is one full movement of the exercise. When you do multiple repetitions, it's known as a set. Once you complete a set, you take a break for about a minute and repeat the set. You should do 2–4 sets of any single exercise. If you're just starting out, keep it to one set of each exercise for the first week or two. Lift the heaviest weight you can safely handle with good form. If you can easily get to 12 repetitions, increase the weight by 10%; if you can't get to 8 reps, decrease it by 10%.

I've divided the body into 4 parts—upper-body pushing, upper-body pulling, hips and thighs, and power core. Work each part 2–3 times a week, and give yourself 48–72 hours of rest in between. Listen to your body here; if you're still sore, take an extra day of rest. You should never be sore to the touch, at a joint site, or for multiple days. If you are, dial it back a bit—your body is trying to tell you that you're overdoing it. Focus on multi-joint exercises like push-ups rather than single-joint exercises like triceps extensions—you'll get far more metabolic bang (build more muscles, burn off more calories) for your exercise buck.

Examples for each of the body parts:

Upper body pushing: push-ups, chest press, overhead press, dips
Upper body pulling: pull-ups, lat pull-downs, 1 arm rows, upright rows, bent-over rows
Hips and thighs: squats, lunges, step-ups, leg press
Power core: sit-ups, back extension, Swiss ball exercises

Here are some resistance-training guidelines:

- Warm up before starting
- Do 2–4 sets of each exercise
- Do 8–12 repetitions
- Take a 60-second rest break between sets
- Rest for 48–72 hours before you work that body part again
- Work each body part 2–3 times per week

FAST, FUN, AND DONE IN 15 MINUTES OR LESS

If you want the one-two punch of bursting and resistance training all in one workout, try my free 4x4 (find it here: http://jjvirgin .com/4x4workout). The 4x4 is fast, fun, and done in 15 minutes. It's a full-body workout that incorporates the two absolute best ways to develop lean muscle, burn more fat, and boost your metabolism, *all day long*. Each workout combines four bursts for each of four body parts (upper body pulling, upper body pushing, hips and thighs, and power core) done in a circuit. Do 4x4 just 3 times a week; you'll be astonished at the difference you see and feel fast!

PUTTING IT ALL TOGETHER

The bottom line is that I'd like you to move more every day. You'll supercharge your Sugar Impact Diet results and your health overall. And when you add the exercises we've talked about here, you'll transform your body through fast fat loss, stable blood sugar, hormone balance, low stress, and more. Set your burst training to 4 to 8 total minutes, 3 times a week, and resistance train each body part 2 to 3 times a week. Don't forget to reward yourself after a workout with a Sugar Impact Shake—it's great for recovery!

Conclusion

SWEET FREEDOM

If you ever had a moment's doubt that Sneaky Sugar is public enemy No. 1, you're past that now, aren't you? You're a believer. There's no way to have been on the journey you were on and come out the other side skeptical in any way about the lethal powers of that drug. And getting off it has transformed your life—it's tamed your sugar cravings, helped you regain control of your appetite, filled you with strong, steady energy, and sharpened your focus and brainpower.

You've transcended the limits of what you believed was possible. Tell me the truth: you never really thought you could kick sugar, did you? You can cop to that now! Because you've done it—you've forever changed the relationship you have with food. You'll know now to always look at its Sugar Impact (SI), so sugar will never get its hooks in you again.

One of the things that amazed me the most after *The Virgin Diet* came out was how generous everyone was in sharing the secret to their success. People couldn't wait to pay it forward, and a movement began. Well, you're part of that movement now, and I hope you won't keep it to yourself. Go out and help transform the health of your family, friends, and future generations.

You may have already started by pulling some high-SI foods

from your family's table or sharing some swaps with your BFF. Well, don't stop there! Everyone can benefit from what you know; this information has the power to change the world. And if you don't share, we might all be headed for some serious trouble. Think I'm overselling it a bit? Not so much.

The health care industry is on life support. Costs are skyrocketing, mostly because of the exploding rates of diabetes and obesity. We're all feeling that pain. Obesity in the United States took off from the starting line with high-fructose corn syrup in the 1970s, and it never looked back. Remember—sugar cravings start in the womb!

We need change. And no one will ever say it better than Mahatma Gandhi did: Be the change that you wish to see in the world. You can't sit on the sidelines for this one, not as one of the enlightened. So get engaged, jump in! We have to aim high and set our sights on changing industry—because we can, and nothing else will do. Sugar is going to take our country down and us with it; we can't stand by and watch.

But at the same time, there's good news—we can control it! Diet is the biggest *controllable* threat to our health. You can do this! You just have to be always sleuthing out where it hides. And for that, you have to be tough as nails.

MENTAL TOUGHNESS

The Sugar Impact Diet was never intended to help you break the vicious circle created by sugar and then just dump you at the curb. You'd be holding a "Will Work For Candy" sign in minutes! It's really about your success for life, and that means giving you the support you need.

But when I'm not feeling very motivated, I'm reminded that I'm in charge of that. I'm in charge of my own physiology. My mentor, Brendon Burchard, author of the *New York Times* bestselling book

The Charge, likes to say, "A power plant doesn't have energy; it generates energy." You've got to produce your own energy. You've got to create your own enthusiasm.

YOU'VE GOT TO SET NEW GOALS THAT KEEP YOU FIRED UP!

Your goals—the ones that really matter to your life in the end—should be stretch goals, aspirational goals. Remove the limitations in your own mind. You can chase down your simple goals by keeping your low-SI life fun and interesting forever. But what would you really go for if you knew you couldn't fail? What would really change everything for you?

Think about the things that inspire you and keep you jazzed up for the long haul. The things that always bubble up to the top of your wish list in a quiet moment. The Sugar Impact Diet will help you get there.

YOUR PRESENT TO YOU

Let's put a bow around this so you can go off and enjoy your new low-SI life. Before you go, though, take one last look at your Sugar Impact Quiz, your weight chart and measurements, and your journal pages. Look how far you've come! Don't you love the view from here? Every bit you put into the Sugar Impact Diet has come back to you and more, and it was so worth it.

First, you made the commitment to break your addiction to sugar. That meant an unflinching look at how much sugar you were really eating and what it did to you. Now you've reclaimed your sugar sensitivity, and you've retrained your taste buds. You can sense when things taste too sweet! It's a miracle. Stay in this place of being able to appreciate natural sweetness and emphasize savory and spicy flavors in your food.

You can really design this program for *your* life. Ask yourself what you want that life to be. What do you want to do with all this information? Maybe it's enough to have gotten a handle on sugar. Maybe you want to intensify your fitness.

It's time to build on your success, to go further. Kick up your heels with that extra energy and think about where you'll go from here. Believe anything is possible, and will it into your life. Stop negative feedback loops about how little weight you think you can lose, that your knees will always hurt, or that you'll never have the energy you had in high school. Now you know it doesn't have to be that way.

You're here, with the dots connected. Make your next move a big one. Decide what your life will look like and make it so. You've earned it! Congratulations!

ACKNOWLEDGMENTS

This book started as a good idea and turned into my full-blown mission. As the idea grew, I realized I was going to need a lot of help—both to create the book and bring it out to the world. This idea would never have gotten off the ground without the help of an amazing group of people.

First of all, none of this would have happened without the insight of my incredible agent Celeste Fine, who saw the enormous need for this book and helped me find the perfect publisher—one who really got the vision. Jamie Raab, your enthusiasm inspires me! I am so fortunate to be able to work with you and the amazing team at Grand Central. And how lucky was I that they brought in my *Virgin Diet* editor, Sarah Pelz, so she could work her magic again on this book? Karen Murgolo, Matthew Ballast, Sonya Safra, Brian McLendon, Emi Battaglia, Andrew Duncan, Stephanie Sirabian, and Jane Lee—thanks for getting behind this project in such a big way and making sure that it gets major attention!

When I decided to write this book, the first thing I did was review all of the brilliant work that has been published on the topic. I am so fortunate to have had such amazing pioneers to be able to reference, including Dr. John Yukdin (in memoriam), Dr. Robert Lustig, Gary Taubes, Michael Moss, Dr. Mark Hyman, Nancy Appleton, Dr. Joseph Mercola, Dr. Timothy Johnson, Dr. Pamela Peeke, and David Gillespie. I also want to send a shout-out to Michael Fishman for his wisdom on how best to research and frame the book.

Speaking of framework, I have to extend special thanks to Camper Bull, the president of my company, the "king of framework," who helped me create the framework and test the model with nearly 1,000 people. And, of course, big thanks to Ellyne Lonergan, who helps me nail the messaging in my books and PBS shows, and to Jason Boehm, who hunts down the research to back up my ideas and helps me put out incredible blogs. Dr. Sara Gottfried, my sister (yes, I've adopted you), thank you for painstakingly reviewing this manuscript to ensure we were spot on with the science. Donna Gates, thanks for the insider info on using fermented foods to blow through those sugar cravings!

I know you can eat deliciously on this program, because I have a secret weapon—the talent of chefs Marge Perry and David Bonom, who translate my messy recipe ideas into simple delicious delights. Also, thanks to Suzanne Griffin, who helps us build our community cookbooks. Big thanks to my pals at So Delicious Dairy Free (Hilary Martin, I adore you), Randy Hartnell of Vital Choice, and Betsy Foster of Whole Foods Markets for supplying awesome ingredients for us to work with. Jonathan Lizotte, it's good to be home again—so happy to be working with you on all of my product formulations.

Of course, none of this matters if you don't know about it! Thanks to my primo "pubbie" Barbara Teszler of Tezsler PR and Mike Danielson of Media Relations for connecting me up with great product lines to support the program. Mary Agnes Antonopolous—you are the Queen of Social Media. I pinch myself daily that you are supporting the mission. Liana Chaouli, best stylist ever, thanks for making sure I show up on brand and looking fabulous! Victoria LaBalme, thanks for making sure that when I am speaking I am creating an incredible experience and communicating a bigger vision. Kathy White and Patsy Wallace, thanks for taking such good care of the Virgin Lifestyle community. Lacy Kirkland, cutest human being on the planet, thank you for being such amazing support for all of our partners, and all of you in the Mindshare Collaborative—thank you for supporting my programs and mission and being such courageous pioneers in health. My favorite thing to do is spend time with all of you, especially if it involves dancing and great wine. Alan Foster, thanks for all of the great coaching and for convincing so many PBS stations to air my show.

I can't mention coaching without thanking my mentors and coaches. Brendon Burchard, you continue to push me and inspire me to go to the next level. Joe Polish, you are the best connector on the planet, I feel so fortunate to be the "minnow" in 25K. Babs Smith and Dan Sullivan of Strategic Coach, thanks for helping me get my life back and learn how to impact more people while still being able to be a mom and have a life! And Jon Walker, thanks for all of your incredible wisdom on launches and being so generous with your time.

Of course, when you get that message out there, you get a lot of questions, and my amazing customer service team is incredible at taking care of everyone—big thanks to Rose, Nadiya, Sigourney, and Brandy for your amazing grace and positivity! And a shout-out to our advisory circle as well for giving us such valuable feedback so we know how best to serve the community.

One of the key ways we get our message out there is through the online world, and we have a true master heading that up— Travis Houston. And thanks to his adorable wife Joy, who jumps in to help on projects as well. And thank you Traci Knoppe, who runs our tech. Ben Clark, our incredible designer, makes us look so good, as does my fabulous photographer Lesley Boehm. Susan Tafralis puts together most of the cool handouts and e-books, but that's just one of the hats she wears—she's been with me for over 14 years now and has run every part of my business. She is truly my right hand; I would be lost without her! Thankfully, we also have Kim Ward now as that job got way too big for one person.

Kim, you are the first person I've ever relinquished my calendar to; thanks for being so uber-organized so that I can show up where I need to relaxed and prepared.

Aahh legal and finance....thank you all for your protection and advice so that I can make sure that I can continue to serve at the highest level. Darryl Sheetz and Peter Hoppenfeld—I feel like you two are my legal white knights. Michael Ross, thanks for the massive attention to detail, and Mary Ann Guillory, thank you for making sure those orders go out every day, no matter what.

And I saved the best for last—my amazing family. Mom, thanks for always believing in me, and I forgive you for raising me on Pop Tarts and Captain Crunch. John Virgin, you are an incredible dad, you allow me to be able to go out and do what I have to without worrying (too much) about my kids. Bryce Virgin, I wonder how I scored such an incredible son—you are brilliant, talented, and so kind. In 17 years you have not given me one reason to punish you nor have you said one mean thing to me. You blow my mind. Grant Virgin, you are the epitome of a victor—to have survived the unsurvivable with the most amazing positive attitude—you make me so proud. You show people what is possible with the right mind-set. Thank you all for supporting me so that I can truly have it all—be the mom of two beautiful young men while fulfilling my mission to empower people worldwide to take control of their health so they can go out and do the big things they were put here to do.

REFERENCES

Chapter 1: Break Free from the Sugar Trap

S. Basu et al., "The Relationship of Sugar to Population-Level Diabetes Prevalence: An Econometric Analysis of Repeated Cross-Sectional Data," *PLoS One* 8, no. 2 (2013): e57873.

C. Colan et al., "Excessive Sugar Intake Alters Binding to Dopamine and Mu-opioid Receptors in the Brain," *NeuroReport* 12, no. 16 (2001): 3549–52.

D. Gillespie, *Big Fat Lies: How the Diet Industry is Making You Sick, Fat and Poor* (New York: E-penguin, 2012). Kindle edition.

R. Johnson, *The Fat Switch* (New York: Amazon Digital Services, 2012). Kindle edition.

K. Keskitalo et al., "Same Genetic Components Underlie Different Measures of Sweet Taste Preference," *The American Journal of Clinical Nutrition* 86, no. 6 (2007): 1663–9.

M. Lenoir et al., "Intense Sweetness Surpasses Cocaine Reward," *PLoS One* 2, no. 8 (2007): e698.

K. Heritage, "Study links sugar intake to stress," *The Oracle: University of South Florida*, last updated February 9, 2010. http://www.usforacle.com/study-links-sugar-intake-to-stress-1.2144586#.UwUCbRbSOdJ/

Chapter 2: Track Your Impact

R.K. Johnson et al., "Dietary sugars intake and cardiovascular health: A scientific statement from the American Heart Association," *Circulation* 120, no. 11 (2009): 1011–20.

D. Kessler, *The End of Overeating* (New York: Rodale, 2010).

L.C. Martineau et al., "Anti-diabetic properties of the Canadian low-bush blueberry Vaccinium angustifolium Ait," *Phytomedicine* 13, 9–10 (2006): 612–23.

D.J. Pettitt et al., "Prevalence of diabetes in U.S. youth in 2009: The SEARCH for diabetes in youth study," *Diabetes Care* 37, no. 2 (2014): 402–8.

J.A. Welsh et al., "Caloric Sweetener Consumption and Dyslipidemia Among US Adults," *The Journal of the American Medical Association* 303, no. 15 (2010): 1490–7.

M. Thomassian, "The Many Names for Sugar," *Dietriffic* March 27, 2009, accessed May 15, 2014. http://www.dietriffic.com/2009/03/26/names-for-sugar/

Chapter 3: The Sugar Impact Plate

D.M. Arble et al., "Circadian Timing of Food Intake Contributes to Weight Gain," *Obesity (Silver Spring)* 17, no. 11 (2009): 2100–2.

A. Ascherio et al., "Trans-Fatty Acids Intake and Risk of Myocardial Infarction," *Circulation* 89, no. 1 (1994): 94–101.

M. Hibi et al., "Nighttime Snacking Reduces Whole Body Fat Oxidation and Increases LDL Cholesterol in Healthy Young Women," *American Journal of Physiology: Regulatory, Integrative, and Comparative Physiology* 304, no. 2 (2013): R94–R101.

M. Journel et al., "Brain Responses to High-Protein Diets," *Advances in Nutrition* 3, no. 3 (2012): 322–9.

M.B. Katan et al., "Trans Fatty Acids and Their Effects on Lipoproteins in Humans," *Annual Review of Nutrition* 15 (1995): 473–93.

D. Mozaffarian et al., "Trans Fatty Acids and Cardiovascular Disease," *New England Journal of Medicine* 354, no. 15 (2006): 1601–13.

W.C. Willett et al., "Intake of Trans Fatty Acids and Risk of Coronary Heart Disease among Women," *Lancet* 6, no. 341 (1993): 581–5.

"Hypoglycemia." National Diabetes Information Clearinghouse, accessed February 19, 2013. http://diabetes.niddk.nih.gov/dm/pubs/hypoglycemia/

University of Washington Study. 2002. Reported in *Integrated and Alternative Medicine Clinical Highlights* 4, no. 1: 16.

Chapter 4: Be Gone, Grains, Roots, and Fruit

N. Barnard, *Breaking the Food Seduction: The Hidden Reasons Behind Food Cravings—and 7 Steps to End Them Naturally* (New York: St. Martin's Press, 2010).

C.S. Berkey et al., "Milk, Dairy Fat, Dietary Calcium, and Weight Gain: A Longitudinal Study of Adolescents," *Archives of Pediatric and Adolescent Medicine* 159, no. 6 (2005): 543–50.

J. Boyer and R.H. Liu, "Apple Phytochemicals and Their Health Benefits," *Nutrition Journal* 3, no. 5 (2004).

E.A. Brinton et al., "A Low-Fat Diet Decreases High Density Lipoprotein (HDL) Cholesterol Levels by Decreasing HDL Apolipoprotein Transport Rates," *Journal of Clinical Investigation* 85, no. 1 (1990): 144–51.

L. Calabresi et al., "An Omega-3 Polyunsaturated Fatty Acid Concentrate Increases Plasma High-Density Lipoprotein 2 Cholesterol and Paraoxonase Levels in Patients with Familial Combined Hyperlipidemia," *Metabolism* 53, no. 2 (2004): 153–8.

C. Catassi et al., "Non-Celiac Gluten Sensitivity: The New Frontier of Gluten Related Disorders," *Nutrients* 5, no. 10 (2013): 3839–53.

W. Davis, *Wheat Belly: Lose the Wheat, Lose the Weight, and Find Your Path Back to Health* (New York: Rodale, 2011).

W. Davis, "Wheat Belly: Frequently Asked Questions." July 26, 2011. http://www.wheatbellyblog.com/2011/07/wheat-belly-frequently-asked-questions/

M. Hadjivassiliou et al., "Gluten Sensitivity: from Gut to Brain," *The Lancet Neurology* 9, no. 3 (2010): 318–30.

J.V. Higdon et al., "Cruciferous Vegetables and Human Cancer Risk: Epidemiologic Evidence and Mechanistic Basis," *Pharmaceutical Research: The Official Journal of the Italian Pharmaceutical Society* 55, no. 3 (2007): 224–36.

A. Hsu et al., "Promoter De-methylation of *Cyclin D2* by Sulforaphane in Prostate Cancer Cells," *Clinical Epigenetics* 3, no. 1 (2011): 3.

J.C. Hsu et al., "Indole-3-Carbinol Mediated Cell Cycle Arrest of LNCaP Human Prostate Cancer Cells Requires the Induced Production of Activated p53 Tumor Suppressor Protein," *Biochemical Pharmacology* 72, no. 12 (2006): 1714–23.

M. Hyman, *The Blood Sugar Solution: The UltraHealthy Program for Losing Weight, Preventing Disease, and Feeling Great Now!* (New York: Little, Brown, 2012).

M. Hyman, "Three Hidden Ways Wheat Makes You Fat," Huffington Post, February 18, 2012. Accessed February 19, 2014. http://www.huffington post.com/dr-mark-hyman/wheat-gluten_b_1274872.html

A. Keys et al., "The Diet and 15-Year Death Rate in the Seven Countries Study," *American Journal Epidemiology* 124, no. 6 (1986): 903–15.

D.W. Lamson and M.S. Brignall, "Antioxidants and Cancer, Part 3: Quercetin," *Alternative Medicine Review: A Journal of Clinical Therapeutics* 5, no. 3 (2000): 196–208.

C.M. Matthews, "Exploring the Obesity Epidemic," *Proceedings (Baylor University Medical Center)* 25, no. 2 (2012): 276–7.

F. Perez-Vincaino et al., "Endothelial Function and Cardiovascular Disease: Effects of Quercetin and Wine Polyphenols," *Free Radical Research* 40, no. 10 (2006): 1054–65.

J.M. Seddon et al., "Dietary Carotenoids, Vitamins A, C, and E, and Advanced Age–Related Macular Degeneration. Eye Disease Case–Control Study Group," *Journal of the American Medical Association* 272, no. 18 (1994): 1413–20.

Q. Shao and K.V. Chin, "Survey of American Food Trends and the Growing Obesity Epidemic," *Nutrition Research and Practice* 5, no. 3 (2011): 253–9.

F.L. Soares et al., "Gluten-Free Diet Reduces Adiposity, Inflammation and Insulin Resistance Associated with the Induction of PPAR-alpha and PPAR-gamma Expression," *Journal of Nutritional Biochemistry* 24, no. 6 (2013): 1105–11.

A.P. Toft-Petersen et al., "Small Dense LDL particles—A Predictor of Coronary Artery Disease Evaluated by Invasive and CT-based Techniques: A Case-Control Study," *Lipids in Health and Disease* no. 10, 21 (2011).

XJ Yan et al., "Indole-3-Carbinol Improves Survival in Lupus-Prone Mice by Inducing Tandem B- and T-cell Differentiation Blockades," *Clinical Immunology* (Orlando, Fl.) 131, no. 3 (2009): 481–94.

"Magnesium," Linus Pauling Institute Micronutrient Research for Optimum Health, accessed February 19, 2014. http://lpi.oregonstate.edu/infocenter/minerals/magnesium/

"Vitamins," Linus Pauling Institute Micronutrient Research for Optimum Health, accessed February 19, 2014. http://lpi.oregonstate.edu/infocenter/vitamins.html

"Vegetables and Fruits: Get Plenty Every Day," Nutrition School at the Harvard School of Public Health, accessed February 19, 2014. http://www.hsph.harvard.edu/nutritionsource/vegetables-full-story/

"Phytonutrient FAQs," United States Department of Agriculture, accessed February 19, 2014. http://www.ars.usda.gov/aboutus/docs.htm?docid=4142#classes/

Chapter 6: So Long, Sweet Drinks and Dressings

M.H. Alderman, "Salt, Blood Pressure, and Human Health," *Hypertension* 36, no. 5 (2000): 890–3.

G.A. Bray, "Soft Drink Consumption and Obesity: It is All About Fructose," *Current Opinion in Lipidology* 21, no. 1 (2010): 51–7.

J. Calissendorff et al., "Alcohol Ingestion Does Not Affect Serum Levels of Peptide YY but Decreases Both Total and Octanoylated Ghrelin Levels in Healthy Subjects," *Metabolism* 55, no. 12 (2006): 1625–9.

E.A. Dennis et al., "Water Consumption Increases Weight Loss during a Hypocaloric Diet Intervention in Middle-aged and Older Adults," *Obesity (Silver Spring)* 18, no. 2 (2010): 300–7.

G. Fagherazzi et al., "Consumption of Artificially and Sugar-Sweetened Beverages and Incident Type 2 Diabetes in the Etude Epidemiologique aupres des femmes de la Mutuelle Generale de l'Education Nationale-European Prospective Investigation into Cancer and Nutrition cohort," *The American Journal of Clinical Nutrition* 97, no. 3 (2013): 517–23.

J.A. Greenberg and A. Geliebter, "Coffee, Hunger, and Peptide YY," *The Journal of the American College of Nutrition* 31, no. 3 (2012): 160–6.

M. Inoue-Choi et al., "Sugar-Sweetened Beverage Intake and the Risk of Type I and Type II Endometrial Cancer Among Postmenopausal Women," *Cancer Epidemiology, Biomarkers and Prevention* 22, no. 12 (2013): 2384–94.

C.S. Johnston et al., "Vinegar Improves Insulin Sensitivity to a High-Carbohydrate Meal in Subjects With Insulin Resistance or Type 2 Diabetes," *Diabetes Care* 27, no. 1 (2004): 281–2.

R.J. Johnson et al., "Sugar, Uric Acid, and the Etiology of Diabetes and Obesity," *Diabetes* 62, no. 10 (2013): 3307–15.

S. Kuriyama et al., "Green Tea Consumption and Mortality Due to Cardio-vascular Disease, Cancer, and All Causes in Japan: The Ohsaki Study," *Journal of the American Medical Association* 296, no. 10 (2006): 1255–65.

S.E. Lakhan and A. Kirchgessner, "The Emerging Role of Dietary Fructose in Obesity and Cognitive Decline," *Nutrition Journal* 12, no. 114 (2013).

F. Macrae, "A Cheap Weight-Loss Tip that Really Does Hold Water: Drink Two Glasses Before Every Meal," *Daily Mail Online,* August 24, 2010. Accessed February 19, 2004. http://www.dailymail.co.uk/health/article-1305575/A-cheap-weight-loss-tip-really-does-hold-water.html

Y. Matsuda et al., "Coffee and Caffeine Improve Insulin Sensitivity and Glucose Tolerance in C57BL/6J Mice Fed a High-Fat Diet," *Bioscience, Biotechnology, and Biochemistry* 75, no. 12 (2011): 2309–15.

N. Ogawa et al., "Acetic Acid Suppresses the Increase in Disaccharidase Activity that Occurs during Culture of Caco-2 Cells," *Journal of Nutrition* 130, no. 3 (2000): 507–13.

A. Riedel et al., "Caffeine Dose-Dependently Induces Thermogenesis but Restores ATP in HepG2 Cells in Culture," *Food and Function* 3, no. 9 (2012): 955–64.

S.M. Tieken et al., "Effects of Solid versus Liquid Meal-Replacement Products of Similar Energy Content on Hunger, Satiety, and Appetite-Regulating Hormones in Older Adults," *Hormonal and Metabolic Research* 39, no. 5 (2007): 389–94.

L. Wang et al., "Alcohol Consumption, Weight Gain, and Risk of Becoming Overweight in Middle-aged and Older Women," *Archives of Internal Medicine* 170, no. 5 (2010): 453–61.

A.M. White and C.S. Johnston, "Vinegar Ingestion at Bedtime Moderates Waking Glucose Concentrations in Adults With Well-Controlled Type 2 Diabetes," *Diabetes Care* 30, no. 11 (2007): 2814–5.

M.R. Yeomans, "Alcohol, Appetite and Energy Balance: is Alcohol Intake a Risk Factor for Obesity?" *Physiology and Behavior* 100, no. 1 (2010): 82–9.

"How Alcohol is Metabolized in the Human Body," HAMS: Harm Reduction for Alcohol. Accessed February 19, 2014. http://www.hamsnetwork.org/metabolism/

Endometrial Cancer 2013, World Cancer Research Fund and American Institute for Cancer Research. Accessed February 19, 2014. http://www.aicr .org/assets/docs/pdf/reports/2013-cup-endometrial-cancer.pdf

Chapter 7: See Ya, Sweeteners and Added Sugar

M.B. Abou-Donia et al., "Splenda Alters Gut Microflora and Increases Intestinal p-glycoprotein and Cytochrome p-450 in Male Rats," *Journal of Toxicology and Environmental Health, Part A* 71, no. 21 (2008): 1415–29.

R. Blaylock, *Excitotoxins: The Taste That Kills* (New Mexico: Health Press NA, 1996).

H. Carter, "Vanilla Dulls Sweet Craving," *The Guardian*. July 23, 2000. Accessed February 19, 2014. http://www.theguardian.com/uk/2000/jul/24/ helencarter

W.J. Chen et al., "The Antioxidant Activities of Natural Sweeteners, Mogrosides, from Fruits of Siraitia Grosvenori," *International Journal of Food Sciences and Nutrition* 58, no. 7 (2007): 548–56.

R. Curi et al., "Effect of Stevia Rebaudiana on Glucose Tolerance in Normal Adult Humans," *Brazilian Journal of Medical and Biological Research* 19, no. 6 (1986): 771–4.

R. Di et al., "Anti-Inflammatory Activities of Mogrosides from Momordica Grosvenori in Murine Macrophages and a Murine Ear Edema Model," *Journal of Agricultural and Food Chemistry* 59, no. 13 (2011): 7474–81.

A. Ferland et al., "Is Aspartame Really Safer in Reducing the Risk of Hypoglycemia During Exercise in Patients With Type 2 Diabetes?" *Diabetes Care* 30, no. 7 (2007): e59.

E. Green and C. Murphy, "Altered Processing of Sweet Taste in the Brain of Diet Soda Drinkers," *Physiology and Behavior* 107, no. 4 (2012): 560–7.

J. Hiebowicz et al., "Effect of Cinnamon on Postprandial Blood Glucose, Gastric Emptying, and Satiety in Healthy Subjects," *The American Journal of Clinical Nutrition* 85, no. 6 (2007): 1552–6.

J. Hiebowicz et al., "Effects of 1 and 3 g Cinnamon on Gastric Empty-ing, Satiety, and Postprandial Blood Glucose, Insulin, Glucose-Dependent Insulinotropic Polypeptide, Glucagon-Like Peptide 1, and Ghrelin Concentra-tions in Healthy Subjects," *The American Journal of Clinical Nutrition* 89, no. 3 (2009): 815–21.

Y. Horio et al., "Aspartame-Induced Apoptosis in PC12 Cells," *Environmen-tal Toxicology and Pharmacology* 37, no. 1 (2013): 158–165.

B.J. Horowitz et al., "Sugar Chromatography Studies in Recurrent Candida Vulvovaginitis," *The Journal of Reproductive Medicine* 29, no. 7 (1984): 441–3.

M. H. Hsieh et al., "Efficacy and Tolerability of Oral Stevioside in Patients with Mild Essential Hypertension: A Two-Year, Randomized, Placebo-Controlled Study," *Clinical Therapeutics* 25, no. 11 (2003): 2797–808.

P. Humphries et al., "Direct and Indirect Cellular Effects of Aspartame on the Brain," *European Journal of Clinical Nutrition* 62, no. 4 (2008): 451–62.

M. Ishikawa et al., "Effects of Oral Administration of Erythritol on Patients with Diabetes," *Regulatory Toxicology and Pharmacology* 24, no. 2, Pt. 2 (1996): S303–8.

T. Just et al., "Cephalic Phase Insulin Release in Healthy Humans After Taste Stimulation?" *Appetite* 51, no. 3 (2008): 622–7.

J. Kawanabe et al., "Noncariogenicity of Erythritol as a Substrate," *Caries Research* 26, no. 5 (1992): 358–62.

J.Y. Kim et al., "Aspartame-Fed Zebrafish Exhibit Acute Deaths with Swimming Defects and Saccharin-Fed Zebrafish have Elevation of Cholesteryl Ester Transfer Protein Activity in Hypercholesterolemia," *Food and Chemical Toxicology* 49, no. 11 (2011): 2899–905.

N. Lailerd et al., "Effects of Stevioside on Glucose Transport Activity in Insulin-Sensitive and Insulin-Resistant Rat Skeletal Muscle," *Metabolism* 53, no. 1 (2004): 101–7.

Y. Liang et al., "The Effect of Artificial Sweetener on Insulin Secretion. 1. The Effect of Acesulfame K on Insulin Secretion in the Rat (Studies in vivo)," *Hormone and Metabolic Research* 19, no. 6 (1987): 233–8.

K.K. Mäkinen, "Long-Term Tolerance of Healthy Human Subjects to High Amounts of Xylitol and Fructose: General and Biochemical Findings," *Beiheft* 15 (1976): 92–104.

K.K. Mäkinen, "Similarity of the Effects of Erythritol and Xylitol on Some Risk Factors of Dental Caries," *Caries Research* 39, no. 3 (2005): 207–15.

V.S. Malik, et al., "Intake of Sugar-Sweetened Beverages and Weight Gain: A Systemic Review," *The American Journal of Clinical Nutrition* 84, no. 2 (2006): 274–88.

P.T. Mattila et al., "Increased Bone Volume and Bone Mineral Content in Xylitol-Fed Aged Rats," *Gerontology* 47, no. 6 (2001): 300–5.

T.J. Mayer and R.J. Wurtman, "Possible Neurologic Effects of Aspartame, a Widely Used Food Additive," *Environmental Health Perspectives* 75 (1987): 53–7.

M.Y. Pepino et al., "Sucralose Affects Glycemic and Hormonal Responses to an Oral Glucose Load," *Diabetes Care* 36, no. 9 (2013): 2530–5.

W.H. Redd et al., "Fragrance Administration to Reduce Anxiety During MR Imaging," *Journal of Magnetic Resonance Imaging* 4, no. 4 (1994): 623–6.

S.E. Swithers, "Artificial Sweeteners Produce the Counterintuitive Effect of Inducing Metabolic Derangements," *Trends in Endocrinology and Metabolism* 24, no. 9 (2013): 431–41.

A. Uittamo et al., "Xylitol Inhibits Carcinogenic Acetaldehyde Production by Candida Species," *International Journal of Cancer* 129, no. 8 (2011): 2038–41.

Q. Yang, "Gain weight by 'going diet?' Artificial Sweeteners and the Neurobiology of Sugar Cravings," *Yale Journal of Biology and Medicine* 83, no. 2 (2010): 101–8.

J. Zabner et al., "The Osmolyte Xylitol Reduces the Salt Concentration of Airway Surface Liquid and May Enhance Bacterial Killing," *Proceedings of the National Academy of Sciences of the United States of America* 97, no. 21 (2000): 11614–9.

Chapter 8: Cycle 1: Taper

K. Casavva et al., "Myths, Presumptions, and Facts about Obesity," *New England Journal of Medicine* 368, no. 5 (2013): 446–54.

C.A. Helman, "Chewing Gum is as Effective as Food in Stimulating Cephalic Phase Gastric Secretion," *American Journal of Gastroenterology* 83, no. 6 (1988): 640–2.

J.F. Hollis et al., "Weight Loss During the Intensive Intervention Phase of the Weight-Loss Maintenance Trial," *American Journal of Preventive Medicine* 35, no. 2 (2008): 118–26.

D. Jakubowicz et al., "High Caloric Intake at Breakfast vs. Dinner Differentially Influences Weight Loss of Overweight and Obese Women," *Obesity (Silver Spring)* 21, no. 12 (2013): 2504–12.

H. Randall, ed. *Inflammation in the Pathogenesis of Chronic Diseases* (New York: Springer, 2007).

C. Swoboda and C.L. Temple, "Acute and Chronic Effects of Gum Chewing on Food Reinforcement and Energy Intake," *Eating Behaviors* 14, no. 2 (2013): 149–56.

Chapter 10: Cycle 3: Transformed!

T. James–Todd et al., "Urinary Phthalate Metabolite Concentrations and Diabetes among Women in the National Health and Nutrition Examination Survey (NHANES) 2001–2008," *Environmental Health Perspectives* 120, no. 9 (2012): 1307–13.

Chapter 11: Low-Sugar Impact Recipes

G. Finlayson et al., "Low Fat Loss Response After Medium-Term Supervised Exercise in Obese is Associated with Exercise-Induced Increase in Food Reward," *Journal of Obesity* (epub 2010): 615624.

Chapter 12: The Final Frontiers

J.P. Little et al., "Low-Volume High-Intensity Interval Training Reduces Hyperglycemia and Increases Muscle Mitochondrial Capacity in Patients with Type 2 Diabetes," *Journal of Applied Physiology (1985)* 111, no. 6 (2011): 1554–60.

B.J. Rolls et al., "Salad and Satiety: Energy Density and Portion Size of a First-Course Salad Affect Energy Intake at Lunch," *Journal of the American Dietetic Association* 104, no. 10 (2004): 1570–6.

D.M. Thomas et al., "Why Do Individuals Not Lose More Weight from an Exercise Intervention at a Defined Dose? An Energy Balance Analysis," *Obesity Reviews* 13, no. 10 (2012): 835–47.

E.L. Thomas et al., "The Missing Risk: MRI and MRS Phenotyping of Abdominal Adiposity and Ectopic Fat," *Obesity (Silver Spring)* 20, no. 1 (2012): 76–87.

F.B. Willis et al., "Frequency of Exercise for Body Fat Loss: A Controlled, Cohort Study," *Journal of Strength and Conditioning Research* 23, no. 8 (2009): 2377–80.

"How to burn more fat, with less effort," University of New South Wales Australia, January 23, 2007. Accessed February 20, 2014. http://newsroom.unsw.edu.au/news/how-burn-more-fat-less-effort/

INDEX

ABOUT THE AUTHOR

JJ VIRGIN, CNS, CHFS is a highly regarded fitness and nutrition expert, public speaker, and media personality. Her book *The Virgin Diet: Drop 7 Foods, Lose 7 Pounds, Just 7 Days* has appeared on numerous bestselling nonfiction lists, including the *New York Times, USA Today,* the *Chicago Tribune,* and the *Wall Street Journal.* Her second book *The Virgin Diet Cookbook: 150 Easy and Delicious Recipes to Lose Weight and Feel Better Fast* is also a *New York Times* bestseller.

Internationally recognized as an expert in helping people overcome "weight-loss resistance" (a term she uses to describe the condition of people who do everything right according to current dieting strategies but still can't lose weight), JJ has helped hundreds of thousands of people achieve fast fat loss by addressing food allergies, food sensitivities, and other food intolerances. Clients feel better in days and achieve fast, lasting fat loss when they drop the seven highly reactive foods she has identified.

JJ's recent media appearances include PBS, *Access Hollywood, Rachael Ray, The Doctors,* and *The Today Show.* She is a frequent blogger for Livestrong.com, the *Huffington Post,* and *Prevention* magazine. JJ has been interviewed in numerous publications, including *Fox News Magazine, Women's World, Health, LA Weekly, Cosmopolitan,* and the *Los Angeles Times.*

High-performance athletes, CEOs, and A-list celebrities seek out JJ to deliver the results they need and expect. She has worked with Nicole Eggert, Tracie Thoms, and Tamara Johnston-George, and she helped Brandon Routh get in top physical form for *Superman Returns.*

For two years, JJ was the nutrition expert on the top-rated *Dr. Phil* show, and she spent two seasons as co-host of TC's *Freaky Eaters.* She has one of the top pledge shows on PBS, *Drop 7 Foods, Feel Better Fast!* based on the Virgin Diet principles. She is also the bestselling author of *Six Weeks to Sleeveless and Sexy* and creator of the 4x4 workout series.

JJ is a lifelong learner and has completed 40 graduate and doctoral courses in the areas of exercise science, nutrition, functional medicine, and psychology. She is a board-certified nutrition specialist through the American College of Nutrition, board certified in holistic nutrition, and a certified health and fitness specialist through the American College of Sports Medicine.

Most importantly, JJ is the mom of two amazing teenage boys. One of them survived a near fatal auto accident, and JJ used her knowledge, expertise, and peer network to take him from comatose to thriving. Every day JJ wakes up with gratitude to be able to spend another day with her children and to help more people live fuller lives by achieving better health.

For more information, please visit JJ at jjvirgin.com.